News

in Public Memory

Toby Miller
General Editor

Vol. 6

PETER LANG
New York • Washington, D.C./Baltimore • Bern
Frankfurt am Main • Berlin • Brussels • Vienna • Oxford

News

in Public Memory

An International Study of Media Memories across Generations

Edited by
Ingrid Volkmer

PETER LANG
New York • Washington, D.C./Baltimore • Bern
Frankfurt am Main • Berlin • Brussels • Vienna • Oxford

Library of Congress Cataloging-in-Publication Data

Volkmer, Ingrid.
News in public memory: an international study
of media memories across generations / edited by Ingrid Volkmer.
p. cm. — (Popular culture and everyday life; vol. 6)
Includes bibliographical references and index.
1. Communication, International. 2. Globalization. 3. Mass media--History. I.
Volkmer, Ingrid. II. Series: Popular culture & everyday life ; v. 6.
P96.I5N486   302.2—dc22   2005029928

Bibliographic information published by **Die Deutsche Bibliothek**.
Die Deutsche Bibliothek lists this publication in the "Deutsche
Nationalbibliografie"; detailed bibliographic data is available
on the Internet at http://dnb.ddb.de/.

Cover design by Lisa Barfield
Cover art Ingrid Volkmer

The paper in this book meets the guidelines for permanence and durability
of the Committee on Production Guidelines for Book Longevity
of the Council of Library Resources.

© 2006 Peter Lang Publishing, Inc., New York
29 Broadway, New York, NY 10006
www.peterlang.com

Printed in the United States of America

To Neil Postman—because media not only deconstruct childhood, but reconstruct a collective perception of the world.

Table of Contents

Acknowledgments 100

Preface 1
    Ingrid Volkmer

I. Local Profiles in Cross-Generational Analysis

Introduction 13
    Ingrid Volkmer

Australia 27
    Christina Slade

Austria 35
    Theo Hug

Czech Republic 53
    Jan Jirák

Germany 69
    Gebhard Rusch and *Ingrid Volkmer*

India 95
   Keval J. Kumar

Japan 119
   Reiko Sekiguchi

Mexico 139
   Margarita Maass, Daniela Rivera, and *Andres Hofman*

South Africa 159
   Ruth Teer-Tomaselli

USA 177
   Matthew D. Payne, Jill Dianne Swenson, and *Thomas W. Bohn*

II. Comparative Analysis Across Generations and Cultures

Perceptions and Memories of the Media Context .195
   Christina Slade

Construction of Memory 211
   Keval J. Kumar, Theo Hug, and *Gebhard Rusch*

Memory and Markers: Collective Memory and Newsworthiness 225
   Ruth Teer-Tomaselli

Globalization, Generational Entelechies and the Global Public Space . .251
   Ingrid Volkmer

About the Authors 269

Appendix: Tables of Focus Groups 273

Notes 297

Index 303

Acknowledgments

This book is a product of exceptional international teamwork. The project, Global Media Generations, was established in 1998 by the editor, Ingrid Volkmer. The initial goal was to gain an understanding of the transformations in the first mass-media century, in view of different media cultures and generations.

The idea—the challenge—was to study the other side of the news-flow spectrum: to conduct research that would reveal the impact of the new transnational infrastructure of political media on societies, cultures, and lifeworlds of various generations.

The turn of the century and the new millennium appeared to be an ideal time to establish an international project designed to detect some of the crucial aspects of the first mass-media century, the 20th century, and to listen to the voices of those who have lived through critical decades in various world regions.

The focus of the research project was to listen to individuals' memories of the media, across three generations living in various world regions. The project involves media memories of the generation that has experienced the radio as entering and "colonizing" their family life, and their perceptions of the news media during the worst crisis of the last century—the first "global event"—the Second World War. On the other hand, our research also involves the key moments of Marshall McLuhan's Global Village through the eyes of the baby-boom generation, experiencing the first satellite age and the first global news event—the moon landing. Finally, our research might help to refine the concept of news based on a completely different view of the media by the "Generation Net," which does not perceive media any more along the lines of separate technologies, such as television, radio, and print. Instead, they perceive the news media as a simple network of options: a collage of information with entertainment as background noise. The reality of this perception is sometimes ignored by journalists.

This book presents the results of this international comparative study. During the first meeting of the research group in 1998, which was hosted by New York University professor Neil Postman, the members of the group discussed their own media biographies and learned about many common and nation-specific aspects of our shared media world. At this first meeting, the group decided to conduct a qualitative study, in order to allow for cultural depth, for nuances and details, which are increasingly relevant in today's dimension of global communication and very easily overlooked.

As the coordinator of this study, I owe thanks to those who participated in this research. Over the years, the group not only has become truly a team but also friends. I owe my deep thanks to this core team, which I would like to list here in alphabetical order: Theo Hug, Jan Jirák, Keval Kumar, Margarita Maas, Matthew Payne, Gebhard Rusch, Reiko Sekiguchi, Christina Slade, and Ruth Teer-Tomaselli. I thank them for their trust, their time and effort, and for believing in my idea.

This project could not have been established without the great support from Carlos Arnaldo of UNESCO, Paris, who has helped to create the organizational structure.

I am thankful to those who have continuously supported our group. I am especially thankful to Dieter Czaja: Department of Standards and Practices, RTL Television, Cologne, Germany, for generously funding our project meetings and greatly supporting our research. Others I would like to mention are the Goethe Institute, New York; and Mechthild Appelhoff and Dr. Joachim Gerth, Broadcasting Authority, North-Rhine Westphalia, Dusseldorf, Germany, for inviting us to the Medienforum 2000 in Cologne, Germany, to present first results.

I would also like to thank the Joan Shorenstein Center on the Press, Politics and Public Policy, John F. Kennedy School, Harvard University, where I was invited as a fellow in 2002 and had the opportunity to review and discuss various aspects of project results.

Last but not least, the authors of this book owe gratitude to all focus-group participants, who must remain unnamed. Their willingness to participate and their openness provided us with a new perspective on lifeworld and the "order of things" in a sometimes very personal way. Without them this project would not have been possible.

Our entire research team would like to dedicate this book to Neil Postman. He has not only supported our research, but seemed to have enjoyed the overall theme of the project, in which media-related memories not only deconstruct childhood, as his work on the *Disappearance of Childhood* (Vintage, 1994) suggests, but reconstruct common grounds of perceiving the world, despite national differences and sometimes artificial borders. His death in 2003 has left an irreplaceable void in academic discourse. It is an honor for us to dedicate this book to him and his memory.

INGRID VOLKMER

Preface

The role of the news media, as information platforms and active mediators of world representation, seems to have gained complexity and pace within the advanced, globalized media infrastructure at the beginning of the twenty-first century. This increased complexity and pace not only shapes political identity and transforms national public spheres, but also creates a new global public space.

One could argue that nations live not only on "media time," as Carey claims (Carey, 1998: 44), but in new, varied, multi-directional flow-frameworks of time/space coordinates: Spectacular political affairs take place in global media prime time, are formatted as "breaking news," and are delivered into living rooms around the world via a network of about 400 satellites, instantaneously and continuously demanding actions and reactions. Industrial nations, developing as well as transitional nations, governments, and individuals live in a new global symbolic space, which refines former notions of "distance" and "proximity" by a constant presence of crises and conflicts, associated by a never-ending stream of "contest-," "conquest-," and "coronation-" type media events (Dayan and Katz, 1992).

Considering this advanced stage, not only of globalization as such, but in particular the globalization of political communication, I claim that the changing flow of political information from gate-kept "distribution" (from point A to point B) to new, unregulated, and transnational network-type flow formats in conjunction with the increasing relevance of "mediated" communication, constitutes a new global public space. This global public space, in a postmodern/constructivist viewpoint transforms the specifics of "historical time" into a broad sense of "hyperreality" mode (Baudrillard, 1988) and reroutes political discourses in democratic as well as totalitarian states within a new transnational political territory, with varying centers and peripheries.

Of course, from the perspective of globalization critics, these developments represent just another argument for the elimination of not only the conventional construction of nation-states, but, increasingly, of national sovereignty, i.e., of internal, national political communication. In the perspective of a sociological terminology, which is deeply embedded in the traditions (and ideals !) of "modernity" and "modern" social structures, the dynamics of globalization appear as new "external" pressure on national/state politics (see for instance, Beck, 1992).

However, what these approaches tend to overlook—as do various debates even *within* the field of communication/media studies—is that global communication does not only refer to a new structure of information flow and a variety of new transnational channels. Instead, the increasing network density and network character of global political communication, within new time/space coordinates, require a revised set of terminologies, which serve to describe and define most current dimensions and phenomena as well as the changing role of (political) media. These descriptions should be made not only in terms of "risks," but also in view of potentials. The potentials are described in regard to news-media balances, to "global" journalism, as well as to concepts of "communicative competence" (Baacke, 1973), and "communicative action" (Habermas, 1987) on the lifeworld discourse level within such a new political space.

A review of recent debates within the field of international/global communication reveals that approaches to mapping these new coordinates of global political communication are based more on paradigms of modern information flow, and less on paradigms of globalization in the sense of differentiating globalization approaches (Robertson, 1992; Robertson and White, 2003) and/or network paradigms (Castells, 2000; Wiley, 2004).

By examining various lines of argumentation within a broad discourse of global political communication, the following concepts can be distinguished: The first approaches of international communication, in the true sense of "inter-national" (i.e., as communication between nations) have been debated in view of "development communication" (Lerner, 1958). The purpose of these concepts was to systematically "modernize" traditional (i.e., developing) societies by means of media. These first approaches have been developed in the U.S. (particularly at MIT, Cambridge, MA) during the height of the Cold War (see Lerner, 1958, Schramm, 1968).

Roughly one decade later, these debates have inspired an entirely new set of theories, which transformed "development" communication not only into an active concept, but also into a critique of Western news flow. The demand for a New World Information and Communication Order (NWICO) by countries of the Southern Hemisphere was coordinated by UNESCO and provided the platform for a call for a "balanced" flow of international information and communication. This NWICO has on one hand created an overall UNESCO policy, still in place today (see the UNESCO Initiative "International Commission for the Study of Communication Problems, 2003"), as well as subsequent initiatives in relation to new technologies. Some of the conventional lines of argumentation of "media imperialism," which have been raised within this conceptual framework since the late 1970s, are occasionally re-voiced in current discourses of global political communication (Fejes, 1986; Nordenstreng and Schiller, 1993; Mattelart, 1993; Thussu, 1998).

Other lines of argumentation have diversified. Some have been absorbed by very specific debates, for instance by studies of the "Digital Divide," relating to the Internet as a global medium (Norris, Bennett and Entman, 2001); others by new notions of media as "weapons" of "cultural conquest" (Said, 1994); on in-flows of "imperial" media in particular world regions (Meyer, 1988); as well as by critical reviews of the traditional concepts of media imperialism (Tomlinson, 1991).

Besides these traditional and more current approaches of media imperialism, a second line of debate within global political communication can be best categorized as "global media relativism." These approaches emerged around the mid-nineties of the 20th century and were less influenced by the paradigm and ideal of "modernity" than by emerging and differentiated approaches of globalization that developed in other neighboring disciplines, particularly in sociology. Concepts of global media relativism focus on a comparison of various media cultures in a relativistic globalized viewpoint. Examples for this approach are comparative studies of the perception of news from the viewpoint of different cultures (Lull, 1988; Jensen, 1998), studies on the impact of CNN on the global public sphere (Volkmer, 1999), as well as a new approach of "de-Westernizing media studies" (Curran and Park, 2000).

Another, third, discourse stream within global political communication has arisen in relation to global journalism and global-conflict communication relating to recent types of world crises. Though only recently developed, these discourses represent another line of argumentation within global political communication. Issues within these debates are the growing influence of global news media on (national) foreign policy, for instance in conjunction with various debates of the "CNN Factor" (Robinson, 2002), the impact of the news media in shaping world conflicts (Ammon, 2001; Gilboa and Davidson, 2002), as well as new forms of journalism in world crises (Hachten and Scotton, 2001; Zelizer and Allan, 2002).

"Globalized audiences" categorize the fourth dimension of discourse. These approaches attempt to detect new supra- and sub-national political communities such as "diasporic" groups (Cunningham and Sinclair, 2001).

The fifth category of discourses within global political communication could be described as "Global Media Infrastructures and Policies." Debates within this discourse field focus on new transnational media policies (Raboy, 2003) and transnational media. A sixth dimension of conceptual frameworks can be roughly described as "Theories of Global Communication," which relate global communication structures to political theories (Mowlana, 1997).

However, given the network format of the global public space, global political communication enters the lifeworld directly, shaping an almost Habermasian sphere of "interpenetration" (Habermas, 1987, 1981). This interpenetration occurs not so much in the Habermasian dualism of "system" and "lifeworld," but in the format of a colonialization of the lifeworld by the global public space.

Habermas's crucial concept involves communication and related concepts of rational communicative action. I argue that from the viewpoint of the interpenetration, in the sense of a colonialization of global public space and lifeworld, the inside of the lifeworld is defined by the view from the outside of the global public space. In other words, the colonialization process within this network-framed global political space is constituted not so much by the sheer presence of media in lifeworlds, as in the early days of television, but by the switch of the "mediation" process in defining the relationship between the "world" and "me."

Reviewing these processes of colonialization of the lifeworld and global/transnational media across various decades of the 20th century reveals that media have conveyed very specific notions of the world as a common place, along various notions of unity and difference, of distance and proximity.

The first decade of the 20th century was still dominated by colonial internationalization, which was based on communication via telegraph, cable lines, and telephone. Technologies supported the needs of the colonial motherlands, such as Great Britain, France, and Germany, to preserve communication to their colonies worldwide. For example, Great Britain dominated the world telegraph system. Governmental (colonial) internationalization also influenced the international news flows provided via transpacific and transatlantic cable lines, facilitating rapid communication across vast territories and oceans. The emerging news market, also shaped after these world territories of colonial internationalization, was associated by the commercialization of news (Boyd-Barrett, 1980; Baldasty, 1992).

Just one decade later, in the early twenties, the radio became a new household medium in many countries around the world. The radio allowed sharing, within the family context, somewhat "live" political and cultural events, taking place within regional proximity. Whereas the newspaper can be viewed as a unidirectional medium, since news selection required editorial gate-keeping processes, the radio provided first occasional niches of "extraterritorial" political information, which are today overlooked in many discourses about global news flow.

This unique extraterritorial dimension was made possible by coincidental transborder radio distribution in close border regions, as well as by short-wave channels. The BBC World Service, which commenced its operation in 1931, is one of the most prominent examples, particularly during world crises such as WWII. This unique extraterritorial news flow already challenged totalitarian regimes and contributed to a new sense of internationalization and the relativity of political perspectives.

Television refined this notion of internationalization in a new—as I claim—dual way after the middle of the century, particularly in industrialized countries, where television replaced the radio as the dominant medium on the family center stage. On one hand, the availability of regional news pools in various world regions (such as "Asiavison" throughout Asia and "Eurovision" in Western Europe), which could be used by international stations for their foreign news coverage, enabled a new constant foreign news flow, even for those broadcasters who could not afford their own international crews. However, foreign news was not directly accessible to audiences, in that they were edited, selected, and domesticated for local (in those days, basically national) markets and the national mass audience. Even live satellite feeds of major events of these decades, such as the moon landing, were reedited by national editors and tailored for the information needs of a clearly defined national audience. Whereas the radio provided a multidirectional program flow, as described above, television in the sixties and seventies can be best described as practicing a domesticated internationalization, which has created concepts and formats of foreign news still in use today.

Due to the commercialization of the former public-service satellite industry in conjunction with new distribution technologies, such as cable systems and direct-to-home satellite delivery, the phase of "global" television began in the early nineties of the 20th century. Within this era, new transnational news channels have been established, such as CNN, which began to challenge national markets and domesticated television coverage by directly entering lifeworlds via direct-to-home satellite technologies. The Internet, as a new point-to-point platform, has almost eliminated former notions of "domestic" and "foreign," and creates a communication infrastructure without centers or peripheries.

Magnifying the Habermasian dimension of interpenetration in conjunction with these new colonialization processes allows us to (1) identify the arising sphere of mediation, of world representation within this lifeworld dimension of the global public space; and (2) detect the meaning of varying degrees of global news media flow in lifeworld perspectives.

To gain an insight into these processes, the Global Media Generations project was launched in 1998. Given the fact that the 20th century has been the first mass-media century, where media were available to the emerging middle classes, the underlying idea of the research was to capture and compare media and news-related memories of different generations, who have lived through very particular phases of colonialization of their lifeworlds by media, in various countries worldwide. Despite the very different societal and cultural context of the three age cohorts involved in this international study, it can be argued that media and the increasing global news flow has, in fact, created very similar generational experiences in the nine countries involved. The results show that the assumed colonialization of lifeworlds by media has shaped generational-specific worldviews and very particular notions of the global public space across the decades involved.

The methodology of the project has been based on the theory of generations, as proposed by the German sociologist Karl Mannheim, whose theory on the "Sociology of Knowledge" is widely ignored in current media-related debates. Mannheim's definition of generations is based on "generational knowledge," which defines each generation's "identity of location" within a given society (Mannheim, 1951: 292). According to Mannheim, individuals who belong to the "same generation," who "share the same year of birth," are "endowed, to that extent, with a common location in the historical dimension of the social process"(Mannheim, 1951: 290).

Based on this methodology, three generations who have experienced very particular media during their "formative" years have been involved in this research: (1) the "print/radio" generation, born 1924–1929, their formative years being 1935–1945; (2) the "black-and-white–television generation," born 1954–1959, whose formative years are between 1965–1975; and (3) the "Internet generation" born 1979–1984, their formative years being 1989–1999. In the focus of this comparative project are generational perceptions of their respective lifeworld—specifically their media environment, but also of the meaning of media-transmitted political events in nine countries.

The study identifies a generation-specific degree of the colonialization of the lifeworld by globalized media, conveying very particular notions of distance and proximity held by each generation. Results reveal the specific meaning of news events and the relevance of the media environment for generation-specific perceptions of the world, despite national, cultural, and societal differences.

A qualitative method was chosen, in order to allow for an elaborate in-depth articulation of childhood/youth-related media memories in a "life-world logic." Results reveal that this approach has succeeded in detecting interesting specifics and details of meaning in the childhood/youth media environment as well as news memories, which would have been inaccessible by quantitative methods.

The research project brought together distinguished academics of media and communication studies from different world regions in order to jointly map the meaning of media and news memories in the minds of people living in diverse cultures across the globe, such as Australia, Austria, Czech Republic, Germany, India, Japan, Mexico, South Africa, and the United States.

The detection of specific "entelechies," as Mannheim phrases the underlying structure of common experiences of each generation (Mannheim, 1951) in view of media and political information, is important in order to understand the potential and opportunities of this new global public space. Given the complexity of the new crises of the still-young 21st century, it seems to become not only an important task but also a responsibility for communication studies to help to bridge gaps, to detect similarities of "fate" and "togetherness" (Heidegger, 1935)—to enable communication for the new generation of world citizens within our new public space.

INGRID VOLKMER
University of Otago, New Zealand
March 2004

Bibliography

Ammon, Royce (2001). *Global Television and the Shaping of World Politics: CNN, Telediplomacy, and Foreign Policy.* Jefferson, NC: McFarland.

Baacke, Dieter (1973, 1980). *Kommunikation und Kompetenz: Grundlegung einer Didaktik der Kommunikation und ihrer Medien.* [Communication and Competence: Basics of the didactics of communication and the media] München: Juventa.

Baldasty, Gerald J. (1992). *The Commercialization of News in the Nineteenth Century.* Madison, University of Wisconsin Press.

Baudrillard, Jean (1988). *Selected Writings.* ed. Mark Poster. Cambridge, UK: Blackwell, Polity.

Beck, Ulrich (1992). *Risk Society: Towards a New Modernity.* London: Sage.

Boyd-Barrett, Oliver (1980). *The International News Agencies.* London: Sage.

Carey, James (1998). "Political Ritual on Television: Episodes in the History of Shame, Degradation and Excommunication." In *Media, Ritual and Identity,* ed. Tamar Liebes, James Curran, and Elihu Katz, 42–70. London, New York: Routledge.

Castells, Manuel (2000, 2nd ed.). *The Rise of the Network Society.* Oxford: Blackwell.

Cunningham, Stuart and John Sinclair, eds. (2001). *Floating Lives: The Media and Asian Diasporas.* Boulder, CO: Rowman & Littlefield.

Curran, James, and Myung-Jin Park, eds. (2000). *De-Westernizing Media Studies.* London, New York: Routledge.

Dayan, Daniel, and Elihu Katz (1992). *Media Events: The Live Broadcasting of History.* Cambridge, MA: Harvard University Press.

Gilboa, Eytan, and Alistair Davidson, eds. (2002). *Media and Conflict: Framing Issues, Making Policy, Shaping Opinions.* New York: Transnational Publishers.

Fejes, Fred (1986). *Imperialism, Media and the Good Neighbor: New Deal Foreign Policy and United States Shortwave Broadcasting to Latin America.* Norwood, NJ: Ablex.

Habermas, Juergen (1987, 1981). *The Theory of Communicative Action.* Boston: Beacon.

Hachten, William, and James Francis Scotton (2001). *The World News Prism: Global Media in the Era of Terrorism.* Jefferson, NC: McFarland.

Heidegger, Martin (1935). *Sein und Zeit.* 4th ed. Halle A.D. S.: Niemeyer.

International Commission for the Study of Communication Problems (2003). *Many Voices, One World: Towards a New, More Just, and More Efficient World, Information and Communication Order.* Boulder, CO: Rowman & Littlefield.

Jensen, Klaus Bruhn (1998). *News of the World: World Cultures Look at Television News.* London, New York: Routledge.

Lerner, Daniel (1958). *The Passing of Traditional Society: Modernizing the Middle East.* New York: Free Press.

Lull, James (1988). *World Families Watch Television.* London: Sage.

Mannheim, Karl (1951). *Essays on the Sociology of Knowledge.* London: Routledge & Kegan Paul.

Mattelart, Armand (1993). *Multinational Corporations and the Control of Culture.* Brighton, UK: Harvester Press.

Meyer, William H. (1988). *Transnational Media and Third World Development: The Structure and Impact of Imperialism.* Westport, CT: Greenwood Publishing Group.

Mowlana, Hamid (1997, 2nd ed.). *Global Information and World Communication.* London: Sage.

Nordenstreng, Kaarle, and Herbert I. Schiller (1993). *Beyond National Sovereignty: International Communication in the 1990s.* Norwood, NJ: Ablex.

Norris, Pippa, Lance W. Bennett, and Robert Entman, eds. (2001). *Digital Divide: Civic Engagement, Information Poverty and the Internet Worldwide.* Cambridge: Cambridge University Press.

Raboy, Marc (2003). *Global Media Policy for the New Millennium.* Luton, UK: University of Luton Press.

Robertson, Roland (1992). *Globalization: Social Theory and Global Culture.* London: Sage.

Robertson, Roland, and Kathleen White (2003). *Globality and Modernity.* London: Sage.

Robinson, Piers (2002). *The CNN Effect: The Myth of News Media, Foreign Policy and Intervention.* London, New York: Routledge.

Said, Edward (1994). *Culture and Imperialism.* New York: Vintage.

Schramm, Wilbur (1968). *Mass Media and National Development: The Role of Information in the Developing Countries.* Palo Alto, CA: Stanford University Press.

Tomlinson, John (1991). *Cultural Imperialism: A Critical Introduction.* Baltimore: Johns Hopkins.

Thussu, Daya, ed. (1998). *Electronic Empires: Global Media and Local Resistance.* London, New York: Arnold.

Volkmer, Ingrid (1999). *News in the Global Sphere: A Study on CNN and Its Impact on Global Communication.* Luton, UK: University of Luton Press.

Wiley, Stephen B. Crofts (2004). "Rethinking Nationality in the Context of Globalization," *Communication Theory.* February: 78–96.

Zelizer, Barbie, and Stuart Allan, eds. (2002). *Journalism after September 11.* London, New York: Routledge.

PART I

Local Profiles in Cross-Generational Analysis

Ingrid Volkmer

The following articles present results of the qualitative project from nine national perspectives. We have chosen this approach because qualitative methods provide in-depth insights as well as a variety of nuances, which are relevant for internationally comparative research. Although a quantitative study would have allowed us to compare broad trends, such a survey would not have brought detailed subjective "lifeworld" contexts and meanings to the surface—aspects that have been considered crucial for this research.

The study is based on focus-group interviews with members of three generations in each of the nine countries, and focuses on media-related memories of childhood and youth. The study follows Anderson's argument that "while reception studies of television have questioned assumptions about the passive spectatorship of TV viewers, memory studies provide a way of looking at historical reception, what people remember of history, the ways it is made useful in their lives" (Anderson, 2001: 20, 21). Given this framework, memories of the media as technologies as well as their meaning in the construction of the lifeworld still have relevance for today's media usage. Particularly formative news memories seem to provide a framework for today's world perception. Anderson argues that viewed "as a component of cultural memory, the past is less a sequence of events than a discursive surface, readable only through layers of subsequent meanings and contexts," and for him, the process of understanding is best described as an "archeology in which the goal is not simply to uncover something that has been buried, but to discover how and why additional layers have been built on top of it" (Anderson, 2001: 23).

In our research, we attempted to uncover first segments of such an archeology of media memories, being aware that reconstructions of the past are not only dynamic and interactive, but also produce collective "communicative pragmatics"; that is, "criteria for remembering are seen to be contingent upon the action to which the talk is oriented" (Middleton and Edwards, 1990: 29). This process produces interesting nuances of generational-specific "intersubjectivity" regarding the perception of the media.

Three generations have been selected for this research project, each of which has experienced very particular roles of the media as mediators of the world, as well as very specific news cultures during their "formative" years, during childhood and youth:

1) **The Radio Generation:** born between 1924 and 1929, with their formative years being between 1935 and 1946.
2) **The Black-and-White Television Generation:** born between 1954 and 1959, with their formative years being between 1965 and 1975.
3) **The Internet Generation:** born between 1979 and 1984, their formative years being between 1989 and 1999.

We are aware that in some countries, for instance South Africa and India, television has entered the media sphere with some delays in comparison to many other countries. However, these overall generational-specific categories serve as a description of the leading media culture during the childhood/youth years of each generation.

The focus of this comparative project is on generational perceptions of the lifeworld, i.e., media environment, but also the meaning of media-transmitted political events in nine countries worldwide.

In each of the nine countries, one focus-group discussion has been conducted with six members of each of the three generations involved. In each country, three focus-group sessions brought together eighteen individuals. Given this basis for our research, this study can be viewed as an "explorative" study or an experiment that simply attempted to find new dimensions of the role of the (news) media within the symbolic parameters of the phenomenology of lifeworlds, and the various integrative modes of media within very specific social criteria.

However, given this very specific angle, the study, does reveal interesting results; for instance, the transformation of the media from so-called mediators of national affairs to a globalized media world across the genera-tions. It became apparent that media are not simply media, that is, tech-nologies, but are deeply embedded in the symbolic territory of the family as "the economy of the household" and "provide, actively, interactively, or passively, links between households, and individual members of house-holds, with the world beyond their front door, and do this (or fail to do this) in complex and often contradictory ways" (Silverstone, Hirsch, and Morley, 1992:15). The authors further argue: "For information and commu-nication technologies define both some of the main routes along which the biographies of ideas and meanings, information and pleasures, are con-structed, but also they themselves, as objects and as things, have their own biographies, as they too become domesticated into the distinct cultures of families and households." (Silverstone, Hirsch, Morley, 1992: 19).

Focus groups were organized in the "snowball" method, by bringing together those individuals who share a somewhat common collective view and, in some cases, are acquainted with each other. By using this method, it was possible to quickly advance to in-depth questions, simply because the group atmosphere was open and individuals trusted each other, which allowed very subjective and honest responses. Given the explorative nature of this study, this approach brought up responses that helped in building further models for methods of comparative international research. This snowball method proved to be exceptionally relevant for the oldest cohort, who had to talk about memories of one of the most critical phases of their lives: the Second World War. In Germany and Austria, interesting results were produced, which help to provide a new view of the role of the media during the Nazi period. As Reiko Sekiguchi notes, in Japan, members of the oldest generation are reluctant to publicly discuss any memories of the traumatic events of Hiroshima and Nagasaki. With the snowball method, it was possible to create an atmosphere of trust, which particularly helped members of this oldest generation to respond in elaborate ways.

Each of the focus-group sessions lasted at least forty-five minutes, and some lasted about two hours. Each focus-group interview was taped and later transcribed. All of the focus-group sessions have been conducted in original language and have been interpreted based on a common scheme by each national member. This method permitted focus-group members to respond in their own native language, which encouraged more elaborate communication than an interview in a second language would allow.

The first segment of the focus-group session was focused on the percep-tion of media during their childhood and youth years. This segment con-structed the collective environment for further memories and encouraged otherwise-hidden reflections. Results show that focus-group members described their specific memory of the media in very different nuances: as colonizers of family space, as reproducing family power structures in regards to the "gatekeeping" of media, or the particular role of media as educational tools. They were also encouraged to reflect on the role of their parents' media use.

This method also proved to reveal vivid memories of those media, which are forgotten in mainstream media research; for instance, the quite important role of small children's media in Nazi Germany. Although small and focusing on children, these media contained Nazi ideologies, which focus-group members expressed for the first time. They recalled the show-cases having been placed where children would see the stereotyping racist images, and the journals, given to children for free in department stores. Another example of the depth of these interviews was the quite elaborate description of the removal of the Buddhist statue in the living room in a Japanese household in order to make room for the radio, as described by individuals of the oldest focus group in Japan. This identified a meaningful gesture, which could easily be interpreted as the beginning of the new media age in Japan and elsewhere. Interestingly, all these memories have been built into the overall media biography of members of this focus group in Germany and have been raised in the quite extensive focus-group debate.

The second segment was based on this environment and revolved around the very specific news memories, perceived as having occurred during their childhood and youth years. These focus-group segments revealed an interesting interwoven aspect of public and private spheres, by integrating international and national events into their biographical con-texts. These interviews also showed how differently these processes of inte-gration are viewed in the perspective of each generation. Whereas news events can be viewed as lifeworld events in the oldest cohort—being described at some length and revealing various modes of connection to their biographical memory—in the youngest generation, news memories are integrated into broader media memories or "media biographies" that reveal the different perceptions of the media by these generations.

The third segment of the interview sessions asked for responses to ten national and ten international political events. Particularly in view of the ten international events, the goal was to compare memories regarding the depth and meaning of these events. The memories were sometimes shared by the entire generation, although located in different worldwide places and experiencing the same event from varied perspectives. Results for the focus groups of the oldest generation showed only a small number of inter-national events were recalled. The interviews with members of the youngest generation revealed knowledge, though only superficial, of a variety of international events.

The following articles will present findings of the nine national projects. I would agree with Curran that "media systems are shaped not merely by national regulatory regimes and national audience preferences, but by a complex ensemble of social relations that have taken shape in national contexts. It is precisely the historically grounded density of these relationships that tends to be excluded from simplified global accounts, in which theorists survey the universe while never straying far from the international airport" (Curran and Park, 2000: 12). The following articles will reconstruct aspects of this density and reveal the historical development of the role of the media as agents of internationalization and globalization in different societies from diverse lifeworld perspectives.

Tables representing the composition of each focus group are included in the appendix of this book. These tables also identify socioeconomic details of each focus group as well as other relevant factual lifeworld coordinates. Names, which appear in the context of interview quotations, have been recoded. All focus-group members remain anonymous and names are only used for reference purposes.

Bibliography

Anderson, Steven (2001). "History TV and Popular Memory." In *Television Histories: Shaping Collective Memory in the Media Age*, ed. Gary R. Edgerton and Peter C. Rollins, 19–36. Lexington: University Press of Kentucky.

Curran, James and Myung-Jin Park (2000). "Beyond Globalization Theory." In *De-Westernizing Media Studies*, ed. James Curran and Myung-Jin Park, 3–18. London and New York: Routledge.

Middleton, David, and Derek Edwards (1990). "Conversational Remembering: A Social Psychological Approach" In *Collective Remembering*, ed. David Middleton and Derek Edwards, 23–45. London, Newbury Park, New Delhi: Sage.

Silverstone, Roger, Eric Hirsch, and David Morley, eds. (1992). "Information and Communication Technologies and the Moral Economy of the Household." In *Consuming Technologies: Media and Information in Domestic Spaces*, ed. Roger Silverstone and Eric Hirsch, 15–31. UK: Routledge.

· A U S T R A L I A ·

Christina Slade

1. Introduction

As a set of six independent colonies of the British Empire, the Australian states in the 19th century were overwhelmingly British in orientation, and drew their attitudes in general, as well as their particular view of news, from the motherland. The indigenous population, small to begin with, was much reduced in number and was in retreat from the southern and eastern seaboards, where the colonies were growing prosperous as exporters of primary produce. After a process of debate and discord between the colonies, Australia became an independent federation in 1901. It was a wide-flung, sparsely populated country with an imperative to develop a national identity and a defense strategy. When radio was introduced, it was placed under the bureaucratic control of the Department of Post and Telegraph, and given an explicit charter: to develop national consciousness through ensuring access not merely to those within the cities, but also to the far-flung farming communities in the bush.

Although radio had been heard in New York in the first decade of the century, fears of wartime security risks delayed the first public demonstration in Sydney until 1919.[1] Radio was not officially permitted to operate in Australia until 1923, when a variety of commercial groups began transmitting in the larger cities. In 1927, concern that the country listeners were not being included led to the establishment of a new national government radio network, the Australian Broadcasting Company (ABC). At this stage, the Australian nation was still overwhelmingly Anglo-Celtic in origin, and culturally dependent on the mother country, the United Kingdom. Through the 1930s the British Royal family provided the real-life soap operas of the nation, and sporting events hosted by home teams tested the national caliber. With the Second World War, radio and newsreels provided sounds and images to accompany the press. At the same time, events of the war made Australians aware that they could no longer rely on England for protection; Australia began to look to the United States for leadership and to the Asian Pacific for regional relationships.

After the end of the Second World War, Australia's Anglo-Celtic racial mix was leavened by successive waves of immigration, from Europe in the early years, and later from the countries of Asia. The war had delayed the introduction of the new medium, television, and political bickering delayed it still further. Not until 1956 were commercial and government (ABC) channels made available in the larger cities. Commercial channels were dominated by U.S.–based materials, and the ABC was dominated by British Broadcasting Corporation (BBC) product. By the mid-1960s, legislation requiring a certain amount of local content encouraged the production of a number of Australian programs. A period of legislative change in the 1980s and early 1990s led to a rapid change in ownership of the commercial networks.

The introduction of pay TV in Australia was, like the introduction of television, delayed through political debate. The first pay network was not introduced until 1995. However, Australians are notoriously quick to take up new technologies and this has been evident with the Internet.

The Australian study was conducted in Adelaide, capital of the state of South Australia, and in Canberra, the capital of Australia. Both are medium-sized Australian cities,[2] with a typical mixture of the middle-class groupings that this study aimed to investigate. The great majority of the Australian population is raised in the suburbs of one of the coastal cities; this was overwhelmingly true of those interviewed in the experiment. Among the middle classes, home ownership is almost universal. All of those interviewed in this study lived as children in suburban detached homes owned or rented by their parents, except in one case where, on the death of the mother, the father and daughter moved to live in a hotel.

2. Media Environment

Table 1 (see Appendix) summarizes the family environment and availability of the members of the Australian focus groups. Each group was relatively uniform in its social background and there was substantial agreement and similarity in both family background and knowledge of the media. Members of each cohort were by definition middle class, and hence in adequate financial positions to acquire the media of the time. However, there were differences between the cohorts, in part based on historical factors and in part due to the groups that were chosen.

It will be evident that while each cohort was relatively uniform, the education levels of the older (first) cohort and in particular of the women is strikingly high, with two of them having tertiary education. The group was from Adelaide and over their lifetimes had achieved a higher level of socioeconomic status than that to which they had been born. This has consequences for the understanding of world affairs—there was a distinct impression among most of the group that they had reflected on history over their lifetimes. All had traveled outside Australia.

The second cohort was a more typical Australian middle-class grouping with a mix of tertiary and secondary qualifications. There were distinctly mixed political affiliations and, while all had left Australia on occasion, there was none of the sense of reevaluation of their experience that was found in the older cohort. This may be a function of age; certainly the younger group was strikingly unreflective and local in their perspective, with their major concerns being the local football team. This younger group, it should be noted, was not from a central metropolitan area but from the hills around Adelaide, in a commuter community with some small-scale farming.

The most notable differences in perspective, between their views of themselves as children and their views of both their own parents and their own behavior as parents, related to access and control of the mass media. "Who was allowed to do what" was a question of real concern and interest in each discussion—the parental role as guardian of access to the sources of information was noted in all cases. As is evident from the table, the older cohort had access to newspapers, radios, and in some cases, crystal radio sets. Different families had different regimes or practices surrounding the media. For instance, while one member of the oldest cohort reported that children were never allowed to turn on the radio or read the paper before the father had finished, other members reported being allowed to listen as they chose. Another member explained that the radio access in his paternal home was wired from the grandparents' set next door, and they could only listen if the grandparents' set was turned on. One member of the older cohort, whose mother had died when she was young, reported listening to soaps on the car radio in secret, which was possible because the early car radios were not wired into the ignition switch. There was a general sense in this generation of the iconic importance of the radio—in one family the radio (AWA brand) was set on the mantelpiece in the place of honor; in another it was in the dining room.

The iconic import of the television took over from the radio in the middle (second) cohort. There were intense debates about where it was placed, when watching was allowed, and when it first came to their street. Differences in control persist through the generations, with one member of the 40- to 45-year-old cohort reporting that her parents refused to have a television after their first set broke down; while others had the first set in the street, and watched constantly. This cohort was very dependent on their "trannies" (transistor radios) in their teenage years, carrying them along everywhere they went and changing stations to catch their favorite pop tunes. There appeared to be little attempt by parents to regulate the trannies, although they were strictly forbidden (if ubiquitous) at school.

In the third cohort, the younger generation, there appears to be no real control on their access to the media, or any constraints on its use. In response to a query "Who holds the remote control?" the reply was "I don't know. It's usually lost, but. . . ." The only context in which there were limitations was (again) in school, with mobile phones strictly forbidden, and Internet computer access filtered by the school servers. It is impossible to generalize with such limited data, but it does appear to be the case that the larger the family and the less educated, the less the control, and that the newer media are the most regulated, while the older media have been assimilated.

3. Media Interaction

The physical context of media, along with the content of the media memories themselves, is a factor in its impact. All cohorts talked of the importance of the location and access to the electronic media, and the sense of reverence for the newer equipment. In the senior cohort, although the radio was strictly rationed there is little evidence of regulation of the newspapers, except that no papers were available at boarding school. Each member of the senior group talked with reverence of the radio. Among the middle cohort, the excitement of what was then the new medium—television—is apparent. The physical object dominates in the early memories, particularly for those who had a "television set" before their neighbors. For this generation, radios were first important for children's programs such as the Argonauts on the ABC, and later for contemporary music. There appeared to be unlimited access to radio for this generation. Newspapers and magazines were read when available, but were of little importance until the time of the Vietnam War, when this cohort was leaving school.

The younger cohort treat access to television as a given. Many have a television set in the kitchen and each bedroom, and locate events in terms of where they were watching. For this generation, the media are a seamless web and they are accustomed to switching from one form to another. There was some indication that parents were concerned about use of the Internet for this generation. However, the entire group appeared to have unlimited access to television and radio, and the limited range of newspapers and magazines (generally niche magazines, such as motorbike, fishing, and cooking) that the parents bought.

There is a distinct progression from the senior to the younger cohort in the awareness of the media as mediating experience. While the older generation later became aware of censorship during the war, and those who were fighting realized how little they knew, in general, they trusted the media. One woman was first disillusioned about the radio reporting of test cricket during the focus group:

Hilda:	. . . the main thing I remember about the wireless was the test cricket from England.
Eva:	Oh, yes!
James:	All the kids from school would sit up until all hours, depending on the attitude of the parents. And I'm not sure whether we were really listening to a direct broadcast or whether—
Hilda:	No, we weren't. We weren't. They used to knock a pencil on the table for the ball hitting the bat and they had cables coming through, I think.
Hilda:	They reconstructed it and they really made it sound as if they were there. It was very cleverly done.
Eva:	What cheats!
Georgie:	Have you only just found out? (Cohort 1, Australia)

Another example was the advertisements:

Georgie:	I always thought it was the real actresses speaking, you know, saying, "Barbara Stanley uses Lux. 'I always use Lux.'" And I

> thought, "That's Barbara Stanley." I took years before I realized that it was not her at all. (Cohort 1, Australia)

The Vietnam generation is generally far more suspicious of the media, and was more questioning during that time. Throughout the discussion, mention is made of press stereotypes:

> Ric: Well, there has always been that type of stereotyping, if you look back on that, I mean the minute you have a Muslim, they're typically, you know, they're a freedom fighter, so we can say they are an extremist. (Cohort 2, Australia)

There is a constant sense of the fact of mediation:

> Meg: I suppose maybe television was still developing at that stage and still working out its news coverage, you know, and its use of images, its control of images. . . . Newspapers had been at it a lot longer . . . (Cohort 2, Australia)

The younger generation has a wholesale cynicism about all media product. The availability of news is taken for granted, but not given any importance:

> Beth: I listen to the radio all the time.
> Interviewer: So, you get news that way?
> Beth: Yep.
> Interviewer: On the hour or half hour or whatever?
> Beth: Yep.
> Interviewer: And what do you listen to?
> Beth: Triple J.
> Interviewer: They do news every . . .
> Beth: Every hour.
> Interviewer: Every hour. How long? A couple of minutes?
> Beth: Three to five minutes, I suppose. (Cohort 3, Australia)

When they listen to the news, they take it very lightly. At the same time, they question the reliability of the sources. When talking of the O.J. Simpson case, they are dismissive of the media, of O.J.'s innocence, and of the process of the media blitz. What is notable, however, is that cynicism about the media has not led them to question or investigate any issues more deeply through other sources. One has the impression that the cynicism about the media is itself picked up from the media's self-criticism, rather than derived from any examination of different media sources, or of more direct forms of evidence.

4. Media Memories, Prompted and Unprompted

Group dynamics make an enormous difference in the process of gathering unprompted memories. The older Australian cohort knew each other well and the members were very relaxed with each other. They were happy to allow their memories to expand, and would comment and add to remarks made by others. At the other extreme, the group of youngsters, while friends, seemed intent on impressing each other with their cool assumption of ignorance, rather than in remembering itself. Between the two, the middle cohort, who did not know each other before the focus group, trod warily. They were wondering about the political orientation of others in the group, and were perhaps concerned not to betray too much ignorance. Thus the understanding of this data must be put in context: the unprompted memories were memories that members of the group were prepared to admit to in company; the recognition of prompted events may have been a matter of persuasive definition.

There is a striking fact across the generations that several unprompted media memories were of events as they were reported through the older media. The most vivid memories of the major events for the older cohort were pictorial images. For instance, the entire group recalled a range of newspaper images, from the Second World War.

> Oh, I can remember a picture on the front page of the *Advertiser* that I have never forgotten. It was a picture of an Australian airman with his hands tied behind his back, who was beheaded by the Japanese. (Hilda, Cohort 1, Australia)

For this generation, media events were, when remembered, very explicit and highly detailed. They remember dates of attacks in the war, the setting of newsreels, and even particular forms of words used when King Edward abdicated.

> Don't you remember that speech on the radio, I don't know how we heard, how we came to hear that, and he ends up, "I'm prepared to give everything up for the woman I love," and I thought, "Ahhh." (Georgie, Cohort 1, Australia)

On the other hand, the group needed to be prompted on certain events. They explained that they had learned of certain events well after they had occurred—Kristallnacht in Germany, for instance, and the Salt March in India. Films and books clearly played a major role in filling in details of events, even those such as the attack on Pearl Harbor, which were remembered directly as well.

Undoubtedly the strength and force of the wartime memories of this cohort is a consequence of the immense importance of the war for the generation. Their friends died, they fought, and wartime censorship led to a remarkably uniform diet of news. But the consequence was a group with a definite, if somewhat biased, view of the international situation of the time. This group also had a notably uniform set of spontaneously recalled events—certain radio programs, such as *Fred and Maggie,* soap operas, sport matches, the death of King George ("The paper had a black border"), and ABC concerts. As they talked, a wealth of circumstantial details came out about who had known whom, and so on. There is real evidence of a common and mutually assumed media environment.

The middle cohort's memories were much less explicit, less detailed, and with a far wider range of sources. Nearly all the group was aware of the 1968 student revolutions, but while some recalled the image of the shooting at Kent State in a magazine, and others mentioned television coverage of events in Paris, yet others talked of student protests in Japan.[3] There was much less collective memory of the specified events: just one member had detailed memories of the photos of Mars, and only two of Prague Spring. Knowledge about protest movements in Africa, the PLO, and the Cultural Revolution in China was strikingly imprecise, and reinforced by films and later images.

However, at the same time, the group had very precise joint reactions to Woodstock, Watergate ("The Tricky Dickie masks!"), and a memory of the press dealing with the OPEC crisis. Most notable of all was the collective memory of images from Vietnam. Again, these memories were typically of newspaper images, which is the older technology:

Mat:	I can remember quite a few from the Vietnam War, but not only the war but also the anti-war protests in North America, the Kent State University things. Those images are very strong.
Interviewer:	Can you remember the context of that memory, I mean, where you saw them?
Mat:	—the napalm.
Ric:	The napalm.
Unidentified:	Yeah, the napalm kid. Yeah. (Cohort 2, Australia)

The middle cohort also had an amazingly strong set of collective memories of early television and the radio of their youth. They all recalled watching the man walking on the moon on television, however fuzzy the reception:

Ric:	The shoe box in the middle of the road. Two hours of "Khshshshshshshsh." The reception was really awful! [laughter] "And there's the man! He's stepping down!"
Anna:	It was awful: just this blurry white figure that you could hardly see and had to think this is the man on the moon.
Unidentified:	We were all dragged into the school hall. (Cohort 2, Australia)

Each person knew where he or she was for the death of John F. Kennedy. The common culture of this generation consisted of rock music and the perennial interest of challenges to traditional sexual morals.

The younger cohort takes this trajectory further, with no collective knowledge of events except for that of the global soap operas of President Clinton's sex life, O.J.'s trial, and Princess Diana's death (cf. Barnhurst and Wartella 1998; Bourdon, 1992). On those three issues they are unsure about the source of their knowledge, but are quite aware of the media blitz. One says, talking of news:

> You don't, you don't hear it like the first time it comes on, you sort of, it keeps coming on and how it's like full on and you sort of ask what's happened and you know when did this happen sort of thing. You hear about it after . . . (Jill, Cohort 3, Australia)

They are also quite remarkably judgmental about those events they had heard of, whether because of the increasing power of the moral opinion makers on television, or because they felt so familiar and at home with the events, that they felt they had a right to judge.

On the other hand, they had only a vague idea about the ending of Apartheid in South Africa. One girl had a rough idea of who Nelson Mandela is ("Like a prime minister?"). None could discuss the 1989 change of power in the Eastern Block. This may be because the members of the cohort were in the younger bracket of the age group, but when asked:

Interviewer:	Do any of you remember? Do you know what the Cold War was?

The reply—not just a joke—came quickly.

John:	Was it cold? (Cohort 3, Australia)

The reunification of Germany they knew of simply as the basis of a pop song:

Jill:	That one that goes, "Break Down the Wall." [laughter]
Beth:	Peak Boy?
Jill:	I got it. (Cohort 3, Australia)

The Gulf War and the Beijing massacre they knew of in only the most vague terms, and nothing at all about the European monetary union. They were aware of the economic crisis in Asia, but again with very little detailed knowledge.

They did mention three issues on which they were collectively well informed: the local sporting events, especially a Grand Final, the death of Ayrton Senna, and the career of an Australian financial wizard who had embezzled money and then left the country. As a group they seemed surprised to imagine that there were things, other than sport and the global soap operas, about which they might all be informed. This may be a consequence of the increasing volume and the variety of sources of information. This particular group was also clearly and unusually focused on sporting events. But it would, I think, be fair to characterize the group as one with a very high level of knowledge about what would once have been called "private" international happenings, and very little on any of the major "public" events of their era.

Within the Australian context, all of the international media events mentioned were known about indirectly through the media. For each generation, it is evident that mediated memories are reinforced by later reconstructions, fictional, historical, or even musical. This is to say that there is a high degree of intertextuality in the mediated memories. Except for certain media events recalled by the senior cohort, most prompted memories elicited a range of media sources. Even within the senior cohort, the reinforcing effect of movies, reproductions of newspaper images, and repetitions of those images in the historical summaries, was evident. Movies, books, and (notably) songs have a major role in memory. Among the senior cohort, we find the war in Abyssinia recalled by a schoolyard ditty:

Georgie:	I remember the Abyssinian war.
Eva:	And the rude songs they used to sing about it in the schoolyards. [laughter]
Interviewer:	What were they? Come on, sing!
Eva:	Oh . . . I don't know (laugh). What was that Abyssinian song?
Georgie:	Abyssinian became the thing about, "I'll be seeing you." It became, "A be seein' ya!"

For the middle cohort, songs were the major memories of Woodstock, and indeed, snippets of the songs of the 70s came up throughout the interview.

Images have a central role in organizing the memories of the two older cohorts, although they appear to play a much lesser role with the younger group. It is not surprising that particular images, many of which have been often repeated, have such an impact. It is striking, however, how strong the emotional impact of certain images was:

Eva:	We did have those pictures, of course, but they weren't immediate, of course.
Interviewer:	What pictures?
Eva:	That man having his head chopped off, and um er, the men walking-stick-thin building that bridge, you know.
Hilda:	Oh, and the other one—
Georgie:	The bridge of the River Kwai.
Hilda:	The one in New Guinea.
	The Burma railway.
	The Kokoda trail.
Hilda:	Of the Kokoda trail. There was the picture of the Australian serviceman . . .
Georgie:	You know that marvelous fuzzy-wuzzy angel helping
Hilda:	Yes.
Georgie	With mud up to their knees. (Cohort 1, Australia)

That is true, too, of the image of the young girl in Vietnam, whom all of the middle generation recalled, running naked and screaming while covered in napalm. Such iconic images were not mentioned by the younger group: perhaps because of the saturation with images that television offers, which blunts the emotional impact; perhaps because with digital enhancement, the young have grown as suspicious of the veracity of pictures as they are of words.

One other element of this reinforcement of memories is worth noting. As soon as any of the generations began to be precise about the context of their media knowledge, they mentioned talking to people about the events, either directly or by phone. So in the senior cohort, we find:

Well, I was in the RAF at that time and we got a false alarm at the end of the war, when the first bomb was dropped and then I remember that night early hours of the morning, I rang Eva's home. Eva's father answered the telephone and we said, "The war's over. They've dropped an atom bomb. The war's over." He wasn't at all interested because it was about 3 A.M. (Donald, Cohort 1, Australia)

In the younger cohort we find a similar reaction to the news of Princess Diana's death:

. . . then Mum walked in and I told her and she was like, "well," 'cause no one had heard and I rang up Michael and told him 'cause his Dad is um, like . . . English. (John, Cohort 1, Australia)

Talking to and with people about events is a major part of the process of incorporating them as memories, however mediated the events may be.

5. Media Generations in Australia

There is very clear evidence of a change in the conventions and patterns of family regulation of the media, even within a context where different families of each cohort had very different regulatory regimes. It is apparent that as new media become familiar, and the fear of consequences of excessive use became less daunting, parental regulation weakens. There is very little evidence in the Australian study of any control of newspaper access in the senior group, radio use in the middle cohort, or of television use in the younger cohort. At its introduction, however, the new media were strictly controlled.

At the introduction of any new media, the machinery that delivers the service has an iconic status. Radiograms had brand names, shapes, and significance for the senior cohort; television sets were important items of furniture and status symbols for the middle generation; whereas for the younger generation, possession of a television is assumed. High-tech computers have the role of high-status items, to some extent, for the younger generation. The iconic status of the apparatus brings with it an associated set of rituals—rituals that familiarity diminishes—and parental control.

The increasing availability of a variety of media sources has also had clear consequences. The older generation has a clearly defined common knowledge of the mediated events of their youth. The collectivity is evident in their ability to discuss particular pictorial images, date events in the war in Europe, sing songs in common, and review the play of a cricket match of fifty years ago. The sources of knowledge for the older generation were the same; the attitudes that informed their interpretation were also broadly uniform. During the war years they were all nationalistic. Until well after the war, most of Australia was Royalist, Anglo Celtic, and Christian. There was a common culture.

The next (middle) generation had more sources of information, and sources that were much more direct. They did not have to wait for international news while it passed through telegraph lines and censorship, and they had access to a variety of sources. In terms of the collective memories, this has the consequence that there were less common images, less common knowledge. The division in attitude toward the Vietnam War also meant less commonality in interpretation. Some of the group were silent on issues such as the Vietnam demonstrations, presumably because they did not share the strong feelings of others.

However, at the same time, the group shared a repertoire of marker events: pop shows, seeing the man on the moon, the Beatles, Woodstock, Vietnam images, and so on. They could sing the ads of their youth, and the music that introduced the ABC news, recite the formulaic openings of programs, especially the news. News events were seen on one of two television channels—newsreaders were known and revered across the major cities. The common culture of television and radio was evident.

By the nineties, this common culture has evaporated. The beginning of pay television in Australia, delayed until the mid-1990s, coincided with the proliferation of Internet news access. Television programs, songs, and even ads last for a shorter time and are not as generally known as they used to be. Kids phase in and out of programs, depending on their peer groups, and the extent of choice means they have little collective knowledge. Common knowledge about international affairs is limited to *sexual* affairs, in particular those of Princess Diana, Clinton, and O.J.

The pattern of use of the media has also developed, with the younger cohort far more likely to channel surf, and pick what they want from the media, rather than listen or watch attentively. This may not mean that the younger group are less intelligent about the media than their older peers. As Rushkoff puts it:

> The "well-behaved" viewer, who always listens quietly, never talks back to the screen, and never changes channels, is learning *what* to think and losing his own grasp on *how* to think . . . the viewing style of our children is actually more adult. (1997: 49)

Whether or not we accept this view, it is apparent that, while at a superficial level the young appear to have access to a wide range of information, they have far less detailed knowledge of the major international events of their time than either of the two older groups. The senior Australian cohort, who were teenagers through the war years, are, naturally, very well informed about the events of the war. Moreover, they, like the middle group, have had time to reappraise the experiences of their youth, and thereby learn more about events. Nevertheless it is correct to say that new forms of access to information have correlated with less-detailed global knowledge.

"Media relativism" is the thesis that some aspect of human knowledge is relative to the media. Versions of media relativism can be found throughout literature on the media. Eisenstein (1983) developed a sophisticated version of media relativism about print; McLuhan (1964, 1967) talked of radio and television; and Meyrowitz (1985) and Turkle (1995) carefully articulated a view that deals with the Internet in media-relativist terms. Here I do not attempt to chart the literature on media relativism, but to articulate those theses in terms of the global media generations' data.

There are at least three different versions of media-relativist theses that we can derive from the material above. First, it is apparent that the media that are available to us, as much as the content those media represent, have an effect on the ways we perceive events and the fashion in which we remember them. It suggests that how we find out about events is relative to the media and will inevitably color the way we recall them. This is a relativist thesis, if of an anodyne sort. It does not imply that we are limited to the view presented by one form of media. When, as is often the case, we have multiple sources of knowledge, we have multiple colorings. Nevertheless, a variety of ways of seeing an event is still not God's-eye objectivity, of the sort that the non-relativist might aspire to. It is instead a multi-mediated view. As long as the multiple media represent a variety of approaches, seeing events several ways rather than just one is likely to be less biased. This much is, I take it, uncontroversial.

When we speak of the effect of media on the generations, we might propose two versions of a much stronger relativist thesis about the media and knowledge of the world. The weaker claim, which is the assumption of this project, is that as the new media globalize and offer an increasingly homogeneous product to the youth of the entire world, so will the knowledge and memories of the generations grow increasingly similar, particularly with respect to global issues. That thesis awaits comparative analysis. However, the Australian study reminds us that the history of a nation also has an important impact on the global knowledge. Knowledge is relative not just to what we hear in the media but also to the importance of those events in the local context, and the personal impact they may have. Australia fought in World War II and friends and relations of those in the focus group died. They had a strong and personal set of memories of the global events of the time, however difficult access to information was. On the other hand, the major global conflicts and changes of the last ten years have hardly affected Australia. The younger generation, while well informed about global soap operas, was little interested in other major international events, at least until September 11, 2001.[4]

The stronger claim is the view that the media available to us structure our knowledge and understanding of the world. According to this view,[5] the availability of certain media determines the possibility of certain types of intellectual movements. Print, for instance, is claimed to be uniquely suited to logical "linear" thought, while television is emotional and "saturated." Radio lies between the two, with its disembodied voices calling for a certain level of ratiocination. A consequence of this view would be that we should expect a print and radio generation to have more detailed linear knowledge of events than a television or Internet generation. Our evidence does appear to support such a consequence. However, empirical evidence in support of these relativist claims is very difficult to assess, since it requires a stringent understanding of the ways in which people think. The Australian evidence suggests that the first print-to-radio generation, with its command of detail and dates, was more logical than the more impressionistic and visual young. A defense of that argument, however, would require a far broader study, and a more precise definition of ways of thinking, than is possible here.

Bibliography

Barnhurst, K.G., and E. Wartella (1998). "Young Citizens, American TV Broadcast and the Collective Memory." *Critical Studies in Mass Communication* 15: 279–305.

Bourdon, J. (1992). "Television and Political Memory." *Media, Culture and Society* 14: 541–560.

Eisenstein, E. (1983). *The Printing Revolution in Early Modern Europe.* Cambridge, MA: Cambridge University Press.

McLuhan, M. (1964). *Understanding Media: The Extensions of Man.* London: Routledge & Kegan Paul.

McLuhan, M., and Q. Fiore (1967). *The Medium Is the Message.* Harmondsworth, England: Penguin Books.

Meyrowitz, J. (1985). *No Sense of Place: The Impact of Electronic Media on Social Behavior.* New York: Oxford University Press.

Miller, T. (1997). "Radio." In *The Media in Australia: Industries, Texts, Audiences,* eds. S. Cunningham and G. Turner, 47–69. Sydney: Allen & Unwin.

Poster, M. (1994). "The Mode of Information and Post-Modernity." In *Communication Theory Today,* ed. D. Crowley and D. Mitchell, 173–192. Cambridge: Polity.

Postman, N. (1985). *Amusing Ourselves to Death: Public Discourse in the Age of Show Business.* New York: Penguin.

Postman, N. (1993). *Technopoly.* New York: Penguin.

Rushkoff, D. (1997). *Children of Chaos:* Surviving the End of the World as We Know It. Flamingo, New York: Flamingo.

Turkle, S. (1995). *Life on the Screen.* New York: Simon & Schuster.

Theo Hug

1. Austrian Media Context

The history of Austrian media has been similar to other industrial nations in Europe. Daily newspapers were already being circulated during imperial rule (1804–1918) and the first radio programs were aired in 1923. The public interest in these test broadcastings was tremendous. It is therefore not surprising that in 1924 approximately 11,000 radios were already registered.

In the same year, RAVAG,[1] the Austrian radio company, was founded. At first, RAVAG's broadcastings consisted mainly of music, literature, and scientific contributions. Later, the first news programs were introduced. RAVAG considered itself to be politically neutral until 1933. In 1934, the station was taken over by the National Socialists in a coup. Even though this first worldwide radio putsch failed, the station was soon afterward incorporated into the German Reich's radio broadcasting company (German Austrian Radio) in 1938, the same year the German troops invaded Austria.

In 1939, the German Reich's radio broadcasting company took control of all Austrian radio stations and launched an all-Austrian "Reich

Program" network. Each affiliated station was only permitted to overlook the music and foreign-language broadcastings for the bordering regions of southeastern Europe. Nevertheless, every important operational area was managed from Berlin. National socialist talks and reports were broadcast for hours and hours. In addition, collective reception was ordered to occur in schools and public offices. Also, companies and restaurants were forced to enable collective listening to programs relating to national policy. Law forbade listening to foreign stations, especially to BBC programming.

After the end of World War II, four broadcast groups were established, according to the four occupied zones.[2] Between 1946 and 1949, censorship of the radio was obligatory. Radio stations finally became at least partially independent at the end of the fifties. At that time, FM transmitters were introduced. With the signing of the Austrian State Treaty (in May 1955), the stations became property of the Austrian nation. In the same year, the Transport Ministry passed a broadcast law, which provided for a national public-broadcasting monopoly by the Austrian Broadcasting Corporation (ORF).

The ORF launched its radio and television broadcasting operations at the beginning of 1958.[3] During the initial years, the number of television licenses doubled annually. At the beginning of 1963, 400,000 TV sets were registered. Austria's independent press called for the first petition of referendum in July 1964. More than 832,000 Austrians signed the petition and demanded the abolition of political-party control of the ORF. A new broadcasting law came into force at the beginning of 1967. It provided for ORF's total autonomy in program, financial, and personal matters, as well as for an independent director. Within the last twenty-five years, however, the national monopoly of the ORF has been challenged by the in-flow of foreign television programs via cable and satellite platforms.

The first cable-TV companies were established in 1975. In 1990, when 95 percent of Austrian households were able to receive ORF's two television channels, the first satellite dishes appeared. Already in 1994, more than 61 percent of all license holders subscribed to cable systems and received satellite programs.

The new multimedia trends have only been of importance in recent times. In 1999, around 33 percent of the population (2,250,000 people) used the Internet at least occasionally; 22 percent had access from their homes, although 51 percent of all households owned a personal computer (23 percent had a telephone/modem connection). In 2002, about 1.6 million households (of 3.45 million) had access to the Internet (Fachverband der Telekommunikations und Rundfunkunternehmungen, 2002, p. 3).[4]

2. Perception of Media Environments

The Austrian study was conducted in Innsbruck, which is an alpine city with roughly 130,000 inhabitants.[5] At the beginning of the focus-group discussions, the groups were rather chairman oriented. One of the possible reasons for that is the relatively reserved and cautious style, which seems to be a cultural phenomenon—at least in comparison to southern European countries—and a viable way to deal with new situations for many Austrians. And taking part in a research project was a new situation for all the participants. Furthermore, the questions of media environment and media experiences are not questions that are discussed in public or in the current mass media. And of course, we have to take into account the need for social warming-up phases, too, which might have been rather brief.

Nevertheless, the oldest cohort and the middle cohort revealed a high interest in the project. They made every attempt to answer the questions thoroughly and honestly. Subsequently, the discussion in the oldest cohort (Cohort 1) proceeded calmly and was organized, whereas the discussion in the middle cohort (Cohort 2) turned out to be the liveliest, open-minded, and engaged. In contrast to these, the discussion in the youngest cohort (Cohort 3) can be characterized as a "group interview," because the participants tended to answer questions without elaboration and in quick succession. They did not confer with each other very much, although they had been encouraged to do that.

Oldest Cohort

The question of the individual importance of the media during childhood and youth was answered spontaneously although in different ways:

> Albert: I have to say that I cannot remember any interesting mass medium. There were no mass media. (Cohort 1, page 5, line 286)
>
> Robert: We entertained ourselves [general agreement). (Cohort 1, page 6, line 287)

It seems that respondents had difficulty perceiving media as "mass" media in those days. The relevance and concept of mass media has changed much throughout their life spans. As children, these individuals had access only to the media that was available in their family households. Since most members of this focus group stated that they grew up in low-income households, the number of media was limited. What were remembered are broader details of the media.

One participant remembered a radio station up on a hill; Anna remembered a so-called detector:

Anna: I can remember such a big box, you had to put wires [cables] together. First you heard wauwauuuwaaauuwwaauuu and then there was something to hear. It was very exciting for us children. (Cohort 1, page 6, line 325–327)

This machine was very special, not only for children but also for adults, simply because it was the first machine that played music. In ordinary households, it was not common at that time to own a standard radio set. However, some time later a more simplified and affordable radio receiver, called the "Volksempfänger" (popular wireless) became available. Its low price allowed even low-income families to purchase it.

Some participants remember that their radio set had been modified by family members to enable "short circuiting." This term refers to a common practice of technically altering the radio so that short-wave programs could be received. However, this practice was considered by the government to be illegal. It was, indeed, prohibited during World War II, because it allowed one to listen to foreign "enemy" radio programs. Nevertheless, a lot of people risked the heavy penalty and listened to these foreign stations, as did, for example, Anna's family.

Middle Cohort

In this cohort, the radio sets (stationary as well as portable) and newspapers were the most important media of their media equipment during childhood and youth (in this focus group, only two families owned a television set).

Radio was the newest mass medium during their teens. However, parents limited the listening time for children and even selected radio programs for their children. Other participants were allowed to listen to radio whenever they wanted.

Maria describes her limited access to the radio: she was only allowed to turn the buttons of the radio—it was her mother who decided on the program. Other radio-related memory is quite vivid, even in details:

Maria: Well, I remember it quite well, especially the first ten years we had a wireless [Volksempfänger] in the kitchen and later my

mother was given a radio in a box and that one was always
making funny noises. (Cohort 2, page 4, line 191–193)

Furthermore, the difference between the "popular wireless" and new models seemed to be important:

Beate: Yes, but not an ordinary wireless, we had one of those modern
                  shiny radios (laughs). (Cohort 2, page 4, line 233)

Television spread in the late sixties and early to mid-seventies. The two
individuals of the focus group who had access to a television set at home were
only permitted to watch certain shows, for instance *Kasperle* (similar to *Punch
and Judy*), U.S. productions such as *Lassie* and *Fury*, and some sport shows:

Markus: . . . in this sense we had no access to television. It was the same
                  in all families. Watching TV in the evening was an exception
                  and at 8:15 we had to go to bed (general agreement). (Cohort 2,
                  page 6, line 320–322)

Watching TV in the evening was only permitted on special occasions. The
relevance of television and the desire to use this new medium is represented in one individual's remark, who stated that he, not being formally
allowed to watch, made attempts to grasp images of a prime-time show
through the keyhole of the living-room door.

Youngest Cohort

In the youngest cohort, the most important medium in the first ten years
was television. Children's books and audiotapes were also of some significance. In the later childhood, reading gained increasing relevance.

Audiotape recorders mainly were used to listen to children's chants and
fairy tales, almost replacing family members, "since parents or older brothers
and sisters could not always read out stories" (Cohort 3, line 106 f).

The radio, however, is only remembered in connection with the radio
show *Traummännlein*. It was a kind of everyday checkpoint for them in the
sense of a ritual before going to sleep. Otherwise they were not interested in
the radio, because—as one participant put it—typically, somebody was just
talking on the radio and little children are not able to understand that. Later
on, the radio was of relative interest as a source of information. TV was much
more important for them, and only one individual mentioned the computer
as the most important medium. This was in 1999, but due to the widespread

access to the Internet the importance of the use of computers for different purposes has changed for the juvenile in the meanwhile.

Media and media interaction provide co-orientation rituals within the social context of the family. The use of media within the family context requires rules of organization, action patterns, status, and control. Although participants of this youngest cohort had limited access to television during their childhood and early-youth years, they created patterns of family co-orientation to increase their limited TV consumption:

> Christa: Yes, when the parents watched TV, you join in, because you have nothing better to do, and then you watch a bit with them and then you get a bit more [knowledge]. Then you watch more often together with them and you begin to read newspapers and you take a look at them if you are interested in something special, and it happens to be more often. You watch it on your own. (Cohort 3, page 4, line 144 ff)

Another individual described her situation in a different way: her two younger sisters were in a way "forced" to read the magazines she owned. They, too, had to listen to the radio program as she did (cf. page 4, line 156). Her younger sisters were allowed to watch television with her in the afternoons as well as evenings.

Paul remembers comparable circumstances:

> Paul: My situation was right the opposite. Every time they did something, I joined in. The longer they watched TV, I attended too, until I was kicked out some times. You just do what the others do. (Cohort 3, page 4, line 161 ff)

Asked who kicked him out, Paul answered, "Yes, the parents" (Cohort 3, page 4, line 165).

Bernd also remembers family situations like this:

> Bernd: My situation was similar to Paul's situation. I remember watching *X-Large* together with my brother, when I was three or four years old, which is not so good at that age. (Cohort 3, page 4, line 166 f)

Another individual, Beatrix, perceived her siblings' media use as less problematic, due to the small age difference between herself and her siblings.

Beatrix : Yes, my siblings' [ages] are not far from each other—about a year or so—and therefore it was not a big problem, when one joined in watching. So, when my sister came along and joined in, that was totally the same. (Cohort 3, page 4, line 169 f)

The process from strict regulation to more and more self-determination and self-organization is not only a question of media socialization. It also seems to be a question of generational-specific learning (Titze, 2000), which is based on historical processes of turnovers of generations. This type of learning does not refer to intentional or informal learning processes in the courses of the lives of individuals; it rather refers to corresponding effects of emergence, to structural changes, contexts of experiences and lifeworlds, and to regulated inter exchanges of all sorts of accomplishments in institutions. In this sense, being part of the younger generation means experiencing the lifeworld as media world.

The juvenile participants reflected media equipment as personal property (the stereo belongs to himself or to herself). When members of the oldest cohort, however, mentioned their "own" equipment, they meant that the whole family possessed a wireless or a TV set. It seems to be more important for the younger generation to individually own media equipment than share with their family. Besides the self-control of access, the control of the access of others—especially the family members—and the power to freely use media, is important.

The members of Cohort 3 do not notice any deficiency in the variety of media access and programs they are exposed to. Members of Cohort 1 and 2 claim that the young generation today does not have the experience of media-related community that they themselves had.

3. Media Interaction and Marker Tags of Meaning

The importance of face-to-face communication has been emphasized in all three cohorts. More than that, face-to-face communication seemed to be most important regardless of the media involved. Remarkably, all the associated arguments, which were articulated in the focus-group discussions, are characterized by one distinction: they follow the pattern of "natural communication as it is" versus "media-influenced communication." The question of where the concept of "natural communication" might come from was not discussed. It was taken for granted in a typical manner of everyday theory, and not scrutinized in terms of mediated conceivability or cultural aspects of concepts of nature. It seemed that nobody had ever experienced serious irritations in the context of "facts and fiction" or "reality and virtuality." The often-quoted college student who took part in Sherry Turkle's study and who once said, "RL [real life] is just one more window, and it's usually not my best one" (Turkle, 1995, p. 16) would have had great difficulty trying to explain what he is talking about to participants in these focus groups.

Oldest Cohort

In the oldest cohort, the relationship between financial conditions and personal relations was emphasized. All participants claimed that poverty enhances human relations. Another argument was that neighborhood and community experiences brought people closer together because there was no distraction by the mass media, as appears to be the case today. Information was shared by means of face-to-face interaction:

Anna: Yes, it was very interesting, because we were all poor then. And it was not important for us children whether we wore shoes or not. (Cohort 1, page 2, line 97–98)

Anna: If something was shared in the family, then it was automatically shared in the neighborhood too, because we were all part of the same community. (Cohort 1, page 2, line 102–103)

The discussion of this cohort revealed a very critical view on the current media. Media are perceived as a cause for specific problems within society at large:

Sabine: The root of all evil, which makes everything sick, is ungodliness and the turning away from the Ten Commandments of God. (Cohort 1, page 15, line 787–788)

This sentence expresses a strong religious orientation, which describes the Ten Commandments of the Christian religion as an indispensable guide for personal and social development. Simultaneously, this sentence served as a universal explanation for today's problems. It was supported through the following statements:

Bernd: The negative phenomena, which are complained about today, are traced back to the lost old standards, which were thrown overboard. (Cohort 1, page 15, line 809–811)

Bernd: This falling away of the standards has naturally a huge loss of social security as a consequence, the closer standards are, the safer I feel. (Cohort 1, page 15, line 814–816)

These statements were held with conviction and general validity. They faulted the current rank of faith and the church, which in their view could not be compared with the rank and meaning in earlier times.

Middle Cohort

Members of the middle cohort recalled local dimensions of the media, such as an earthquake, a church weekly, and discussions in the youth center of Sigmund Kripp, and national dimensions such as TV shows with Peter Alexander or *Familie Leitner*. The participants of this discussion had very specific and vivid memories. The most important radio programs were *Autofahrer Unterwegs* and the *Totzenhacker*.[6] They remember that *Totzenhacker* conveyed a feeling of being part of a larger social network. To listen to the program meant to take part in social life.

It was not only the content of the television programs that is remembered; issues of the unstable technical equipment were raised. One participant remembered the constant danger of lightning hitting a television antenna during a thunderstorm. Whenever there was a thunderstorm, radio and TV sets were unplugged to avoid damage. Technical appliances sometimes have been handled as if they were "sacred relics." This treatment of media as something quasi-religious placed the media equipment and the handling of it rather high in the symbolic order (see also the comment on media being put in shrines in the chapter on Japan by Reiko Sekiguchi). TV had an especially high symbolic value. This can be seen in the fact that some families who were not very affluent and who hadn't much money, purchased a TV set before they bought a refrigerator. Although these actions may seem very irrational to us, they underline the importance and placement in the symbolic order of the society.

Youngest Cohort

In this youngest cohort, the discussion was dominated by short responses. Memories became vivid and elaborate, however, when the issues of the fall of the Berlin Wall and the deaths of Princess Diana and Mother Theresa were raised (Cohort 3, page 9, line 361 ff).

Beatrix: Yes, the cases of Diana and Mother Theresa, I was shocked a little bit, because I've heard of it when I was on vacation . . . at first I couldn't believe it. Then I read it in the newspaper and I thought: Is that possible overnight? I was totally shocked, because so many famous people died at once [general agreement]. (Cohort 3, page 9, line 391 ff)

The participants remembered that these issues have been discussed among friends and family and in school. During the group discussion they compared meanings of the deaths:

Beatrix:	Yes, the story with Diana . . . she still is admired in London . . . also on pictures. In school we have talked about it and also have seen a film. You have heard a lot. (Cohort 3, page 9, line 397 ff)
Christa:	. . . there was much more fuss about Diana than about Mother Theresa. I cannot understand that, because Mother Theresa was at least as important, even more important. (Cohort 3, page 9, line 399 ff)
Anton:	Yes, the difference is that Mother Theresa simply died, and in the case of Diana it was an accident. (Cohort 3, page 9, line 402 f)
Christa:	OK, yes, that is true, all the circumstances, because about Diana you heard all the time, all the time—on the radio, on TV, in the newspapers—during the first year after her death. In the case of Mother Theresa it's just one year ago she died and that's it. (Cohort 3, page 9, line 404 ff)
Nora:	Yes, that's gone without a trace. (Cohort 3, page 9, line 407)
Christa:	Yes, and that is something I don't understand. (Cohort 3, page 9, line 408)

In the previous quotes, it becomes clear that there is a conflict in attaching meaning. With reference to implicit criteria of importance, the death of Mother Theresa should be as relevant as the death of Princess Diana. But that was not the case, whether in the public reports or in the subjective experience of the juveniles. Furthermore, Nora (with reference to the intensive reporting) remarked the following about the question of meaning: "It's as if you would know somebody personally" (Cohort 1, page 11, line 455).

4. Media Use across Generations and Media Memories

The meaning of the media, but also the use pattern of media, is specific in each of the three generations.

Oldest Cohort

The reason why radio represented a special medium in this cohort can be ascribed to the fact that radio was a new, and therefore attractive, medium during their childhood and youth years. Newspapers and books were already conventional elements of the media environment in this cohort. Radio had been associated with news and music programs. Especially during the time before World War II started, people received most of their political information from the radio. The declaration of World War II was *the* non-prompted event that was discussed with high involvement and in detail.

Most of the members of the cohort group bought the newspaper regularly or when they had enough money. Children used the infrastructure of their surroundings in their free time.

Furthermore, a gender-specific media-use pattern already became apparent in this generation:

Sabine: Girls read fairy tales. . . . (Cohort 1, page 10, line 408)

This difference still seemed to be more or less normal to the participants after all the years. In the context of children's books, Karl May, Jules Verne, and Wilhelm Busch were mentioned.

Spontaneous memories referred mainly to political events such as the radio reports in general and the death of Federal Chancellor Engelbert Dollfuss (1892–1934), the talk "Gott schütze Österreich" of Federal Chancellor Kurt Schuschnigg (1897–1977) shortly before the annexation to the German Reich, and also the bomb attack on Hitler.

With respect to the prompted events, the participants talked with comparatively low collective involvement about the war in Spain and the Berlin Olympics. In contrast, when, after prompting, Reichskristallnacht, Auschwitz, Pearl Harbor, Nagasaki, and Hiroshima were discussed, the discussion was characterized by high involvement on the level of individual statements as well as on the collective level. The source of knowledge was in all cases personal communication and family radio, or collective reception of radio programs related to national policy.

Middle Cohort

The newest and most important mass medium for this generation was the radio. Their families owned one or two radios. Parents limited and selected radio programs for their children. Only some of the participants were allowed to listen to the radio whenever they wanted. Most of them did not have access to TV programs in their early childhood, but they were able to recall special radio programs easily:

Maria: . . . at six o clock, we always listened to *Wer ist der Täter*, a crime series. . . . I always had to listen to *Wer ist der Täter* with my mother. At exact seven o'clock we listened to *Traummännlein*. (Cohort 2, page 4, line 197–200)

Maria: . . . I was fond of listening to that program after coming home from elementary school and secondary modern school. (Cohort 2, page 4, line 226–227)

Markus: . . . in this sense we had no access to television. It was the same in all families. Watching TV in the evening was an exception and at 8:15 we had go to bed [general agreement]. That was right in this way. (Cohort 2, page 6, line 320–322)

One participant, who had limited access to television and who was free to listen to the radio, pointed out that he and his sister "didn't go too far in the use of the radio" (Cohort 2, page 8, line 423–424).

Spontaneous memories referred to *Traummännlein* (a special radio broadcast for kids), TV commercials, and TV broadcasts like *Familie Leitner, Lassie,* or *Einer wird gewinnen, Kasperle, Mickey Mouse,* and the Olympic Winter Games in Innsbruck (1964 and 1976). Furthermore, they made comments on Prague Spring, the moon landing (Apollo 11), the Apollo 13 accident, and (after prompting) Woodstock and Watergate. In spite of prompting, and mainly because they were too busy talking about the other events and topics, the participants didn't make comments on events such as the rise of the Palestine Liberation Organization, the war in Vietnam, the cultural revolution in China, the sleeping tablet "Contergan" which caused a medical disaster, hunger in Biafra, the 1968 students revolution, and the OPEC crisis.

Youngest Cohort

It is noticeable that, with the exception of TV, access to other media (books, records, audiotapes) was more or less unlimited. As soon as one was able to handle or purchase the media, one could decide what, when, and how much to consume. There are manifold reasons for that. First of all, the findings of the Austria study confirm the assumption that the newest media are always the most regulated media (see, for example, the chapter on Australia, by Christina Slade). At least on the level of family interaction and education, this seems to be a constant factor across generations and also across countries and continents. Furthermore, there are other relevant factors, such as new concepts of education in general, more tolerant views of bringing up children, new types of family configurations, consequences of neo-liberal tendencies, and economic constraints such as lack of time to take care of what the children are doing:

> Christa:　　Yes, you had been independent, you simply had to take a book and look at it, or so. With TV you had to ask first and the parents didn't like it so much. (Cohort 1, page 3, line 101–102)

Audiotapes and children's books were often chosen and handled without restriction or control by the parents. In comparison, television consumption was more controlled and restricted. Media use is also strongly related to sibling succession. The youngest siblings learned earlier from the older ones, and the older ones referred to parents or friends:

> Nora:　　I can remember, in the beginning I put the tape into the recorder on my own, until my first sister came and then I could read, and then the second sister came, and then one was reading to them and making music and playing with them. The older I got, I always had two younger sisters with whom I played or watched TV. They had started earlier as I did. If I listened to the radio, they had to listen, too. And if I bought booklets, they looked at them, too, even though they were three, respectively, six years younger. They watched TV in the afternoon, and I was allowed to watch TV in the evening and in the afternoon I watched together with them. (Cohort 3, page 4, line 153–159)

Furthermore, to have your own equipment was very important for them.

> Nora:　　Yes, when I was 10, I got my own stereo set. (Cohort 3, page 5, line 195)
>
> Christa:　　I still know when my brother got a TV set, his own. I was jealous, because I wanted to possess also something on my own. (Cohort 3, page 5, line 203–204)

Media ownership seemed to convey an image of less dependency on parents or siblings:

Paul:　　　　Yes, I still know when we got our first computer. A very old one, I was enthusiastic and I watched my brother all the time as he did something. I was very pleased with it until I understood it myself, than I adopted it. That was really an ingenious event. I was in the last class of primary school and I was so happy when we got the computer in the afternoon. Life was beautiful! (Cohort 3, page 5, line 181–186)

He watched his brother handling it and was fascinated without understanding anything. Being there and being allowed to participate in the scene was relevant in this case.

This family factor seemed to be similar with respect to news on TV. Newscasts were watched together with the family and subsequently discussed, inside and outside of the family:

Paul:　　　　I still can remember when the United States took the offensive against Iraq. Because we had watched that all together at home and my brother thought that now the third world war would start. But nobody believed that. (Cohort 3, page 6, line 251–253)

Nora:　　　　I sat down, too, and watched the news, because I wanted to know, what actually was going on; I did that and I also read the newspaper. My parents watched the news every evening and I stayed with them and watched it too. (Cohort 3, page7, line 270–273)

Spontaneous memories were related to the Gulf War (1990–1991); the fall of the Berlin Wall; "Ötzi," who died about 5,000 years ago in the Schnalstaler glaciers; *Traummännlein*, TV broadcasts for children (especially *Mini-Zip*, a kind of TV news for kids), and children's books. After prompting on a list, the participants also made short comments on Nelson Mandela's release, the BSE scandal, the European Monetary Union, O.J. Simpson, President Bill Clinton's sex life, and particularly on the death of Princess Diana and Mother Theresa. In addition, topics like Rodney King, the Exxon Valdez oil spill, Estonia, and the poison-gas assault in Japan (AUM-sect) were prompted, but received no comments.

5. Comment on Generations and Conclusion

Comparing the generations, it can be argued that in all three the role of children's books is quite significant. Even in the youngest, so-called multimedia generation, children's books are an important element in their quite-diversified media world. Other print media, in particular daily newspapers, became more relevant for the participants when they grew older. As soon as it was introduced and widespread, the major medium for the youngest and the middle cohort was, and still is, TV. TV is major as a source of information, but also with regard to the organization of family life and communicative stabilization of peer-group positions.

The transcribed conversation protocols offer a multitude of starting points for theoretical reflections on knowledge. The question of objectivity arose mainly in Cohort 3 (youngest cohort) and partly in Cohort 1 (oldest cohort). The basic idea was that the media could and should be objective:

> Bernd: I think it is important that you get information through different media, because it happens that media are less objective. (Cohort 3, page 12, line 516–517)

In all cohorts, the influence of the media is assumed. Whereas the oldest generation remembers the censorship policies during World War II, the youngest generation reflects this issue based on their experiences with more current information policies and political events.

In comparison to the oldest and middle cohort, the memories of the youngest cohort seem to have a rather vague nature. Whereas in Cohort 1, for example, vagueness could mean that someone could not exactly recall the code name in a report and then connected this with suppression, the memories of Cohort 3 seemed to have, without exception, a rough nature (see especially the findings of the German and the Australian study). Most of the answers were short answers (one sentence) and in the subtext they seemed to tell us "OK, that's it! Why ask for more details? If there is a need to search for details or coherences, one can do it and also find what he or she or needs":

> Nora: If we read it, we will certainly remember it. (Cohort 3, page 7, line 287)

With reference to Princess Diana, she says at another point:

> Nora: Everybody had known her somehow, everybody had known about her. (Cohort 3, page 10, line 426)

This statement also caused general agreement in the group. The "somehow" points to the speculations and sundry aspects in their descriptions.

Memories of personally important events of a local, national, or global nature show varying degrees of fragmentation. Knowledge often has the nature of a sporadic instant knowledge. Implicit structural knowledge, which contains criteria for truth, reality, significance, and so on, most often goes hand in hand with such knowledge of the world.

If we assume that generations have varying global knowledge, and if we further accept that media surroundings are of highest relevance for the generations' feeling of being part of the world, as well as for the corresponding processes of accumulating knowledge, then the following question arises: To what extent can global knowledge be regarded as a variation of instant knowledge (cf. Hug, 1999; Hug & Perger, 2003)? A possible answer is based on the "variations concept" (cf. Goodman, 1983; Goodman & Elgin, 1988). If we focus on the three criteria—context dependency, fragmentation, and claim to explanation—then the global knowledge fragments can be characterized as absolute instant knowledge. Global knowledge fragments are understood in the sense of keywords and stereotypes, which suggests a global timeframe for parallelism of actions and in such a manner produce a frame for the image of a global community:

- As far as the focus "context dependency" is concerned, the difference from the other types of instant knowledge is due to the event semantics, to the social receptive situation, to biographical aspects, and to the specifically cultural differences.
- Concerning the focus "fragmentation," the contrast lies in the mix of global knowledge components and their connection to national and regional aspects.
- And concerning the focus "claim to explanation," a difference can be demonstrated in simplified portrayals with special relative importance to global associations and their integration in everyday theories.

However, this does not yet appear to me to be the answer to everything, since this desired global knowledge can be depicted not only as immediate knowledge, but also as unproblematic applied knowledge. In this sense, it has a higher potential for reflection. As condensed, "sedimentary" knowledge, it can also be described as action-directing background knowledge. Global media generations' global knowledge would then be that section of collective, conceptual assumptions and ideas (Rusch, 1987, p. 243) that is of outstanding importance to certain generations. Let us conceive the "general world knowledge" as being the quintessence of our ideas of the real makeup of the world, of our concepts of objects, situations, events and their consequences; as well as being the quintessence of our ideas about space and time. If we assume this, then the generations' global knowledge exists in those media-delivered, partially synchronized assumptions of reality. Also, culturally specific standardizations characterize the generations' basic feeling of being in the world and the generations' understandings of regularities, as well as their modalities and abilities to differentiate between relevant and nonrelevant events.

Therefore, in the sense of a figure-reason relation, global knowledge can be conceived of in two ways, or, expressed in athletic terms: global knowledge can be considered to be both a "support leg" and a "free leg." The free leg would then be the fragmented instant knowledge of global media events, and the support leg would be the conceptual background knowledge that makes up a generation's thematic and media horizons. This conceptual background knowledge also contains typical ways to establish relations to reality, meanings, and patterns of orientation. This background, or commonsense knowledge (Feilke, 1994), is therefore not to be understood in the sense of a general world knowledge that is true everywhere and at any time for both sexes. It is rather a type of universal knowledge that is based on a relational combination of different perspectives without reference to epistemological "solid groundwork" and without dissolving those perspectives in a free-floating mess of signs.

Bibliography

Fachverband der Telekommunikations und Rundfunkunternehmungen (2002). *Telekom. Der Telekommunikationsmarkt in Zahlen (Österreich und International). (Telecom. The Telecommunications Market Numerical—Austria and Internationally).* http://wko.at/telekom/inter/tk_statistik.pdf [12–20–02].

Fabris, Hans H. and Kurt Luger, eds. (1988). *Medienkultur in Österreich. Film, Fotographie,Fernsehen und Video in der Zweiten Republik. (Media Culture in Austria. Film, Photography, TV and Video during the Second Republic).* Böhlau, Wien [a.o.].

Feilke, Helmuth (1994). *Common sense–Kompetenz. (Common sense Competence).* Frankfurt/M: Suhrkamp.

Geretschläger, Erich (1997). *Mass Media in Austria.* Vienna: Federal Press Service. (See also http://www.austria.gv.at)

Goodman, Nelson (1983). *Ways of Worldmaking.* Indianapolis, IN: Hacket Publishing Co.

Goodman, Nelson and Catherine Z. Elgin. (1988). *Reconceptions in Philosophy and Other Arts and Sciences.* Indianapolis, IN: Hacket Publishing Co.

Günther, Johann, and Clemens Hüffel. (1999). *Die Massenmedien in unserer Gesellschaft. (Mass Media in Our Society).* Zahlen–Daten–Fakten. Krems: Donau-Universität Krems.

Hug, Theo (1999). *Approaches to Instant Knowledge and the New Media Technologies.* http://homepage.uibk.ac.at/~c60357/[12–20–02].

Hug, Theo and Josef Perger, eds. (2003). *Instantwissen, Bricolage, Tacit Knowledge . . . Wissensformen in der westlichen Medienkultur. (Instant Knowledge, Bricolage, Tacit Knowledge . . . Forms of Knowledge in Western Media Culture).* Innsbruck: Studia.

Rusch, Gebhard (1987). Erkenntnis, Wissenschaft, Geschichte. *Von einem konstruktivistischen Standpunkt. (Cognition, Science, History: From a constructivist Viewpoint).* Frankfurt/M: Suhrkamp.

Sieder, Reinhard, Heinz Steinert, and Emerich Tálos, eds. (1995). *Österreich 1945–1995. Gesellschaft–Politik–Kultur. (Society—Politics—Culture).* Wien: Verlag für Gesellschaftskritik.

Titze, Hartmut. (2000). "Wie lernen Generationen?" *(How Do Generations Learn?) Zeitschrift für Erziehungswissenschaft* No. 1, 131–144.

Turkle, Sherry (1995). *Life on the Screen: Identity in the Age of the Internet.* New York: Simon & Schuster.

Jan Jirák

1. Historical Overview

The political, social, and cultural development of the Czech society within the last century is definitely under the strong influence of the geopolitical location of the country.[1] As a "newborn" independent state founded after the First World War, the former Czechoslovakia was a state of two national majorities, the Czechs and the Slovaks. There was a democratic, parliamentary system, but strong national tensions, especially between the Czech majority and the German minority. Historically, the country was divided into two major parts: Bohemia and Moravia on one side, and Slovakia on the other side. One of the crucial forming factors of the Czech society was an intensive national identity with an immense focus upon Czech language, and its specific culture, as fundamental integrating features.

During the late eighteenth and all of the nineteenth century, the "national uprising" formed the self-image of the Czech nation, within the political framework of late Austrian monarchy. Establishing an independent state seemed to be a quite natural culmination of the development of the Czech nation.

In the first period of its existence, from its foundation in 1918 to the forced change of the state border as a consequence of the so-called Munich Treaty in 1938, the Czech nation was a parliamentary democracy dominated by five democratic parties, a strong leftist movement (including a strong Communist Party), and a fairly stable economy, which was weakened during the Depression in the early thirties. During the thirties, the political development in neighboring Germany inspired the German minority in Czechoslovakia, most of whom lived close to the border between Germany and Czechoslovakia. The representatives of this minority expressed a strong will to belong to Germany. The political demands of this minority gave Hitler an excuse to increase pressure on Czechoslovakia as well as on its European allies. In autumn 1938, he succeeded in annexing the areas of Czechoslovakia inhabited by the German minority with Germany. Representatives of Great Britain, France, Italy, and Germany, in the Munich Treaty, confirmed the success of this takeover.

In the period from 1938 to the end of the Second World War in May 1945, the democratic character of the country was weakened at first and then completely suppressed. The country was then split into two parts. Czechoslovakia was forced to surrender all the land inhabited by the German minority to Hitler's Germany. In March 1939, the German Nazi Army invaded Bohemia and Moravia. Hitler declared the invaded part of the country a *protektorát*—a land under German protection. New officials, installed by Nazi authorities and pro-Nazi loyal Czech representatives, began to create an atmosphere of fear, terror, and death. In a parallel move, the Slovaks founded their independent Slovak State, and declared loyalty to Nazi Germany. The bifurcated status of this country lasted until early 1945, when Allied Armies liberated the inhabitants of the whole country (this liberation ended in May 1945 when the Soviet Red Army entered Prague). Czechoslovakia was immediately re-declared an independent state of Czechs and Slovaks. Within the first two years, most of the members of the German minority were transferred to Germany by consensus with the winning Allies.

The short "interlude" of restoration of Czechoslovakia to its democratic character took place in the three years after World War II (from May 1945 until the beginning of 1948) and ended with the victory of the Communist Party of Czechoslovakia in a parliamentary election. There followed, at the beginning of 1948, a severe governmental crisis during which the Communist Party became the dominant power.

The period of Communist Party rule can be divided roughly into two periods, with one short but significant interlude. The first period (from February 1948, when the Communist Party seized power, until the beginning of "Prague Spring" in 1968) can be characterized as a harsh totalitarian regime with a strong, spectacular, and orchestrated "class struggle" against all kinds of "enemies of the people and the republic." This period witnessed big political trials with death penalties and political figures sentenced to prison or working camps for many years. However, beginning in the late 1950s, some changes could be seen. Step-by-step the toughness of the regime was softening, and the public sphere became more complex and diversified—a process that culminated in the second part of 1960s and especially after January 1968. At the same time, the economical power of the country was weakening and the shortage of everyday goods became painfully visible, particularly in comparison with the neighboring welfare states of West Germany (BRD) and parts of Austria.

The short interlude called Prague Spring (from January 1968 until August 1968, when the Warsaw Pact armies invaded) meant a remarkable experience of liberalization of the public sphere, political discussions, traveling abroad, and a generally high level of freedom of expression. During this period, Czechoslovakia also was declared to be a federation of two republics: the Czech Republic and the Slovak Republic.

Then the period of "normalization" began, starting at the end of 1960s and lasting until the end of the 1980s. During this time, the power of the Communist Party was fully restored under the protection of Warsaw Pact armies. Political opponents were labeled "anti-Communist" and "anti-Soviet," and tracked down (especially among CP members) in a long and elaborate process. Many intellectuals and representatives of various professions were forced to leave their positions, and some had to leave the country. "Charta 77" represented the internal opposition, however weak and isolated. This was a loose association of people who signed a charter stating that Czechoslovakia, as a country whose government signed the Helsinki agreement, should not violate human rights.

In 1989, with the end of the "Cold War," and the political and economical fall of the Soviet Union and the entire "Eastern Bloc," the last time-period for this study began. Until 1992, Czechoslovakia remained a federation of two republics and the democratic character of the regime was under restoration. It openly declared being strongly inspired by the growth in personal freedoms that occurred between the periods of war. Massive privatization of industry and agriculture took place, and democratic institutions were newly established. On January 1, 1993, Czechoslovakia split into two independent republics: the Czech Republic and the Slovak Republic. The Czech Republic, at this writing, has about 10 million inhabitants, who share a free-market economic environment in the country. Most of industry, the banking sector, the media, and land have been privatized. The main legislative body is a two-chamber parliament and the leading players on the political playground are political parties on a close orbit around the political center. The Czech Republic is a member of the North Atlantic Treaty Organization and became a member of the European Union in spring 2004.

Following the previous brief overview of historical development, we can characterize the Czech media—in the period of establishing the former Czechoslovakia—as a highly developed media landscape with a variety of print media, mostly political dailies and magazines, including "prestige" titles, and various lifestyle magazines. Human-interest dailies were nonexistent at the beginning of the century and never became a really strong segment of Czech media performance. The "normative" framework of media performance was under the influence of the cultural and political "nationalization" of Czech society. Media were considered a formative factor that possessed an ability to contribute to the strength of the nation by cultivating the language and enriching the national cultural wealth.

During the two decades between WWI and WWII, independent Czechoslovakia copied the media development in the rest of Europe. Almost immediately after establishing the independent state, a national press agency was founded. In 1923, the first regular radio broadcasting started. The network of cinemas was developing very quickly, especially during the 1930s. However democratic Czechoslovakia was, the press was operating under some limits and under constant danger of being censored, whenever the "defense of the republic" was at stake.

The media were highly controlled during Hitler's *protektorát* (from March 1939 until May 1945) and after the Munich Treaty in 1989. After the Nazi Army invasion of Bohemia and Moravia, a strong system of media control was installed. The Nazi invaders forced media professionals to serve the Nazi propaganda goals. Many journalists decided to cooperate with the Nazi administration, and many had to leave the country or disappeared in concentration camps. Simultaneously, an important underground press developed, distributing communist and non-communist leaflets and periodicals. People got in the habit of listening to broadcasters operating abroad, mainly in London and Moscow, however dangerous such prohibited listening was.

During the years between 1945 and 1948, the free democratic media were restored to the public sphere and most political papers were published. Journalists who had cooperated with the Nazi administration were forced to leave the media. Some of them were imprisoned, and even sentenced to death. The Czech Radio played a very important role in the last days of WWII, announcing the beginning of the so-called Prague Uprising on May 5, 1945, and organizing willing participants to protect from the Nazi Army the building that housed the Czech Radio station. The movie industry was one of the first sectors nationalized by the president of the republic and financed from the state budget.

After 1948, when the Communist Party took political power, the media system was rebuilt according to the main doctrine of the role of media in the "Soviet model." Media were understood as one of the ideological and educational forces that could support the dissemination and integration of communist ideas.[2] Under the control of the Communist Party, media were centralized and operated under an elaborate system. The principle of personal responsibility of editors and directors was one of the main tools of censorship. However, the media development was comparable with the development in other countries, especially in the 1950s and 1960s—regular television broadcasting started in 1953 and was spreading quite quickly during the1960s.

In the 1960s, the overall process of liberalization of the public sphere, which kept pace with the students' movement in Western Europe, helped Czech media to develop a more independent and free media environment. The popular culture of the society was widely concentrated around leading critical and art magazines. The movie industry freed itself from state control, but was still financed from the state budget, constituting a unique framework for the development of the Czech "new wave." The press articulated the demands of the Prague Spring and became a leading social and cultural power in the society. In August 1969, during the invasion of Warsaw Pact armies, Czech Radio played an important role once more, mobilizing people and distracting the attention of the invading armies.

After the military invasion in August, the process of "normalization" took place in the media, too. Media professionals who did not show enough loyalty toward the pro-Soviet regime, especially those who expressed any kind of disagreement with the invasion, had to leave their profession; some of them decided to or were forced to leave the country as well. Meanwhile, the media system was developing. Dailies were launched, published by political parties organized under the umbrella of the National Front. Many magazines were available for readers. Czech state television started to broadcast on two channels and shifted from black-and-white signals to color broadcasting. There were four important national dailies published by main political parties and by the Socialistic Union of Youth. The trade union movement and various ministries, such as the Ministry of National Defense, published some other dailies. There was also a well-developed system of regional press published by regional Czechoslovak Communist Party committees, and a local press published by various local authorities.

Some types of dailies were missing, for instance any form of "yellow press." Also, the audiovisual media (radio and television) were controlled by the state—the Czechoslovak Television and the Czechoslovak Radio. Private media did not exist, not surprisingly, because the amount of advertising was very limited in such a quasi "market" situation.

There were some attempts to publish and distribute illegal print media, but these efforts became more significant at the end of the 1980s with the process of Glasnost and the weakening Soviet regime. On the other hand, people in the former Czechoslovakia were used to listening to foreign radio broadcasting in their Czech language (mainly Radio Free Europe, Voice of America, and the BBC) and were able to "read between the lines" of official media and to understand hidden messages.

The deep social and political change at the end of 1989 caused a complete restructuring of the whole media system. The ownership of existing print media quickly changed. Nowadays most of the dailies are in the hands of foreign owners (mostly based in Germany). New titles appeared, too, and some of them disappeared within two years. Some of them, of course, survived, but mostly without any brilliant market success. Only one sensational daily is continuously in third place among dailies, according to circulation figures.

Currently, there are five important national dailies in the Czech Republic and three of them existed before 1989. The pre-1989 structure of magazines collapsed almost completely, and currently Czech versions of foreign titles dominate the market. The range of titles was "completed" by erotic and pornographic magazines, upper-class lifestyle magazines, and other publications. In the field of audiovisual media, the so-called dual system of public service and commercial media was introduced, such as elsewhere in Europe. The radio and television controlled by the state were changed into public-service media, and commercial media have been established. Almost immediately, the private radio stations appeared. Most of them were local entertainment stations with a high percentage of music and "phone-in" shows, but there were new nationwide stations as well. The public Czech Radio operates three national channels, one network of regional channels, one joint news channel (with Radio Free Europe), and one channel for broadcasting abroad. In television broadcasting, the public Czech Television operates two nationwide channels: one with more mainstream programs, and one with more alternative programs. Commercial television appeared first on the regional level, for instance in the metropolitan area of Prague and in local cable networks. In 1994, the nationwide private television, TV Nova, appeared and almost immediately won about three-fifths of TV viewers as well as a substantial share of the advertising market. TV Nova was assigned to the slot of the former first (federal) channel of state television.

A high level of stability and concentration of ownership were coincidental features of the contemporary media situation at the beginning of the new century. There were six nationwide dailies on the market, controlled by five owners, in addition to one regional daily in each bigger city, all of them run by one owner. There is an ever-changing number of lifestyle magazines (controlled by two major foreign publishing houses) and quite a large number of radio stations. There is a dual system in broadcasting media, and public-service media are under very tangible political pressure. The number of mobile-phone users has increased remarkably, as has the number of Internet users.

2. Media Environment and Media Interaction across Generations

Probably due to post-war developments, there is a significantly low difference in media experience between the age groups that were the subject of the research project.[3] In all three age groups, the first experience with media in childhood depended mostly upon the family's environment and the media available in the household. The importance of school as a media environment was only mentioned in the youngest age cohort.

The first experiences with books and newspapers were based upon books and newspapers available in the household. The penetration of so-called new media refers to radio for the 65- to 75-year-old cohort, and television for the 40- to 45-year-old cohort, and took place through family activities, such as visits with friends. All households represented by the members of each cohort experienced average media saturation, with the following remarkable similarity: all households subscribed to a daily and one or more magazines.

"Newsreels" additionally enriched the media environments of the 40- to 45-year-old and 65- to 75-year-old focus groups. The newsreel, that is, a short film that provided the latest news before the feature film begins in a cinema, was introduced to the Czech media landscape before WWII, and remained a standard part of movie-theater features until 1989.

All families were equipped with the common mass-media appliances. The radio set was mentioned as an exceptional part of a household during their childhood by members of the oldest age group, but as an obligatory part of household by all other groups. Television was mentioned as an exceptional part of a household during their childhood by the middle age group, but considered as a normal part of the childhood household by members of the youngest group. Consumption of traditional mass media was regarded as an ordinary activity primarily related to adults and orchestrated by members of all groups involved in this study.

The richness of images and the quality of memories of events and their representation in media seem to be strongly supported by the wider context of perception, especially when reinforced by parents and teachers. The memory is much stronger in those cases, where events have been discussed in the family or at school.

Generally, most media memories mentioned spontaneously were related to the Czech Republic. Most participants agreed that it was difficult to recall older events, because they are "overlapped" by newer ones. According to their observations, media have a "counterproductive" influence on one's memory (see "Construction of Memory" by Kumar, Hug, and Rusch in this volume).

In spontaneous responses, there was a remarkable lack of interest in magazines and journals. Only members of the youngest cohort mentioned magazines for children and teenagers as a relevant part of their media experience during their childhood years.

The middle and oldest cohorts, on the other hand, shared nostalgic feelings about viewing newsreels with great enthusiasm. Media in general were recalled (from the "use and gratification" point of view) as a source of information about political issues.

The media messages probably had a strong influence upon the nature of the recalled memories. There was a remarkable progression from verbal associations related to topics to image associations, according to age. Members of the 65- to 75-year-old cohort were able to quote headlines, names, and even statements. Members of other groups were able to describe different pictures and images, but were hesitant about quotations, names, and statements.

An evaluation of these findings from the perspective of agenda-setting processes reveals that, despite the age, the strongest "memory traces" were related to catastrophic and/or sensational events, especially if the events had some kind of political dimension. The concept of news values seems to also have had an influence on the structure of memories. A remarkable number of "media memories" are related to various international sport events, such as the Olympics, and championships in soccer.

After analyzing the resultant data collected in each age group, we came to the following findings:

- In the 65- to 75-year-old age group, the first experience with media mentioned by all participants was the fact that during their childhood, the main sources of media experience were print media, especially newspapers, magazines, and radio.

- Most of the participants remembered the title of the newspapers their fathers were reading (newspapers were associated only with fathers!).
- The oldest-age cohort was able to even relate the newspaper title to their father's attitudes and social background: "My father was a farmer, and he read newspapers for farmers."[4]

Some of the participants remembered the *Hvezda* magazine (a *Star* magazine for young women).

The responses revealed that access to radio broadcasting was very limited until the beginning of the 1940s. The radio set represented an exceptional phenomenon in middle-class households in which most of the respondents were raised. Memories about the "radio set in the family" were located in the mid-1930s (particularly in 1934 and 1935). The first recalled experiences with radio broadcasting were connected to collective listening in the home of a radio-set owner: "In our village, our priest had a radio, so we were listening to their football and ice hockey matches. . . . All boys were coming there . . . but the parents were not going there."

Others recalled the school as the center of radio use: "I can remember that we were allowed to listen to a fairytale in the classroom and we took part in the quiz show for children—we were supposed to draw an illustration of that fairytale."

In the 40- to 45-year-old cohort, the first experience with media mentioned by all participants was the fact that during their childhood, the main source of media experience was the family. School was mentioned as the second most important "space" of media experience. Due to social, political, and ideological reasons, the most frequently mentioned medium was the daily *Rudé právo*,[5] followed by the other dailies (*Lidová demokracie* and *Vecerní Praha*).[6] However, dailies were used mostly for entertainment purposes, rather than gathering political information. In this sense, dailies provided sports news as well as crime stories. Radio broadcasting was mostly perceived as a source of "white noise," not as a source of serious information. All participants remembered their first contact with television, and especially visits to the cinema, as special social events. Each participant had some nostalgic feeling in relation to cinema, including newsreels: "Oh, yes, that was extremely boring and we did not pay any attention to it . . . maybe it was pity. Anyway it was part of the whole socializing."

In the focus group of 15- to 20-year-olds, the first experience with media revealed that their main source of media experience was the family,

that is, their parents. Parents habitually watched the evening news on television and then discussed the issues with their children. Respondents in
the group aged 17–18 years recalled their experience with print media.
Parents played the decisive role selecting the household print media: "I
read newspapers especially thanks to my parents—they bought them regularly, and therefore I got them."

The *Mladá fronta Dnes* daily was mentioned most frequently.[7] Male
respondents remember preferring the sport section[8] at the beginning,
before they read the other sections later on. In contrast, females recalled
beginning their consumption of the daily paper with the cultural pages.
Mladá fronta Dnes was still the most popular daily among participants, but
some replacements could be accepted, most frequently *Lidové noviny.*[9] There
was a remarkable lack of experience with print media among respondents
in the 15–17 age group.

The main source of information and the number-one medium mentioned
repeatedly was television. Some of the participants mentioned the Internet as
"one of the first sources of information I put my hand on." This phenomenal
media priority could be partially viewed as "Internet snobbism," that is, a
particular social status attached to the Internet by this age group.

3. Media Memories

The proliferation of radio sets increased from the beginning of the 1940s and
resulted in the role of the radio changing from an entertaining to an informing
medium. More elaborate memories of the oldest cohort revealed various
"serious" events, like concerts of symphonic orchestras. Some of the participants, however, mentioned the cinema and newsreels as part of their media
experience, too. The structured discussion led to some other memories of
media: their experience with anti-Semitic newspapers, the patriotic tone of
newspaper articles in 1938 and 1939, and especially, listening to foreign broadcasting from London and Moscow during World War II. The invasion of
Ethiopia, the Civil War in Spain, and the assassination of Reinhard Heydrich
in Prague were the events mentioned spontaneously, followed by some sport
events, such as the World Soccer Championship Finals in Italy. One of the participants was not able to develop any memory related to media.

As to the richness of media images remembered, various events within
the childhood and youth years of the oldest cohort, were, indeed, mentioned in the spontaneous discussion and confirmed by the rest of the
group. Most images were related to the invasion to Ethiopia, the Civil War
in Spain, the funeral of president Masaryk, as well as photos from Soviet

battlefields during World War II. The images of events were more associated with words (especially headlines), and much less with pictures. The mainstream of media communication was based upon written text, not upon visual information in the respective period. A specific set of memories was related to images offered by Nazi propaganda during World War II, especially posters depicting "the Danger of Soviet Communism."

During the group discussion, the leading event was the Civil War in Spain, however, the respondents returned to the invasion of Ethiopia several times and complained that Ethiopia should be on the list of prompted events in this study.

Though the Civil War in Spain was viewed as the leading event among events from the moderator, respondents had no image in their memory related to the event. They could recall Alcazar ("Alcazar, that was something . . .") and some artifacts related to the Civil War, such as Karel Čapek's drama *Matka* (*The Mother*), Bertold Brecht's dramas, and Picasso's *Guernica* painting. They could not recall a single image, or a single headline related to the event.

When speaking about Prince Edward's abdication, respondents were able to tell the time of the event and to quote the headline: "They just wrote 'Left the Throne Because of Love.' She was Mrs. Simpson, wasn't she?"

The image of the Berlin Olympic Games was not very clear. Respondents were able to recall that Czechoslovak athletes were somehow successful but had a lot of difficulty when asked to attribute this knowledge to any image offered by media. Finally, one of the participants recalled pictures of gymnasts in the newsreel when he went to the cinema. The names of American sprinter Jesse Owens and German boxer Max Schmeling were mentioned, but no media images were associated with them.

All participants were aware of the *Kristallnacht* events, but recalled no pictorial or other images related to it stored in their memories. The respondents did not recall the fall of Singapore and all the answers related to this event were negative. There were no historical facts mentioned, not even additional post-war memories. Also, the respondents very weakly mentioned the attack on Pearl Harbor. "Americans lost it there," was the only positive response that can be referenced into the proper time as a real media experience. One of the participants mentioned that he recently watched the movie *Pearl Harbor*. The event at the time, and the subsequent memories, were probably very unclear because of Nazi propaganda: "I can remember the name of Pearl Harbor from those days . . . and I was quite confused why people spoke about it—I know nothing but the name."

Respondents associated the nuclear bomb in Hiroshima with nuclear tests that took place later on. Two respondents recalled a newsreel showing the destroyed roof of a church in Hiroshima. One of the participants spoke about the "picture of the completely destroyed metropolitan area."

Members of this oldest focus group stated that they heard about Auschwitz only after WWII. These answers can be considered quite logical, given the fact that concentration camps were not on the agenda of the Nazi-controlled media landscape at that time. The Czech lands and Moravia, the contemporary Czech Republic, were "under protection" of Nazi Germany.

Most of the participants in the 40- to 45-year-old cohort remembered that they watched the main evening news on state television during their childhood. The dominant event of the period under discussion was the Prague Spring and the years 1968 to 1969.

In the spontaneous part of the discussion, the events of August 1968 and the invasion of Czechoslovakia by the Warsaw Pact armies was the first event mentioned spontaneously. This was followed by memories of the picture of Alexander Dubcek, the Prague Spring leader and political icon of those days. However, the oldest cohort's media-related memories were international events, such as President Kennedy's funeral, Yuri Gagarin's first flight into space, and the military takeover in Chile. All other memories were related to Czechoslovakia and its national sport representation during the Olympic Games in Grenoble and Mexico, as well as the World Championship in ice hockey.

The generational, defining national event in this age cohort was one of the most important political crises of the Cold War, the Prague Spring. For the researchers, there was a methodological difficulty connected with this result. The events of the Prague Spring and the whole context of the political crisis during the 1960s were heavily revised by the media at the beginning of the 1990s, just after the fall of the Soviet Bloc. For this reason, it was not possible for the participants to make a clear distinction between "genuine" media experience in the 1960s and "revised" media experience in the early 1990s.

Participants did not relate the photo of Mars to any image offered by media. All of their information about Mars had been gathered from other sources, for instance at school and in textbooks.

This cohort associated the Cultural Revolution in China with the specific pictorial image of crowds of people waving with "red booklets," the identity cards of Communist Party members. Most of the participants were able to recognize and identify the communist leader Mao Tse-tung.

When the student movement/revolution of the late 1960s was referenced, the participants had no image related to this event. They associated this movement with France, and recalled that Charles de Gaulle was the president of France at that time. The lack of any memory of the student movement could have been caused by the overwhelming national impor-tance of the events of the Prague Spring, which occurred at the same time.

The first spontaneous memory related to the Prague Spring was the image of Soviet tanks invading Czechoslovakia in August 1968. This image was closely connected to radio broadcasting and not visual: "We were out of Prague with my mother and I can remember her listening to the radio at six in the morning."

The visual images that were recalled were photos of consequences of the invasion, especially damage to public buildings such as the National Museum. The participants remembered the political leaders of the Prague Spring, especially the reforms leader Alexander Dubcek and his companion Josef Smrkovský. Other memories were loosely related to the feeling of free-dom of expression and to the democratization of political discourse. In recol-lection of formerly banned issues, for instance, there was the memory of a TV documentary about the suspicious death, in 1948, of the former foreign secre-tary Jan Masaryk, who was the son of the first president of Czechoslovakia.

The references to the independence movement in Africa were extremely hesitant. One of the participants referred to the increase of African students in Czechoslovak universities ("Blacks in the universities, that is all . . .") and knew about the existence of Patrice Lumumba University. No supporting media images were related to the issue.

The oil crisis was also not supported by any spontaneous media-related association. Respondents vaguely associated articles in newspapers about "Westerners" desperately saving fuel, and after that there were some remarks about photos of deserted filling stations.[10]

The Vietnam War was recalled second after the Prague Spring in terms of richness of media experience. Respondents felt that they knew quite a lot about Vietnam and that they also had a great number of media images. However, the discussion revealed that this notion was not accurate. It seems that the Vietnam War also can be considered a formative event of this generation. The first image participants recalled was the photo of the running girl (after the napalm attack). The topic of Vietnam was closely associated with napalm: "The word *napalm* appeared in my head immedi-ately, but I cannot see any visuals from television, nothing like that . . ." With some guidance, however, other images appeared; for instance, fighter aircraft shooting missiles above the Vietnam jungle.

The respondents had no concrete, spontaneous association with Watergate, but all participants know about the event and offered some description. However, they were not sure about those who were involved, including Richard Nixon, and none of them knew why the scandal was called "Watergate." During the guided discussion, one of the respondents finally mentioned Nixon and his resignation speech. However, no image associated with the event appeared in the discussion.

The first expression related to Woodstock (1968) by the rest of the group was "flower-power children" and the first medium associated with the event was not television or radio, but a record album, *Woodstock,* featuring songs from the concert. The album was illegal but available, even in Czechoslovakia, due to the number of people who smuggled it in from the West: "I can see the records in front of me. . . . There were three records in the box. So what? A record is a medium, too, isn't it?" The album was the main experience related to Woodstock, and all the other images and experiences were somehow derived from the strongest one: Jimi Hendrix and "musicians, lots of musicians, Woodstock was about music, wasn't it?"

In the youngest age cohort, the first media-related memories were related to national events of the Czech Republic. All participants mentioned the events of November 1989: "Parents called me, because there was a 'live' broadcast of demonstrations on TV. . . . We watched it the whole day. Next day, it was in the papers and 'live' news on TV."

When addressing the richness of remembered media images, various events were mentioned in spontaneous discussion. It was very clear that it was easier for the participants to remember images of catastrophic events, such as the crash of two jumbo jets during the Gulf War. Sensational events, such as Princess Diana's death or the Clinton-Lewinsky affair were also easier to remember.

Many images recalled by respondents were remembered not so much because of their media representation but because of frequent discussions within the family: "All I can remember is Saddam Hussein, since my parents were speaking about him all the time."

The discussion of prompted international events revealed that those events were primarily recalled in a few details that refer directly to Central Europe. There were almost no images or memories related to foreign events, such as O.J. Simpson or Rodney King, the economic crisis in Asia, and the liberation of Nelson Mandela. The only exception was the Gulf War: "It is the fate of our times that an event is viewed as most attractive if it looks more like a videogame than reality." Participants had only very general notions of these events: "I can remember some articles in newspapers . . . how much money Americans spend on average per day and how much money an average Asian spends, maybe it was somehow related to this crisis."

The fall of the Eastern Bloc was represented predominantly by various images from the former Czechoslovakia and from Prague, especially the week of demonstrations that started on November 17, 1989. Generally, the emblematic image of the end of Communism seemed to be the fall of the

Berlin Wall. One participant was able to associate the fall of the Berlin Wall with the assassination of Ceaucsescu in Romania. The reunification of Germany was not reflected in visual images, but a lot of images were related to the exodus of East Germans to West Germany in October 1989. This was probably because of the fact that most fleeing East Germans traveled across Czechoslovakia and stayed on the premises of the West German Embassy in Prague. The image of dozens and dozens of East German "Trabant" cars left in parking lots became an icon for the reunification of Germany.

The Beijing Massacre was not remembered at all by the participants. The image of a man standing in front of the tanks in Tiananmen Square was only mentioned after some prompting from the moderator, but was not related in particular to the events in Beijing during the student revolution.

Most participants recalled Princess Diana's death, either because radio and television programs were interrupted with "unexpected news," or because of the reactions of family members: "I can just remember my mother crying—she liked Diana very much." Another trigger of this partic-ular media-related memory was Elton John's song for her funeral. During the discussion about the death of Diana Spencer, participants started to evaluate the media performance and came to the conclusion that they still have some slight impression of hypocrisy:

> "I can still remember that kitsch sorrow—souvenirs everywhere."
> "She was like Barbie."
> "Nobody said that it is simply dangerous to sit in a car with a drunken driver and let him go at such a high speed."

The liberation of Nelson Mandela was associated only with very gen-eral concepts: "I can just remember that I learned the meaning of the word apartheid when he was freed"; and very general images: "I saw some bus only for white and some bus only for black." The image of Mandela in front of the prison waving to cameras was mentioned only rarely.

The mention of O.J. Simpson caused no reaction from seven partici-pants. There was only one remarkable association with the cartoon series *The Simpsons:* "I watch *The Simpsons* regularly, and there is no O.J.!" One of the participants remembered the name O.J. Simpson from one of the English lessons at school, where a videotape of TV news was used.

The participants identified the Rodney King case with Los Angeles and their memories were supported by images of burning shops and cars.

The European Monetary Union was conceptualized only on the basis of exchange rates and graphics offered by media. The only image attributed to it was the sign "European Union" and drafts of banknotes and coins. The whole process of the unification of Europe seemed to be very abstract for the participants. However, the Clinton–Lewinsky case was recalled by participants in some detail, however without any images.

4. Conclusion

Based upon the responses of the participants in the three age groups involved, any generalized conclusions are quite risky. However, there is at least one important result that was surprising for the researchers. The common belief of a close relationship between a type of political regime and the trust in media, quite frequently mentioned as a lack of trust in the case of totalitarian regimes with well-developed propaganda systems, seems not to work in the case of the former Czechoslovakia in its post-war history. During the whole period covered in this project, media were regarded as an integral part of personal and family life, with or without the possibility that the content of the media was manipulated. The family played a crucial role in developing and stabilizing the patterns of media consumption, and media are an important factor of specific "family mythology." Visual messages—rather than words—were definitely much more effective for stimulating a memory track.

Bibliography

Jirák, J. (2002). *Czech Media: Social and Political Context.* Praha: Karlova univerzita.

_____. *Dejiny zemí koruny ceské II [History of Lands of the Czech Crown].* Praha: Paseka, 1992

Kaplan, K. (1990). *Pravda o Ceskoslovensku 1945–1948 [*The Truth about Czechoslovakia 1945–1948*].* Praha: Panorama.

Mencl, V., M. Hájek, M. Otáhal, and E. Kadlecová (1990) *Kri ovatky 20. století [Crossroads of the 20th Century].* Praha: Naše vojsko.

Siebert, F., T. Peterson, and W. Schramm (1963). *Four Theories of the Press.* Urbana: University of Illinois Press.

· G E R M A N Y ·

Gebhard Rusch and Ingrid Volkmer

As in other world regions, the transformation of the media environment from a local to a globalized media culture is also obvious in Germany. The German media culture, as well as its infrastructure, has undergone tremendous changes across the life span of the generations involved in this research. During the influential or, according to Karl Mannheim's definition of generations, "formative" years (Mannheim, 1951) media experiences of childhood and early youth differ considerably between the three generations involved in this research. Mannheim's approach of a generational-defining "stratification of experience" (Mannheim, 1951: 297) reveals generational-specific definitions of the symbolic environment of the media as well as to media-related "representative" events. The following chapter will provide an insight into the stratification of experience of the three media generations from the German perspective.[1]

1. Histories of Generational-Specific Media Cultures

In the childhood and early-youth years of the oldest cohort, between 1935 and 1945, media were tightly controlled by the Nazi regime. The oldest generation grew up with the radio as the new medium in their household, as well as with newspapers, film, and books. However, in this generation, media were perceived as targeting adults exclusively. The only media available for children were books and films.

The oldest generation was raised in a "closed" media world. Their media world was on one hand restricted by the limitations of media technology—for instance, the limitations of terrestrial airwaves—and on the other hand, by the utilization of media for political propaganda purposes. Hitler's appointment as Reichskanzler (Chancellor of the Third Reich) in 1933 was also the beginning of a media policy of centralization ("Gleichschaltung"), of control, censorship, and propaganda.

Before Hitler came to power, approximately 4,700 newspapers were printed in Germany during the time of the so-called Weimar Republic. There were a variety of perspectives, which represented the diversity of the political party spectrum during this time. By the end of the Second World War, only 900 newspapers were left. They were less politically diverse than in the Weimar Republic, but still locally diverse. Centralization of the media was viewed as a key strategy of the Nazi regime, in order to gain (and to continuously maintain) political influence on the public. The Reichspresseamt, the centralized Ministry of Press Relations, with its director, Joseph Goebbels, had been established as the key instrument for the manipulation of the public and political "guidance," as this process was officially called, of what soon became the propaganda press.

According to the press laws of the National Socialists, passed shortly after their election, newspaper publishers were replaced by state authorities. Besides the creation of a new tightly controlled journalistic infrastructure, other measures were soon taken, in order to gain increasing influence on the process of news gathering itself as well as on journalistic formats. For instance, daily press briefings conveyed precise orders for the selection of news and its degree of coverage. These orders even included the layout and the font size of headlines appearing on the front page.

Besides the press, radio was a major instrument within Hitler's propaganda machine. Radio had already existed in Germany since 1923; however, most of the first receivers (then called "detectors") were built by radio amateurs. Although radios were widely available, many families simply could not afford to purchase a set. In 1933, Hitler's regime ordered the radio manufacturers to merge into one company and to build a more simplified type of radio set, which could be made available to the broad population. This so-called Volksempfänger sold for half the price of a radio and was therefore affordable even for low-income families. Therefore, it is not surprising that the number of radio households who owned a Volksempfänger[2] increased tremendously, and had reached eight million (up from four million) between 1933 and 1938. This was a quite substantial number, given the population of 68 million at that time in Germany.

In 1943, around 16 million Volksempfänger were already officially registered. The frequency band of the Volksempfänger only allowed the reception of German stations. To listen to foreign broadcasts was strictly prohibited and viewed as an act of treason at the beginning of World War II.

However, during the formative years of the oldest generation, between 1935 and 1945, the commercialization of the film industry also began. Whereas in other countries, for instance in the U.S. and also in Mexico, the Hollywood studios created a new American popular-culture zeitgeist, this was less the case in Germany. Shortly after 1933, Hitler had established a strict censorship policy for the import of foreign films. The Nazi regime realized that political messages were the more effective when they were tied to fictional drama. The film studios in Berlin (UfA) began to increase their outputs.

It was obligatory for cinemas to show the *Wochenschau* (newsreel), produced by the film office of the Wehrmacht and the Office of Volksaufklärung, before each feature-film screening. The *Wochenschau* contained several sequences of news and highly emotionalized political issues as well as war reports. The visual impressions were the more spectacular on the large movie screen in the dark room of the cinema.

The Nazis even forced the development of the first television technology. In 1935 the first worldwide television program, though experimental, was launched. A television crew covered the Olympics, held in Berlin in 1936. The games were transmitted to a number of selected places, so-called *Fernsehstuben* (public television rooms) throughout the city of Berlin. Despite all advancements in this technology, it failed simply because of the high costs of a television set (around 3,000 Reichsmark as opposed to 60 for a radio set).

According to the regulation of the Potsdam Conference of 1945, postwar Germany was divided into four political sectors. Western Allied Forces governed three of these sectors, but the fourth was under Soviet control. In all of these political sectors, the broadcasting system and the print media were viewed as tools for de-Nazification and re-education of the German people. It was not until March 27, 1953, that the six German broadcasting stations signed an agreement for an all-German television channel (ARD) in West Germany.

During the formative years of the middle generation, between 1965 and 1975, a second internationalization process of the media took place.[3] This internationalization, for television and film, can be defined on one hand by an increasing European cooperation among public broadcasting systems in Germany, establishing, for instance, Eurovision, the European news program pool. On the other hand, this internationalization can be defined by an increasing inflow of U.S. television series. Particularly these U.S. products, for instance Disney's multimedia empire, began to dominate the German media market and created a previously unknown children's (popular) media culture during the childhood and early youth of this middle generation.

In a viewpoint of German media culture, this middle cohort can be described as a "sandwich" generation in terms of their media world. In their childhood and youth they still had access to the political propaganda environment and ideological world of their grandparents, which was officially banned but still lingered privately in families. However, on the other side, they also experienced the emergence of a new phase of the internationalization of music, film, and the first worldwide events. These were media events that allowed a first glimpse into a new globalized age: the moon landing and other international news. These were aired live worldwide, and conveyed an extended perception of the world.

During the formative years of the young generation, between 1989 and 1999, these links were diversified and widened, and the terms "local" and "global" media content were refined. When the so-called dual system—the process of liberalization of the German TV market—started in 1984, commercial TV became available alongside public service broadcasting in Germany for the first time. Since then, a multitude of upheavals has radically changed the German media systems: the number of TV channels grew from three to around 30; commercial, local, and regional television and radio stations have been established; and satellite as well as cable channels are widely available. Movie theaters have been transformed to multiplex media spaces. Mobile phones soon took an increasing share of the telecommunications market, the personal computer reached a penetration of about 40 percent in Germany, and—above all—the advent of the Internet opened new symbolic territories for global communication, information, and entertainment. For the youngest generation involved in this study, access to a variety of media including the print media, television, and the Internet, was not only a common but also a daily experience.

The fall of the Berlin Wall in 1989 brought about some major changes within the German media system. New affiliated stations of the first public-service channel (ARD) were founded in East Germany.

2. Generational Media Lifeworlds

The oldest cohort remembered the radio as being the center of their family media environment during their childhood years. In this generation, the radio, as the first electronic unidirectional medium, began to slowly occupy and perhaps dominate social family time and living space. From a child's perspective, the radio was not merely a medium as such, but an apparatus that had the authority to attract the attention of adults and created specific interaction modes. Furthermore, the huge size as well as its shape had an impressive impact on children.

Individuals of this age cohort recall the radio also in aesthetic terms, as a "real piece of jewelry." One individual even claimed that childhood memories are closely tied to the radio:

My memory begins with our Nordmende radio, which was quite large. (Ursula: 6)

Others recall their fascination with simply observing the "green eye" come to full color on the radio set. This was a light, which, in phases, indicated the degree of the electrical power level. The authoritative presence of the radio was only enforced by its location in an important space of the family environment, in the living room, where family life took place.

However, despite this admiration, the radio was also perceived as a social competitor, a competitor for their parents' attention:

I remember that my father listened to the news every day. Both my parents worked. I looked forward to their return in the evenings. However, when we finally gathered around the dinner table, we were not allowed to speak for around ten to fifteen minutes, when my father listened to the news. (Ursula: 6)

The radio is associated in the memory of this group primarily with political information, and in today's view, political propaganda. Ursula explains why certain propaganda strategies had such an impact on her as a child:

My first memory goes back to one particular radio content: Liszt's *Le Prelude*, which always lead into the special reports of the Joint Chiefs of Staff of the Wehrmacht. The aesthetically impressive piece has deliberately been chosen by the Nazi regime, because it is particularly effective not just for adults but because the power of the tune also had an attraction on children. (Ursula: 6)

Within this political context, parents choose to act as gatekeepers, in order to protect their children from conflicting political developments and to shield them from any ambiguous news, which might be viewed as "conspiracies" outside the household. This invisible shield between the household (the private space of the family) and the outside, public, and politically controlled world, was quite obvious to this cohort even in their childhood memories. As children they were well aware of this news shield:

> Well, it was quite different in my home. We did not even possess a radio. We did not have a radio set, because it was too expensive. My parents did not have much money. Another reason why we did not have a radio was simply that my parents wanted to be the judge of what their children listen to. (Karin: 7)

After the radio, the newspaper was viewed as a secondary medium in family life in this cohort. The group clearly remembers all newspapers, which were read in their households. Whereas the radio was remembered as dominating family time (the whole family gathered around this medium), the newspaper was in Germany, as opposed to India, for example, an individualized medium in this generation. Individuals of the focus group recalled that once being able to read the newspaper, they had to report the political news as daily assignments at school. This was a strategy of the Nazi regime, to tightly monitor the media use in the private space of the family.

In this generation, film had already become a children's medium. Hitler's propaganda strategy also targeted children at an early age and encouraged the production of films specifically for this age group. Whereas the radio was from a child's view perceived as a family medium, the newspaper was related to schoolwork, and films were viewed in the memories of this cohort as a medium for escapism and adventure. Since school authorities organized film shows, visits to the cinema were as frequent as once every week or two. However, when the group recalled their memory of film, they simultaneously mentioned powerful newsreel images. These images are so vivid that they are still shared today in the group as a form of collective memory:

> I remember these special screenings for children . . . it was crazy. . . . The performance began at 2 o'clock, which was quite cleverly arranged. So parents could have some time off. . . . The newsreel was also shown to children. Of course there were special movies for children. I remember that sometimes after school, we went straight away to the cinema and watched *Der Standschütze Bruggler* and *Der Hitlerjunge Quex*. (Ursula: 9)

In the memories of this oldest cohort, the message of the newsreels and the feature film supplemented each other. As Martin claims:

The feature film conveyed the overall ideology, of course always in relation to the newsreel. This way, the newsreel showed what was actually going on, whereas the film submitted the overall ideology. (Martin: 15)

Other relevant childhood media of this generation were perceived as "niche" media. Niche media were meant to powerfully target children directly in their lifeworld, by deliberately circumventing parental observation. Individuals of the focus group recalled showcases made of glass, which were stuck within children's eyesight on the walls of buildings, primarily in the neighborhoods of schools. These showcases displayed photos and other visual materials especially made for children. This media was a communication platform of the Nazi regime that exclusively targeted children:

On my way to school, I always passed such a showcase. That was the source, where I got a vague idea, what the Nazis are doing to Jews. They displayed distorted faces and so on. Because I am a visual type, I always took a look. However I did not know what really all this was about. On one hand I thought that this was so brutal and mean, on the other I was fascinated by the power of the visual image. There were always some gruesome tales, being told about Jews. (Martin: 18)

However, parents knew about these special showcases and prohibited their children to stop on their way to school and even briefly take a look.

Particular children's magazines can be considered as other niche media, for instance magazines, published by department stores. The focus group also remembered film guides, which presented the latest film releases and included photos of dramatic scenes and brief descriptions. As one participant remembers:

Years later, I came over a copy of such a film guide. I was absolutely struck by the degree of political propaganda even in these film descriptions. (Erwin: 16)

Cigarette pictures were also remembered as media of their childhood. With each package of cigarettes of a particular brand, came a number of pictures, which were part of a whole series. These pictures became collector's items during the childhood of this cohort. As another niche media, cigarette pictures also contained political messages, hidden in the chosen topical series, such as *The Life of the Führer*.

From the childhood viewpoint of this cohort, films and books were the most important media:

Lederstrumpf and *Tarzan* . . . and I have read 35 of the 64 volumes of Karl May, whose fiction stories played in the Wild West. When I was 14, my parents gave me as a gift Hermann Hesse's book *Der Weg nach innen,* which helped me finding my own way. . . . Yes, books were important. (Klaus: 18)

Another individual recalls the relevance of books as a medium of escapism "from the world . . . and escape into history, literature, just to avoid any current ongoings."(Martin: 18)

Whereas these books were particularly attractive for boys in this cohort, girls favored other authors, for instance *Heidi* and Else Uri's *Das Nesthäkchen* (*The Nestling*). Those who lived in families where media use was closely monitored for political and educational reasons read these books secretly.

The available media in individual media environments differed significantly across the three generational cohorts, as did its relevance to their lifeworld. While the oldest generation claimed films, books, newspapers, and the radio were most important in their childhood, the middle generation considered radio, books, tape recorders, record players, and television as having been most influential. All participants of the middle-generational focus group clearly remembered when television entered their household. Interestingly, these memories are very similar to those of the oldest generation, who recalled the advent of the radio set. Whereas the radio set was placed in the center stage of the household during their time, the radio was removed from its place in the family center stage in this middle generation to make room for a new medium: the television set. As one individual recalls:

> Of course I even remember when the technician was called to come and adjust our new television set. I clearly recall how I watched him at work, wondering what it is that he is in fact adjusting. Of course, as a child I was not allowed to even touch the television set. . . . However, I did not watch a lot of television during my childhood. (Susanne: 3)

In the childhood and early youth of this generation, most media were family owned. Although the middle classes had accomplished some degree of prosperity during the *Wirtschaftswunder* years of post–World War II Germany, this newly owned property was in many cases commonly owned by an extended family. In many cases, members of this cohort grew up with grandparents and other relatives in an extended-family environment. This social structure provided additional media outlets for this cohort. Whereas the immediate family controlled the use of certain media, grandparents were more casual concerning media use. As one participant recalls:

As a child, I thought it was fascinating to listen to all my grandmother's records. I listened to recorded speeches of Hitler, Goebbels, Hess, whatever their names were . . . (Martina: 6)

The "sandwich" media world of this cohort becomes obvious in view of another individual:

Until I was ten, my aunt lived in our household, who was ten years older than I. . . . She listened to all music charts, wore a petticoat and all that. She had all those Elvis records. Besides listening to my grandmother's records with these political speeches of the Nazi era, as well as military music recordings, I liked to listen to my aunt's Elvis records. (Claudia: 9)

Focus-group participants remember that their use of the family media decreased over time. In their early-youth years, they obtained their first "own" media, in most cases a transistor-radio set and a tape recorder, which allowed them to tape and replay music.

As in the oldest generation, books played an important role in this middle generation. In the oldest generation, very specific individual and biographically important book titles and authors were recalled; but in this middle cohort, books had already become mass-market products. Inexpensive pocket books and book series, which targeted the emerging mass market for children, divided into sections for boys and girls. The popularity of books such as *Hanni & Nanni* showed that children's books were an attractive media. One of the participants recalls that her interest in reading remained at the level of children's books and comics for a long time and then, during her teen years:

I went straight from reading *Donald Duck* to reading Heinrich Böll. (Claudia: 6)

Besides the new mass market of children's media, such as television series, books, magazines, and comics, film became another important sector of the emerging children's media culture of this generation. However, given the financial struggles of the post–World War II era, children of this cohort did not have the weekly allowances to regularly visit movie theaters. However, continuing the attempts originally initiated by the Nazi regime to offer occasional low-cost film performances for the masses, in this era, educational and important commercial films such as *Lassie Returns* were screened for a small fee. Some individuals in this cohort recall that this film was in fact their first movie experience.

Participants remember their desperation to see other films as well—such as the film version of Astrid Lindgren's *Pippi Longstocking*—but were not allowed to see it because of limited financial resources at home. Most likely for this reason, children's programs on television began to target this age cohort. Although they joined their parents for political debate programs, such as *Internationaler Frühschoppen*, children's programs increasingly became part of their own television experience:

> We watched all the children's programs, such as *Flipper, Kinder aus Bullerbü.* . . . I also remember *Fury* and *Lassie* . . . and all the tears. (Angela: 11)

Members of the young focus group already grew up not only in a well-equipped, but also in an increasingly high-tech media environment. Almost all media, from print to personal computers, were individually accessible to them. In the oldest generation, children and teenagers in some cases personally owned books and children's niche media (see above). In the middle cohort, individual ownership of portable radios and tape recorders was common. However, in the youngest cohort, the individual ownership of media has multiplied. As we have already observed in the middle generation, media that were personally owned were viewed as most important. This is also the case in the youngest cohort:

> Everybody in our family has his or her own TV set. (Niklas: 3)

Thus, radio sets, record players, and tape recorders—the most relevant individually owned media technology of the 70s—were replaced by television sets, videotape recorders, and personal computers in the youngest generation. Most remarkable, however, is the fact that the young recall using electronic media more or less exclusively. Print media were remembered as being less attractive. The fact that cassette tape recorders ranked as the second-most important childhood media of this generation can be taken as another indication of their weaning from print media. The simple fact that fairy tales are no longer read from books but played from a tape by pressing a button on a machine identifies current media experiences as well as future preferences. But there are some other and, with regards to the children's cognitive development, even more important aspects. Children can control (start, stop, rewind, repeat, change cassette) this electronic type of storytelling long before they are able to read. The self-induced use of this equipment—an early and elementary technical media competence—seems to pave the way for a preference of electronic media in later ages. A second aspect worth mentioning is a relative cultural specificity of cassette-tape story content in Germany. Except for *Turtles*, the German version of the US show *Teenage Mutant Ninja Turtles* and Alfred Hitchcock's *Crime Stories for Children*, all other productions are European or German, such as *Benjamin Blümchen*, *TKKG*, and *Drei Fragezeichen* (Three Questionmarks). Books no longer played a dominant role within the entirely electronic media environment of this youngest cohort.

Television has become the center medium, supporting Neil Postman's argument (Postman, 1982, 1985). Individuals, however, recalled that when they were children, television access and exposure time had been tightly controlled by parents, and had in some cases been utilized as a means for sanctions. Almost all individuals of this young age cohort remember restrictions on their television use with respect to either certain content, "children's program only" (K), a certain age, or time limitations. But this fully matches with the importance of TV in the children's lives. Restrictions of children's TV usage—if anything at all—seemed to work for the parents. At the same time, it becomes plausible that television seems to be the only medium that is controlled at all by parents:

My parents allowed me to watch for an hour or so . . . but when they were away I secretly watched what I wanted to. (Katarina: 5)

TV was prohibited after 8 P.M. (Marcel: 5)

My parents controlled what I was watching until I was 12, but then they did not care much about it. (Andre: 5)

Almost all TV programs and most of the comic magazines, such as *Donald Duck* and *Mickey Mouse*, that were recalled as having been relevant during their childhood years, originated in the U.S. There are only two exceptions: *Augsburger Puppenkiste*, a German puppet show, and *Wetten dass*, a popular quiz show that was aired in a Saturday evening primetime slot. All other programs remembered are U.S. made and were aired fully dubbed.

The early media memories of this young cohort begin with preschool television shows, such as the German adaptation of *Sesame Street*, followed by animated cartoons like *The Simpsons* or *South Park* and series such as *Married with Children* and *Knight Rider*. Comparing these memories to those of this age cohort in other countries reveals an interesting transformation of local and national media environments into a global media world, sharing similar media-related memories. This is an important issue because of the transcultural shaping of TV experiences among the young generations worldwide. The homogenizing or parallelizing effects caused by the export of U.S. models of problem solving, humor, and lifestyle, can hardly be over-estimated.

In summarizing these results, we argue that the media environment diversified with the shift of generations. A number of new media—audio-tape recorders, record players, television and computers—come into play. Most striking may be the fact that books, newspapers, and radio totally disappeared from the young generation's list of important media. The findings of this qualitative study were also supported by overall statistical data, which revealed that the leading medium for the young is TV (93 percent, with music and comic channels at the first place), followed by music tapes and stickers. Video, CD, and the Internet show up as newcomers within this generation's media set (see Feierabend & Klingler, 2002: 9–21).

These findings clearly demonstrate that there is a media divide among generations. The lists of important media, as specified by the old and the young, only have one single item in common: the movies. The middle generation seems to bridge this gap in both directions. They share the importance of print media, radio, and cinema with the old, and they relate to the young by their appreciation of TV, music recordings, and the use of the computer. In 1970, TV already reached 73 percent of the 14–19 year olds, while the daily newspapers reached only 64 percent of that age group (see Berg and Kiefer 1987: 202).

The meaning of radio was different in the early 1920s, when the people started to rig up their detectors themselves, or in the decades of the thirties and forties when the *Volksempfänger* became a product for the masses and radio was primarily used for political indoctrination. Similarly, the movies underwent a series of technical improvements: from silent to surround-sound stereo; from black and white to wide-screen digital color; and from the small theater to modern multiplexes. The number of channels, technical quality, program formats, and the genres were expanded in the sixties and seventies. Whereas watching television was a social experience in the sixties, it is an individualized experience for the youngest generation. The middle generation was brought up with three TV channels, but the youngest cohort has to cope with more than 30 channels and a countless number of videotapes and DVDs, all providing a variety of TV-displayed entertainment. In fact, television itself has become a multimedia platform.

3. Generational-Specific Forms of Media Interaction

Within each generation, interaction with and about media is remembered in very distinctive spheres. Given the overall propaganda environment of the oldest generation, which did not allow open debates and political discourses, media interaction is remembered in two ways: in very specific notions of a "public" and a "private" sphere. This cohort was aware of a public sphere[4] in which nonconformist attitudes, if mentioned openly, were heavily sanctioned. Some individuals associate their memory of media with ambiguous threats and personal dangers. As one individual remarked:

> In fact, because of the *Jenaische Zeitung* [a local newspaper in the city of Jena, G.R./I.V.], I soon learned what dictatorship and eavesdropping really meant. . . . One day the mother of a friend of mine appeared on our doorstep and asked, "Tell me, which newspaper do you read at home?" and I responded, "*Jenaische Zeitung*," and she said "Who loves the Führer reads the *Thüringer Gauzeitung*." From then on, I avoided any further contact with her. (Karin: 14)

Sometimes, even from the viewpoint of children, these clearly defined private and public spheres overlapped. For instance, when guests were present at home, one wanted to know who could or could not be trusted. It is interesting to note how differentiated the perception of their own, associated particular roles were (see quotation above) when they perceived their parents as being silent or careful in a certain social context. Even in their childhood, they were aware that public sanctions could even affect intimate interaction in private correspondence. Some individuals recalled their fear when, soon after they had raised criticism of certain Nazi slogans in private letters to their parents, they realized their occasional childish ignorance. They recalled not being aware, at that time, of how this could endanger the entire family. It seems that these fearful situations predominate their memories of private interaction. Indeed, others recall public noninteraction; for instance, in arranged public media events as when the entire school community had to listen to Hitler's speeches, and they all had to sit quietly and listen.

In the private sphere, however, media interaction was remembered quite differently. Individuals clearly recalled their parents' media use very distinctively, even along gender lines. Whereas fathers are recalled avidly reading the newspapers and listening to particular programs on the radio, mothers are remembered as reading books. However, during the time of World War II, this situation changed and news of battles dominated the media use in their families.

In the oldest generation, media interaction was separated into public and private spheres; it could be argued that in the middle generation, media interaction was divided into two spheres: into a "family" and a "peer" sphere.

In the middle generation, the sphere of family interaction was primarily remembered as a collective, that is, social media experience: viewing certain Saturday-night shows together or simply joining a parent or sibling watching television.

Peer interaction, however, was recalled in distinct, differentiated and active terms. One could claim that family media interaction was viewed as a given, where children just passively joined in. Peer interaction is perceived as participatory and selective. Even in their memories, individuals of this focus group recall their active role in this peer media sphere. They recall reasons why they favored a particular radio program, for which purpose they taped music, or which celebrities began to attract their interest. Contrasted to the oldest generation, who recalled media interaction in passive terms, this generation seems to have actively participated in their specific symbolic environment, and media have actively accompanied their transformation from children to adolescents.

Reviewing the responses, it could be claimed that the relevance of family interaction decreased in their early teens, and the peer interaction sphere gained importance. In conjunction with the rising income of middle-class households as well as increasing home ownership, many of the individuals of this cohort moved to their own bedrooms in their early youth. This new individual physical space was soon furnished with a variety of relevant symbolic peer media:

> To have an own room and a cassette tape recorder sometime, was very important to me. (Claudia: 10)

> The tape recorder moved into our new bedroom with us, which I shared with my sister . . . (Angela: 11)

While media use within this peer interaction sphere was highly individualized at home, it was collectively shared on the peer level. Many individuals of this cohort listened to the same radio programs in their bedrooms. For instance, to the music charts aired by the commercial short-wave station Radio Luxemburg, which was based in Luxemburg, or to BFBS (British Forces Radio Station) in Germany. One participant described these music radio shows as "compulsory":

> It was quite tricky to adjust the antenna to Radio Luxemburg. Then they had this English-language program. They already had these Top Twenty shows and so on. . . . I mean on Radio Luxemburg. I think I even learned a bit of English just by listening to their shows . . . and listening to other English programs . . .

later on, of course, BFBS, on Sunday mornings, the Top Twenty on BFBS. . . . That was absolutely compulsory. Beyond other things, television and such . . . these shows were absolutely important. (Ulrich: 7)

In the symbolic territory of this emerging peer culture, media use was also viewed as an indicator of status. One particular medium that was associated with teenage identity in this generation was the print magazine *Bravo*. A commercial magazine that exclusively targeted the teenage market, *Bravo* seemed to serve as a symbolic bonding medium within the peer culture of the middle cohort. When remembering *Bravo* most, individuals do not so much refer to particular content but the tricks they had to employ in order to get a copy of the magazine, which, of course, was prohibited by many parents because of its open discussion of sexual issues.

Some television shows also had the function of symbolic bonding. Many in this group also recalled that they had to undergo various obstacles to be able to watch a show that was prohibited by their parents. Being able to prove to peers that they overcame their parents' objection certainly gained respect in their peer culture. Where media use for the oldest cohort was one directional—media served as a provider of information and entertainment—this one-dimensional role has changed in this cohort: media began to provide a symbolic territory.

In their early teens, individuals of this cohort possessed their own media equipment, which constituted their own, even "closed" media world that was shared with their peers but not with their parents. Although the oldest generation also recalled collective memories of shared media experiences, experiences in this middle generation were different. In the oldest generation, children were mostly observers of their parents' media use (and shared this observation role in their memories), but this generation developed a collective symbolic territory, which was utilized for different interaction processes.

Many in this group also recall that they had to undergo various obstacles to be able to view television shows that were prohibited by their parents:

. . . and we have watched secretly, later, when sleeping at a friend's house . . . when her parents were out for the evening. When I slept in my friend's house, there was a room in the basement with an old black-and-white television set. . . . There we watched shows like *Der Kommisssar* (the commissar). . . . It was so much fun, particularly watching these scary films. (Susanne: 14)

When this cohort was in their teens, the media-related symbolic territory served new purposes of identity building. It can be argued that interaction about media-transmitted political events contributed to their generational identity. Family controversies about the student revolution and the war in Vietnam shaped their individual and generational political identity.

In the youngest generation, the public-versus-private and family-versus-peer spheres are not as obvious, but rather a web of constantly flowing content, which shaped their generational perception of the media. For them, media became omnipresent.

The youngest generation were quite aware of strong media interactions. This generation grew up with a symbolic network of media shows that targeted exclusively children. These shows were associated with merchandising products of their favorite characters such as He-Man, Batman, Pokemon, or the Sesame Street puppets. Generation-defining media experiences were U.S.–made media products like *Knight Rider, The Simpsons, The A-Team, Tom and Jerry, Disney Club,* a television magazine featuring various clips of Disney cartoons and films, Al Bundy, the leading character of the TV show *Married with Children, Spider Man, Saber Riders, Captain Future, South Park,* and so on.

In the middle generation, parents made an attempt to monitor their child's television usage, but this was less the case in this youngest generation. They have had access to a broad variety of programs and content. As pointed out earlier, the active use of media, like the handling of a cassette recorder to listen to stories, music, or dramatic productions, was a dominant early-childhood experience of this generation. Therefore, it is no surprise to find that the young collected videotapes, videotaped television programs, rented videotapes from a video library, and met on weekends for long video nights. Video and computer games only continued this action-oriented mode of media use.

Although this generation grew up in a broad web of symbols, interaction with friends and peers still worked in very specific ways. In the middle generation, the peer culture involved certain "compulsory" media icons, but in this generation, peer interaction is more concrete—specific, but also fragmented. This is a phenomenon that might be caused by the fact that individualized forms like video, audiotapes, and electronic media (such as the computer), less than television and film from public sources, constitute the center of their media worlds.

Media serve in this sense as platforms for this symbolic web, which mutually shaped and was shaped by social interaction and personal communication. Most impressive were the reports about the families' "processing" of the coverage of the "fall of the Berlin Wall." Members of the youngest focus group were too young at that time to fully understand what was going on. They learned the meaning of that event from the behavior and comments of their parents, while watching television. They only realized the importance, or the extraordinary significance, of what they saw because their parents were so excited and fascinated by the pictures that showed people standing on top of the Berlin Wall or crossing the former border check called "Check Point Charlie." Their parents communicated their excitement, commented on the event, and explained it to their children. In this sense, the event was conveyed in representative format rather than a direct format.

4. Media Memories

In the oldest generation, media-related memories were remembered through the perspective of the parents. In this view, media-related political events were remembered based on their meaning to parents. Since media were perceived as family media, located in the living room, the entire family (including children) shared news and radio shows. In many cases, children were present when news broke about political or other events.

In this perspective, it is not surprising that media-related events and programs remembered are usually those that their parents listened to on a regular basis. Furthermore, listening to the radio was viewed as an event. From the memories of this focus group, the radio was a medium for political news. Fathers are primarily recalled as being regular listeners to news programs. The memory of their parents' radio use was very clear and distinct:

> I remember that my father passionately listened to a radio program called *Where Are You, Comrade?* or something like that. That is all I remember. (Erwin: 6)

Radio programs are also remembered due to the fact that they caused exceptional lifeworld adventures:

> My father was a big fan of Max Schmeling. We went to neighbors across the street at night. And I was allowed to join them at night at half past two; I think it was in 1931, when I was only six years old. Because the fight took place in New York, it was already two-thirty at night. (Klaus: 6)

Besides remembering media programs from the perspective of an observing child, other memories referred to social interaction in the context of radio programs, for instance the memory of an uncle's reaction to a Hitler speech.

Remembered events of this generation are media-related events but also lifeworld events. The closed national media environment in which this oldest generation grew up—media covered primarily relevant national events—also affected their lifeworlds in very different ways. In some cases, the relevant events were marked by lifeworld occurrences, which were later covered by the media. The propaganda media also filled the role of providing an official interpretation of what had happened. One of these lifeworld/media events was the attempted assassination of Hitler on July 20, 1944, by Graf Stauffenberg and his group.

> My mother and I went to pick bilberries in the mountains near Jena. When we walked back to the train station . . . they had these loudspeakers . . . and they repeated the message that a group of criminal officers had tried to kill the Führer. However, by providence he is still alive. My mother almost collapsed and I had the feeling that it is a tragedy that this conspiracy was, again, unsuccessful. All this is kept in my memory. However, it was something that we had to hide. At the moment my mother stepped on the train, she had to pretend as if nothing has happened. (Karin: 25)

The strong intertwining of political event into biographical lifeworld memories seems to be characteristic for this age cohort:

> The battle in Stalingrad. . . . I remember it from the newspaper. We did not listen to the radio. Always the newspaper. I still see the newspaper photos of close combat battles in between buildings and ruins. I felt the tension and the feeling 'something will happen—this is a turnaround,' the time of victories is over. (Martin: 33)

Another lifeworld/media-related event was Kristallnacht:

> When I went to school in the morning, I went through streets with broken glass. However, it was a media event, because we immediately learned through the media the official version of what has happened, and why the anger occurred. I remember that we were quite oppressed at school. There was one in our class who tried to show off with telling us that he had wandered through the streets at night and had set the synagogue on fire. However, the rest of us thought it was just horrible. (Martin: 39)

The beginning of World War II was perceived less as an element of the lifeworld than as a media event. The radio became the key medium of this war even at the beginning. Families and neighbors gathered around the radio to listen to the declaration of the war:

> We did not even know that Germany had attacked first . . . only heard on the radio that Hitler promised "we will fight back." (Karin: 40)

International events were remembered only vaguely. If international events were remembered, they were related to the Nazi regime. Even Pearl Harbor, being vaguely remembered from that time, was interpreted in the Nazi perspective. Otherwise, it was of no relevance to political coverage in Germany at that time.

During this time, exposure to any international media was rare, particularly outside of the closed Nazi world:

> We did not know what was happening in Russia, or in the war in the South Pacific and between Japan and the U.S. Of course, we knew about the war in general, but had no idea what was actually happening. (Martin: 34)

Of the prompted events, the war in Spain, Pearl Harbor, and even Hiroshima and Nagasaki were remembered only vaguely and in superficial terms, as well as the abdication of Edward VIII. All knowledge about these events had been gathered later in their lives.

The opening of the concentration camps by the allied forces, which were major news events in other world regions, had also been widely covered by media in post-war Germany. These events, again, represented lifeworld/media experiences. The allied forces had shown films of their horrible findings, and these were associated with the fact that some individuals recall their own experience of being guided through the former camps by allied forces and personally realizing the horror of the Nazi era.

The oldest cohort remembers primarily national events and international events that revealed a relationship to the Nazi regime. In contrast, memories of the middle generation represent a completely different world-news cosmos.

The middle generation can be viewed as the first media generation. Media were perceived as being substantial and quasi-natural elements of their lifeworlds. As described above, media also played a relevant role in their peer culture. Media memories of this generation represent this particular viewpoint. Because television was only permitted at particular times throughout the week, many of their memories are notably collective. Targeting young viewers, these shows were mostly U.S. made, such as *Star*

Trek, Tarzan, and *Flipper.* However, they also joined their families to watch Saturday-night primetime shows, such as quiz shows:

> In fact, it (television) was not omnipresent . . . in my early childhood, I watched just very few, selected shows and still they have left vivid memories. (Susanne: 14)

> For instance, I remember I must have been in kindergarten age, that I watched a show called *Wilma and King,* maybe I was five years at that time. Of course it dealt with a girl and her horse. Later on they showed *Fury* and so on of course . . . these are very intense memories, which show how important all this was. (Susanne: 14).

One of the key generational events in the German middle cohort was President Kennedy's assassination. Given the era of mass media of the sixties and seventies, when only two or three television channels were available in Germany, events of this magnitude were also "social" events. Many of the focus group recalled that neighbors, not media, broke the news of the assassination. Another aspect of the memory of this event was the overall atmosphere of despair and shock. Another formative international event was the landing on the moon, which is also recalled in social terms:

> The landing on the moon was an exceptional event for me . . . even days before everybody was talking about it and somehow all children and our entire class at school felt somehow involved. It was a strange feeling: a combination of something very exciting but also something quite trivial. . . . I clearly remember that strange atmosphere. (Susanne: 27)

Other international events, vaguely remembered, are the the 1972 Olympics in Munich and the 1973 Sinai Crisis. However, these events are not remembered in the social terms of particular reactions in their lifeworld (for example, by parents and neighbors), but as political events, though in very clear terms. In some cases they even remembered the channel on which they listened to these particular news stories:

> I clearly remember . . . it was in '75, the program *Mittagsmagazin* by WDR2. It was a report on the retreat of the U.S. forces from Saigon. How the helicopters were pulled out, something like "the last ones are leaving" and something like that. I was politically quite active in those days and I thought that this is somehow brutal and touching at the same time. (Ulrich: 29)

The war in Vietnam was otherwise remembered by very particular events, such as the bombing of Hanoi and the peace treaty. Where the Cultural Revolution in China and Watergate in the U.S. were remembered in rough terms, the music concert at Woodstock, New York, was another major, international, and generational-defining event for this cohort. The so-called Prague Spring, the Russian invasion of Prague, was another important event for this cohort. Many remembered how scared their parents were, and that as children they did not know the facts of what was happening.

The most prominent event the young generation in Germany first remembered is the fall of the Berlin Wall. They collectively remembered the scenes and pictures ("people on top of the wall"), which they saw on TV or in the papers. Even radio reports are mentioned. They also quite vividly recalled the situations and social contexts—where they were when they first learned about that historical event. The behavior and comments of their parents helped them to understand what was going on and what it might mean. Although this event was spontaneously recalled first, the group members were not very much involved. The background knowledge that they communicated was minimal. The event did not seem to require much communication among the group members. To some extent, this may be due to the fact that the members of this focus group all lived in West Germany and apparently didn't have relatives in the new Laender or any other connections to the eastern part of Germany.

Another prominent event remembered without any prompting is the death of Princess Diana. Again, the social and situational setting when receiving that news was well remembered. Two members of the group even recall some details reported about the first investigations of the accident in Paris:

The driver was drunk. (Katarina: 13)

The driver was said to have lost his memory. It was discussed whether the paparazzi caused the accident. (Niklas: 13)

Andre gave another remembered example of context information:

Most horrible was the song for her by Elton John. (Andre: 13)

A third quite prominent event was a jet crash at the U.S. Airbase in Ramstein, Germany, on August, 28, 1988. The young cohort remembers "horrible pictures of a jet crashing into the crowd of visitors, people watching the flight show" and felt "treated harshly" by the pictures they watched on TV. There are some other unprompted events like the Olympic Games, the Rugby World Championship, and the Superbowl. Only one group member who was heavily involved in sports mentioned each of these events.

Two events from the international list of major media events were recalled spontaneously: the reunification of Germany (1989) and the death of Princess Diana (1997).

The liberation of Nelson Mandela (1990) was only mentioned by a single person:

> . . . imprisoned for political reasons, later president of South Africa. (Andre: 9)

The European Monetary Union (1991) was also covered, with some general remarks, by one group member only. The first war in the Persian Gulf (1991) was remembered much better, by half of the group. They recalled pictures from TV showing tanks and rocket launchers in the desert as well as people in hospitals. Saddam Hussein was mentioned by name, but there was no other background or detailed knowledge. The O.J. Simpson trial (1994) is remembered vaguely, by half of the group; they also remember courtroom scenes broadcasted on TV. The Clinton-Lewinsky affair (1998) was also remembered by half of the group, mostly because of the extensive TV coverage. One member even recalled some context detail, namely a picture in a newspaper showing:

> Kenneth Starr taking the report of evidence out of a van. (Andre: 13)

In the oldest generation, radio did not provide any children's programs but was entirely used for information, news, and the entertainment of adults. In contrast, this generation was the first to grow up in a somewhat multi-channel environment, with children's television shows, and media in their own bedrooms, such as radio and tape recorders. It seems that the web of constant content flow had created a very specific notion of the media. If created at all, generation-formative events are created by extensive coverage and "ceremonial journalism" (Dayan and Katz, 1992).

Conclusion

Putting all the mosaic pieces from the focus-group discussions together, we may draw a picture showing some general traits or trends, at least from the German perspective. The differences we observe across generations, indeed, support the hypothesis of media generations. If the three generational groups are compared along the dimensions of media, content, audience style, memories, and perspectives, very distinctive divides between the generations can be observed.

As we focus on the media divide across generations, we may state that the oldest generation was primarily orientated toward print media and the movies. The new medium of their youth was the radio. The middle generation grew up in the prosperous post–WWII period. Their families could afford up-to-date media equipment, radios, different kinds of print media, and the new medium of the 1960s: television. This middle or "sandwich" generation became familiar with the whole range of electronic analogue media (from stereo sets, record players, tape recorders to television).

The youngest generation was brought up with television as the leading medium—with more than thirty television channels—and highly developed and diversified analogue media. The new medium of this generation is the digital personal computer with its multiple applications in the professional world as well as in home entertainment. The leading and the new media have changed from generation to generation. These different media environments not only induce different experiences, but also correspond to different orientations towards media content.

Comparing the generational orientations toward content reveals a "content divide" between the old and middle generation on the one hand, and the young and the older generations on the other hand. The young very rarely mentioned print media, but did not mention any news format at all. They did not seek out news, but preferred programming like films, sitcoms, music, or TV shows.

The oldest generation was taught a bitter lesson by history. They learned about the value of reliable information during wartime, when they listened to forbidden foreign radio stations or when they observed the increasing difference between the Nazi propaganda and the reality of WWII. Listening or reading news had become an existential issue. Similarly, the middle generation learned about the fragility of the post-war peace that was maintained in a kind of dance on a tightrope, stabilized by the balance of power and deterrence. Several serious crises (from Cuba to Prague) kept their senses highly alert for political information. When the young generation was media-socialized in the 1990s, it was a decade after the NATO Double Treaty and at the time immediately after the Iron Curtain of the Cold War era had disappeared. It was a decade—probably lasting until 9/11/2001—that was seemingly without any external threats, which may have given rise to a media mentality in which young people could completely avoid seeking the latest political information. News-seeking, as a habitual mode of media use, seems to be absent in the young generation.

The mode of media use seems to have changed across generations. What we observed here may be viewed as an "audience divide." The oldest generation's media socialization was driven by the need for (or interest in) information and affection (i.e., mood management in the sense of Zillmann, 1988) and was focused on print, radio, and cinema. For the middle age group, though, the common media experiences were characterized by their use of a broader range of media and technical devices for a diversified range of interests or needs, including information at a top rank. Hence, the middle generation used multiple media and used it intensively from its beginning, which directly correlated to the growing number of media and technological standards. The youngest generation, again, seemed to exhibit an exclusive difference. Although they made use of all kinds of media, like the generation of their parents, their media use seemed to be mainly driven by affection or high involvement in personally relevant issues, rather than politics and most other news topics.

A look at the lists of spontaneously remembered events in the three age groups proved that there is a kind of "media memory divide" across the generations. Not a single event is part of more than one list. Although there were natural borders separating the childhood media memories of the three generations, it would have been possible for the respective later generation(s) to refer to some event from an earlier period. That this was not the case clearly showed that each generation composed their own set of important events based on their own recollections. Each generation had a distinctive media memory.

Furthermore, the way people socially constructed their generational memories also differed across generations, following a kind of "memory elaboration divide." Individuals of the oldest cohort were highly narrative—they told stories about their memories. The middle generation did not tell stories but gave quite comprehensive reports, probably because they were so widely interested and informed. The number of events they mentioned was the highest compared to the other age groups. Lastly, the young generation recalled media-related memories primarily in headlines. Occasionally, some additional statements brought up a few details.

Finally, we turn our attention to the differences in generational perspectives. The recalled memories were derived from mainly local, regional, and national media in the case of the older generation; primarily national and international media with the middle generation; and international or global media in the youngest generation.

Bibliography

Berg, Klaus, and Marie-Luise Kiefer (1987). *Massenkommunikation 3: Schriftenreihe Media-Perspektiven*, Vol. 9. Frankfurt/M: Metzner.

Dayan, Daniel and Elihu Katz (1992). *Media Events. The Live Broadcasting of History.* Cambridge, Mass, London, UK: Harvard University Press.

Feierabend, Sabine, and Walter Klingler (2002). "Medien- und Themeninteressen Jugendlicher. Ergebnisse der JIM-Studie 2001 zum Medienumgang 12- bis 19-Jähriger." *MediaPerspektiven* 1: 9–21.

Habermas, Jürgen (1992). *The Structural Transformation of the Public Sphere: An Inquiry into a Category of Bourgeois Society.* Cambridge, MA: MIT Press.

Mannheim, Karl, (1951). *Essays on the Sociology of Knowledge.* London: Routledge and Kegan Paul.

Postman, Neil (1982). *The Disappearance of Childhood.* New York: Delacorte Press.

Postman, Neil (1985). *Amusing Ourselves to Death.* New York: Viking-Penguin.

Zillmann, Dolf (1988). "Mood Management: Using Entertainment to Full Advantage." In *Communication, Social Cognition, and Affect*, ed. L. Donohew, H.E. Sypher, and E.T. Higgins, 147–172. Hillsdale, NJ: Erlbaum.

Keval J. Kumar

Memories of the events of childhood and early youth are rarely the subject of research in communication studies. Memories of early media experiences receive much less attention. In social psychology and marketing research, "recall tests" comprise major tools, though they are restricted to the short term and related primarily to product and media use, or to "perception studies." Memories are perhaps felt to be too slippery to pin down and to analyze—almost impossible to quantify or to describe precisely. Perhaps that explains why the subjective experiences of childhood memories have yet to become the stuff of scientific (empirical) research, despite contemporary interest in the violence that children are regularly exposed to in films, television, computer and video games, cartoons, the print media, and in recent years on the Internet and the World Wide Web (cf. Carlsson and von Feilitzen, 1998). But recent research suggests that it is the violence in factual television, especially in news programs, that children and young people find most disturbing, and even frightening (cf. Hargrave, 1993; Ralph, Brown, and Lees, 1999). It also appears that violent events in national and international news are remembered for a much longer time than others. Such memories, as recalled, can be stark, vivid, and precise, but sometimes muddled and exaggerated. These "constructions" of the memories of media events of childhood and early youth were the subject of this research effort.

While there has been much research into the violent content of the media, especially on television and film, hardly any research exists on the narratives of remembered violence among media users. Menon and Bhasin (1998) have analyzed women's memories of the real-life violence that occurred during the partition of India. But media memories, in this case, would deal with remembered violence of events reported in the mass media.

The nature of talk about violence in the media of one's childhood and early youth differs remarkably. Barnhurst and Wartella (1998) have looked at the memories of communication students at a U.S. university. Asked about their childhood experiences of television (and not of violence on television), these memories (or "life-histories") were written down in the form of personal essays. The research focused on the media experiences and the written texts of young people's memories. Uchida (1999) has done a close critical analysis of "popular memory" in Japanese society since the Meiji Restoration, with particular attention to the Ministry of Education's songs for ordinary primary-school readers. Schlesinger et al. (1992) have looked at women's discourse about violent scenes in television programs (such as *Crimewatch* and *East Enders*) and a feature film (*The Accused*) in 14 focus groups conducted in community locations in Britain. The 1993 survey of the Broadcasting Standards Council tested "in detail people's attitudes to violent materials in each of news, reconstruction programs and documentaries" (Hargrave, 1993). The research reported here is different in focus: memories of violent events, both national and international, which occurred during the respondent's childhood and early youth, and as narrated in focus groups held in a home environment.

This paper offers some reflections on memories of the media events of childhood, and the global nature of these memories, with particular reference to the respective situation in India. The source of these reflections was three focus groups conducted with three generations (represented by three age-specific cohorts). The main research questions that were addressed are:

- What kind of memories do three generations of Indians have of the events of their childhood?
- What form do these memories take with reference to national events and international events?
- What makes an event international or global?
- What is the possible role of the mass media in such memories?
- Are there any generational differences in memories of media events of one's childhood?

- How are these narratives of childhood events constructed in terms of the geography, chronology and politics of memory?

Media Environment

The print and electronic media were introduced in India at about the same time as they developed in Europe. The press, first the English-language press and later the vernacular press, took root in the late 18th century, and cinema came to India in 1898, barely a few weeks after the technology was demonstrated by the Lumiere brothers in a Paris basement. By the 1920s, several private radio stations had made their appearance in urban India, and by 1959, New Delhi had its first television studio and transmitter.

Today, the Indian newspaper and film industries are the largest in the world, with more than 49,000 registered publications and a total feature-film output of a thousand every year. Radio reaches more than 100 million homes, and television more than 80 million homes out of a total of approximately150 million. Access to the Internet was low except in the large cities, with barely five million subscribers and ten million Net users nationwide (cf. Kumar, 1999, 2000).

The participants in the Indian focus groups had easy access to both print and electronic media. In total, nine men and six women participated in the three focus-group discussions. The youth group consisted of two boys and three girls; the middle-aged group consisted of three men and one woman; and the elderly group consisted of four men and two women. The participants were largely from well-educated middle-class families representing different regions and different cultural backgrounds of India. Except for one Muslim man and one Christian woman, the majority of participants belonged to the dominant Hindu religion. The participants were selected purposefully as the study was an attempt to explore the relationship between memory of childhood events on one hand and the experience of the media on the other.

The researcher facilitated the 15–20 and 40–45 age groups himself; the first at his residence in Pune (India) in late August 1999, and the second at his residence in Bahrain in the Persian Gulf in June 1999. (More than 3.5 million Indians live and work in the countries of the Gulf). The above-70 age group was facilitated by a research assistant at his residence (also in Pune, India) in late August 1999.

At no stage of the focus-group discussions was there an attempt to steer the discussions toward the recalling of violent events, except in the case of international events where a list of ten events were arbitrarily selected for each period. Violent events of the respondents' childhood and early youth were not the subject of the research project, but violence as a major theme emerged from the focus-group discussions as the respondents talked about their media memories. The researcher was struck by the selection of assassinations, wars, communal conflicts, street riots, and political events as the respondents told and retold their childhood experiences.

Media Interaction: The First Generation[1]

Six Marathi-speaking residents of the city of Pune participated in the focus-group discussion conducted for the elderly group (aged 70 and above). Four men and two women from the high-caste Maharashtrian Brahmin community took part. Among the men, two were university graduates who had worked in the field of education, one was an engineer, and the fourth was a high-school–educated clerk in a government department. One of the participating women was a university graduate who had worked as a labor officer in the state government, and the other was a homemaker, educated up to high school. The majority of the participants were in their seventies.

The participants in the focus-group discussion were all members of a homogenous sociocultural class/caste in the western Indian state of Maharashtra. This class has historically been a privileged section of Marathi society. This was the class that pioneered the education movement in Maharashtra in the late-18th and early-19th century. This was also the class that was involved in the social-reform movement during the same period. This same class/caste has therefore dominated the cultural scene of Maharashtra for several decades. This elite class and its culture—often termed "Brahmani" or "Puneri" culture—continues to dominate. Several of the leading personalities in literature, theater, arts, education, and religious or social-reform movements, emerged from this very class. The decades-long hegemony of the class was challenged successfully several times during the last century, though this challenge was raised in the areas of politics and economics rather than in the area of culture.

Media Environment in the 1930s and 1940s

It is against this background that the childhood memories of the six participants should be seen and read. The formative years of the participants coincided with that period (the 1930s–1940s) when the Brahman culture was dominant and unchallenged in the whole of Maharashtra. The most influential newspapers of the time were run and edited by scholars who belonged to the same class.

The participants in the focus-group discussion said that they were listeners to radio broadcasts, though not very regular listeners. This was primarily because their families could not afford to own radio sets. Five out of the six participants bought their first radio sets only in the 1960s (when they were all in their thirties). There were few radio sets prior to the sixties, but almost all alleys and neighborhoods used to have at least one set. As a result, listening to the radio "used to be a social experience" (FG 3, 2). Thus for the majority of participants, listening to the radio was "a special occasion," associated most of the time with some important political event, such as the end of World War II, Mahatma Gandhi's assassination, and the riots that followed it. For most of them, listening to the radio was always a social experience wherein about ten persons gathered around the set to listen together to the news and other programs. In fact, most of their media experiences were social in character—always in a group with the family or with neighbors.

The newspapers that the participants said they'd read regularly during their childhood and early youth were local Marathi dailies, but two of the men said that they also read English newspapers like the *Times of India* and the *Bombay Chronicle*. The families of all the six participants used to subscribe to at least one newspaper. "There used to be many newspapers and we could read them either at home, in school, or at neighbors' homes," said one participant (FG 3, 2).

Traditional Media

Apart from the mass media such as radio and the press, the participants spoke of their exposure to traditional mass media such as public speeches, religious prayer gatherings such as *keertans,* and religious-social events like *Ganeshotsav.* Several well-known public speakers frequently mentioned in the focus-group discussions were also from the same class. The participants dwelt at length on their memories of public lectures they attended. The great orators they mentioned included N.C. Kelkar, Raosaheb and Achyut Patwardhan, Acharya Atre, and Savarkar. The discussion was replete with references to such public speeches. One of the woman participants (FG 3, 3) said:

> Being women, we had a lot of limitations in accessing information through the mass media. Public lectures and keertans filled that vacuum.

Traditional media like *bhajans* (group singing) and *keertans* (religious gatherings) were employed at that time to disseminate political messages.

Those leaders who employed such methods of popular education came to be known as *rashtriya kirtankars* (national prayer leaders).

Public lectures were an effective instrument for political education. Public lectures used to be held in small towns like Ahmednagar. One participant recalled having listened to public lectures given by the Patwardhan brothers, Madan Mohan Malviya, Subhaschandra Bose, and Manavendranath Roy. He said that these public speeches contributed much to his political education (FG 3, 1), adding that these speeches used to be of greater interest than films.

"Mediation" by Significant Others

A vital feature of the participants' media experience was that it was "mediated" by significant others such as grandparents, parents, siblings, and other members of the joint/extended family. The terms and conditions of media exposure were determined by the elders of the family, specifically by the male elders. The participants recalled their fathers taking them to the neighbors' homes to listen to the radio. As young members of the family, it was their duty to read the newspapers aloud for the benefit of all the other members of the family. So, while one person read the newspapers, others heard the news. This tradition of reading the news aloud for the benefit of the family was continued when the participants started their own families. One participant said that much of the credit for the general knowledge and awareness gained by his son (now a practicing doctor) should be traced to this tradition:

> We used to believe the newspapers cent-per-cent during those days. Today, we are not sure about any of the newspapers. They have lost their authenticity. They have been sold to the capitalist forces. (FG3, 1)

Political Environment

The 1930s and 1940s were perhaps the most turbulent period in Indian and world history. The world events of the period included World War II, the rise of Hitler and the Holocaust, the bombing of Hiroshima and Nagasaki, the fall of the British Empire, and the spread of communism. For India too, these two decades were equally turbulent: the rise of Mahatma Gandhi and his movement of nonviolence against the British Raj, the Salt March, the partition of the Indian subcontinent and its aftermath, and the assassination of Gandhi. In addition, there were several national and local movements and events that electrified the nation. The struggle for freedom left few untouched or unmoved. The period witnessed the rise and spread of a variety of political ideologies in India, from rabid fundamentalism to radical humanism. These took on different colors in different regions of the land. In Maharashtra, this spectrum of political ideologies was marked on the extreme right by fundamentalist organizations like the Rashtriya Sevak Sangh (R.S.S.) led by K.B. Hedgewar, and on the left by Dange and his Communist Party. So politically charged was the nation during the 1930s and '40s that even religious celebrations like the *Ganeshotsav* took on political colorations. The focus-group participants therefore recollected political events very vividly.

The "public memory" of the focus-group participants thus revolved around media and politics. Political events and personalities were reported vigorously in the media of the period. Political news dominated the press then as much as it does now, more than fifty years after India's independence. Even the regional media have a strong political orientation. This perhaps explains why the references to political events, rather than the events related to the social, cultural, and economic conditions of the country and their reporting in the media, dominated the focus-group discussions.

Media Interaction: Newspapers

At the very beginning of the focus-group discussion, one of the men participants (FG 3, 1) narrated his experience of reading the editorials in the *Daily Agrani* (Daily Frontier), a paper run by Nathuram Godse, the assassin of Mahatma Gandhi. In his view:

> Agrani used to carry detailed articles on the Hindu-Muslim riots in different parts of India after independence. The coverage of Naokhali riots were especially inflammatory. I used to stay in Ahmednagar at that time and the situation there was very tense. (FG 3, 1)

He vividly recalled the page layout of the *Lokshakti* (a Marathi daily), which carried the news about the bomb explosion during a prayer meeting led by Gandhi, and later his assassination on January 30th, 1948. He also remembered the tense situation in his hometown when Gandhi was arrested during the "Quit India" movement. He recalled how pamphlets were widely and very frequently distributed. As many historians would vouch for, pamphlets were a low-cost and vital medium used by nationalist leaders to spread information about the struggle for freedom throughout the country.

Several memories of the group were associated with Mahatma Gandhi's assassination. There was a definite touchiness/sensitivity about these memories. This is perhaps because the Brahmins of Maharashtra had to face the wrath of the public since Nathuram Godse, the Mahatma's assassin, was a Maharashtrian Brahmin. The participants talked about their experiences of the anti-Brahmin riots in the state following Gandhi's assassination.

International Events

The majority of the focus-group participants could recollect international events of the 1940s (that is, when they were all in their early youth), but only after some prompting from the facilitator. They knew about the bombing of Pearl Harbor, the bombing of Hiroshima and Nagasaki, the end of World War II, but could not associate any media memory with the events. Only one participant could remember seven out of the ten international events listed in the schedule. He said that he remembered the Berlin Olympics, but the memory of that event was etched in his mind because of its Indian context:

> Hitler refused to shake hands with Dhyan Chand and told him: "You are just a colonel there (in India); if you were a German I would have made you a general." (FG 3, 2)

This group of the elders of the city of Pune talked freely about their recollections of the media of their childhood and youth, and of the media of today (especially the press). There were hardly any references to television in the recollections; references to the cinema are few and far between. Going to the cinema was possibly associated with feelings of guilt among the higher castes, while television came into their lives only in the early 1980s when the participants were over the age of fifty. While access to the radio was extremely limited, access to newspapers was widespread. Newspapers were read aloud in most homes so that literate and illiterate, young and old, were kept abreast of happenings in the country and in the world.

However, far more vital than the modern mass media for the participants were the traditional media such as public speeches, *bhajans*, *keertans*, theater, and pamphlets. All of them stressed that these low-cost and familiar media were the main sources of their political information. These provided them with a "political education" during the 1930s and 1940s. Unlike the 15- to 20-year-old group, which lambasted the media, this group was supportive and appreciative of the reporting of national events in the English and Marathi newspapers of the thirties and forties.

They recalled national events such as the freedom-struggle movement, the nonviolence movement of Mahatma Gandhi, without much prompting.

However, they could remember international events such as World War II, the Berlin Olympics, the bombing of Hiroshima and Nagasaki, and so on, only after some prompting from the facilitator. Also, while their memories of national events were narrated in a vivid manner, those related to international events were often unclear and vague, and even distorted.

Media Interaction: Radio and the Second Generation

Two men, both married, and a married couple made up the focus group of the second age cohort, 40–45 years of age. The couple was Hindu, one of the men was Muslim, and the other a Christian. The couple and the Muslim hailed from Karnataka; the Christian from Kerala. All four were well educated and worked as trainers in a professional engineering and management institute.

The media the four participants had greatest access to in their childhood and early youth was the radio, not television. Television entered their lives only in the mid-1980s, when they were well above the age of 25 or so. Radio was indeed the most important medium and also the most favored media. Their memories of the media during their childhood were also related to newspapers and magazines. The names of newspapers and magazines they had read as children and young men came back to them, though several titles had become defunct. For instance, they remembered reading *The Illustrated Weekly of India* (now defunct), a publication of the Times of India Group, and *Sport and Pastime* (also defunct), a sports publication of the Hindu Group in Madras. Only one of the participants recalled that there were any restrictions or controls on their reading, or on their listening to the radio (this contrasts with the experience of the 15- to 20-year-old generation, who resented the control of parents in what they read). Shoba[2] recalled:

> I don't think I had so much freedom to listen to radio or watch TV. There were a lot of restrictions. Timing, what to watch and what not to watch. My father was more like a military officer; everything had to be done at that particular time. (FG 2, 3)

The 70- to 75-year-old group also emphasized the social nature of media experience. They recalled vividly that few families could afford their own radio sets, and therefore they invariably listened to the radio in a group of some families. Further, newspapers and magazines were not isolated individual experiences; rather, they were read aloud by a literate member of the family for the whole family and this was sometimes followed by discussions.

As recalled, this was the source of much "political education" for men and women, and children and adults alike.

The four participants could recall the following national events from the period 1965–75: the Indo-Pakistan War, the pre-Emergency years, the split of the Congress Party, the National Elections in Kerala, Cricket tests, the Jayaprakash Narayan Movement in Bihar and Gujarat, and the Emergency regime of Indira Gandhi (1975–77). The participants recalled these events, often without much prompting from the facilitator, which were widely reported on radio and in the press. But it is noteworthy that radio was experienced primarily as a medium of entertainment, while the press was perceived as a provider of political information.

The Indo-Pakistan War (1965)

The sole Muslim participant in the focus group recalled in particular one program on All India Radio, which catered to the needs of the prisoners of war, especially those who had been taken away to Pakistan:

> This was one program I used to listen to with great interest. Every day I used to listen to that. (FG 2, 2)

He vaguely remembered the 1965 war with Pakistan:

> I think during my childhood days it was radio that played a major role. Not until 1968 I was actually exposed to other media. I was pretty young, though I have a very vague memory of the 1965 war. I was at that time maybe five years old. So I don't really remember those things. My father . . . was a government servant. I don't have very good memories of the 1965 war. (FG 2, 2)

Indira Gandhi and the Emergency

John (FG 2, 1) recalled the emergency regime of Indira Gandhi and the role of the media at the time:

> One strong memory about media events strikes my mind now. During July 1975, when the internal emergency clamped by Mrs. Gandhi. I still remember that very strongly, because then I was a college student. . . . I was in the final year of my studies; we were very active in collecting information about what is happening in the country. At that time, both the radio as well as the press, newspapers, and everything that was possible. And this was a time when

media got so much importance because even people who were not that much really interested in media events, they were interested in reading magazines, newspapers, because that was a terror period in our country. At least that was the feeling I had. (FG 2, 1)

Khan (FG 2, 2) also recalled the JP (Jayaprakash) Movement that preceded the Emergency:

JP [Jayaprakash Narayan] Movement I had heard about, I was only nine at that time. I was too young to follow. . . . What had happened in 1977 [the internal emergency] I was following . . . that was the time Indira Gandhi was humbled and the Janata Party came to power, and Morarji [Desai] became the prime minister. Actually, it was a government of wise people, but could not pull on for a long period of time. (FG 2, 2)

International Events

The international events the participants recalled without any prompting included the Cyprus crisis, man's first landing on the moon, the Vietnam War, and the liberation of Bangladesh. Some prompting brought back memories of the Watergate crisis in Washington D.C., and the Cultural Revolution in China. However, memories of the events and the media reports related to the rise of the Palestine Liberation Movement, Woodstock, the OPEC crisis, the Prague Spring and the 1968 student revolutions, were very faint and vague. As Khan stated:

International events? Especially I remember Vietnam. Watergate, of course, but not much, but then I had followed it up later on the BBC, when they telecast it just before the Clinton scandal; they had carried a series of shows on TV, as to how Watergate took place, how he was trying to bug all information of all opposition members, and then finally how he had been asked to resign. This I followed up much later, but not when it did. (FG 2, 2)

Said Uday:

No, international news I was not interested in anything much, other than science development, technological revolution. I hate all wars. But since it [Vietnam] concerned all of us, I was following it up to some extent. (FG 2, 4)

John (FG 2, 2) summed up his memories of Vietnam in just one word: "Napalm." The television image of the naked girl running across the screen was seared into their memories. He also vividly recalled the landing of the first man on the moon, which he heard about first on radio:

> One of the events I can recollect strongly is the first man on the moon. Apollo, the person, the whole event, I still recollect because of the broken communication and when he landed on the moon the first time and what he said, all those things do come back to my mind. When subsequently, of course, in the early eighties, when we had television in Bangalore, we could see some of the international events. (FG 2, 4)

The main source of Khan's memories of international events was newspapers and magazines. He had access to magazines like *Time, Newsweek,* and later *India Today* (his favorite magazine). He recalled these two international events without any prompting:

> Especially, I was keenly following two international events: one was the Cyprus crisis, the other was the Vietnam War, which was going on during those days. We were especially following the atrocities committed by the Khmer Rouge. . . . We used to read the local newspapers [in *Kannada* and English], reports especially about the 1970–71 Vietnam War, and the way these people used to drive out all these anti-Khmer Rouge. Then there was an event in my college—to have a kind of mock United Nations. So that time I took part in it. The issue discussed the whole thing surrounding the Cyprus crisis. That was one event which really, clearly [is] vivid in my memory. (FG 2, 2)

He also remembered, after some prompting, the Soviet invasion of Hungary and the OPEC crisis, but hardly anything about the 1968 student revolution in Europe and elsewhere.

Khan: Yes, the Soviet invasion and especially I remember. I was not born when in 1956 the Hungarian invasion took place, but I had read about it in *Time* and *Newsweek.* They had the Soviet tanks had rolled into the streets of Budapest, then the way they had suppressed the. . . . Then of course I was reading the novel of Saul Bellow, who was himself a Hungarian, I think. So he had . . . his novel, which got him the Nobel Prize, if I don't remember wrongly, I think . . . *The Dean's December.* In that, he says how he was annoyed by the Soviet presence, how they suppressed human rights and all the things. Then, of course, now I remember in 1984 Nobel Prize literature winner, Gabriel Garcia Marquez.

Facilitator:	Any memories of the OPEC crisis?
Khan:	OPEC crisis? Of course, it was there in 1975, after the Egyptian war, which had failed. Then of course it was the Saudi Prince— King Feisal, I think. He made one open statement: cut all supply of the western countries, especially Japan, U.S. and then the crisis of oil prices, which went up 38 to 39 dollars. This is the thing I remember about that.
Facilitator:	Any memories of the 1968 student revolution?
Khan:	I had heard about it. (FG 2, 2)

Media Interaction: Television and the Third Generation

The third (youngest) age cohort was represented by two boys (FG 1, 1 and 2) and three girls (FG 1, 3, 4, and 5) who agreed to take part in the focus-group discussions; they were all undergraduate students in colleges of the Pune University. One of the boys (FG 1, 1) was from New Delhi; the second (FG 1, 2), from Calcutta. Two of the girls (FG 1, 3 and 4) were from Calcutta; and the third (FG 1, 5) from Jamshedpur. They were from middle-class families. The Delhi boy (FG 1, 1) was from a Panjabi/Sikh family; while the boy (FG 1, 2) and the two girls (FG 1, 3 and 4) from Calcutta were from Hindu families; the Jamshedpur girl (FG 1, 5) was from a Roman Catholic family.

All five participants had good access to the mass media right from their early years. Television and the press were the media they apparently spent the most time with. They were aware of the major national and international events of the 1980s and 1990s, and the source of their information was invariably the media, though word-of-mouth also played a vital role. Of the three age groups, this group was the most critical of the media, especially the press and television. It was also the group that talked (often angrily) about the negative role of the media in fomenting violence and fundamentalism. It was the group that readily recollected incidents/events of violence at the national and international levels.

The major national events the youth group could remember and were eager to talk about were: Indira Gandhi's assassination, Rajiv Gandhi's assassination, the demolition of the Babri Masjid in Ayodhya and its aftermath, the rise of the Bharatiya Janata Party in national politics, the Kargil skirmish, and the killing of Christian missionaries in Bihar. The majority of events remembered—all without much prompting from the facilitator— were intrinsically violent in nature, and largely associated with the political and the religious life of the nation. Further, they were events that were highlighted by the mass media. It is possible that the main source of such knowledge was the mass media, though other sources like the family and the peer group were influential sources too.

Rajiv Gandhi's Assassination: The "Human Bomb"

How did they come to know about these events in the first place? After a brief warming-up session in which the participants listed these events, the discussion focused in the beginning on their memories of the assassination of Prime Minister Rajiv Gandhi at the hands of a suicide bomber near Madras. The assassination took place when the five participants were around ten years old. "DD [India's public-broadcast TV station] flashed the news at 11:00 P.M.," declared Dev (FG 1, 1), though the others in the group contested this: they insisted that the news was flashed at 10:40 P.M. But Meeta (FG 1, 3) remembered that she got the news from her mother the same night:

> I remember I was sleeping at the time. My mother came and told me that Rajiv Gandhi is dead. She had seen some people in a sort of procession. I remember for one whole week all TV programs were stopped. I remember the cremation. Another thing I remember that my father had a magazine . . . that magazine my father showed to my mother. But we were not allowed to see that magazine. My father had kept it in the almirah. We were very curious what was in that magazine. One day my mother was away. I opened the almirah. It said children should not be shown this magazine. Because there were lots of violent scenes. Many pictures were there, but I guess it did not affect me much because I was already hooked into Hindi movies. (FG 1, 3)

Yashwant (FG 1, 2) also associated the news of Rajiv Gandhi's assassination with the same issue of the magazine *Outlook*.

> My father and mother never used to show it to me, and hid it somewhere. My brother and I said we had to see what was in the magazine. My mother and father go out and we climb up the cupboard . . . take it out somehow. I realize I just conked off. My brother asked me what happened. I said, *"kuch nahi hua"* [Nothing at all has happened]. Then I started crying. Then I realized something bad must have happened. I knew about human bombs, because I had always read about suicide bombers of Japan, but this human bomb and the state in which it left the bomber and the bombed was not expected by me. (FG 1, 2)

The other members of the group were also shocked. Dev of New Delhi put it this way:

A gentleman, a lady screamed: Rajiv is dead, Rajiv is dead. My dad was shocked, my mom was shocked. Of course we were also shocked. But we were shocked the next morning. It just gave a shock. (FG 1, 1)

He too remembered the "human bomb" aspect of the news story:

He was blown out by the LTTE [Liberation Tigers for Tamil Eelam]. A lady put a bomb on herself, a human bomb; we were introduced to the concept of explosives. (FG 1, 1)

Nabo of Calcutta remembered that she was in Class V at the time, and that she did not go to school that morning:

It was quite early in the morning when I got up and I heard my neighbors. They were making a lot of noise. . . . Some people came to my house and they said, "Rajiv Gandhi is dead." Oh my God, how did this happen? It was like a stunning surprise. I never used to watch the news first and foremost. That news was very shocking to me. (FG 1, 4)

She also recalled that it was a Tuesday, and that she "wouldn't be able to watch *Chitrahar* (a popular film-based TV program) on Wednesday . . . we were quite frustrated."

But they said they were all happy that schools would be closed and they would have a holiday. Yashwant summed up the feeling:

The first thing that came to my mind when Rajiv Gandhi died: "Thank God school is closed. We can play our guts out." (FG 1, 2)

The Aftermath: Communal Tensions

At least two of the group recalled that in the aftermath of the assassination some tension was present in the community, and that some trouble or riots were expected. This was possibly because of what happened in New Delhi in the aftermath of the assassination of Indira Gandhi six years earlier. Dev, a Panjabi/Sikh from New Delhi, recalled:

There was a big scare that bombings would take place there . . . Delhi being a very crowded place. (FG 1, 1)

Meeta, a Hindu from Calcutta, was more specific:

> The place where I used to stay was a totally Muslim area. It was supposed to be a violent-prone area. I was personally never affected because from the age of four when I went to school, no Muslims commented on us. So the death was a news item, not something personal for me. Because Muslim people used to work in our place, they were economically dependent on us. In our school, the [Muslim] drivers were very nice. I mean I never had a bad experience of [people] killing each other. Maybe it was going on in other parts of the country but not in my life. (FG 1, 3)

Indira Gandhi's Assassination

Memories of Rajiv Gandhi's assassination naturally led to talk about his mother, Indira Gandhi's, assassination at the hands of her own Sikh bodyguards six years earlier, in 1984. The participants were far too young (four or five years old) to remember very much. Dev put it in this dramatic manner:

> As far as I remember, I have no memories of Indira Gandhi being assassinated just other than . . . maybe because I am a Panjabi, the sardars [Sikhs] being burnt alive. That was a very bad scene. One scene I remember, in fact, two scenes. A sardar was simply chopped off right in the middle of the road, and secondly, there is an old man 60 years of age, they put a tire in his neck, put petrol on him, and burnt him off. I saw the man being burnt alive. I was dragged inside. I don't know what state I was in for two or three days. I wasn't sent to school. It was all war going on the road. Manslaughter, total manslaughter, I remember [it is] still very much a part of mind. It was scary. (FG 1, 1)

Demolition of the Babri Mosque at Ayodhya

One memory of violence led to another as the group got into the spirit of the focus-group discussion. There was no stopping them now: their memories were prodded on by others in the group, and the members were all ears ready to share and even to wallow in the experience. Talk about the demolition of the Babri Masjid in Ayodhya, and the riots that followed in Bombay, Calcutta, Delhi and other parts of the country, led naturally to the group remembering their introduction to terms like "Hindu fundamentalism," the names of political parties such as the BJP [Bharatiya Janata Party] and the role of the media.

While Nabo (FG 1, 4) said she "didn't remember anything . . . nothing," Marie associated Ayodhya (in fact she confused it with Lucknow) with being kept indoors all the time, and with having had the same food day and night in her boarding school. "We had Maggie's [noodles] for boarders' night," she humorously recalled. She added:

> Ayodhya . . . I came to know of it very late. I remember the people around us. There were a lot of Hindus around us, so they were also against the Muslims. They shouldn't have done that; that shouldn't have happened. (FG 1, 5)

But Dev, Yashwant, and Meeta had stronger memories of the aftermath of the demolition of the mosque in Ayodhya. Dev recalled that he was studying in a German school in New Delhi at the time:

> It was a cosmopolitan society. Religion never mattered: You're a Muslim, a Hindu, or whatever. It was just our own world to us. They used to come and tell me: "You know who burnt Ayodhya?" We used to come home and used to see the "aunties" [neighbors] talking. Each one had a different version; each one of them had to say something, and perhaps it's not true. It was more of rumors than reality. (FG 1, 1)

Ayodhya and the Mass Media

The violence associated with the event Meeta remembered from the film *Bombay.*

> I saw the violence and all that. I was never affected by this violence. I felt they were exaggerating. I don't think such things happened. (FG 1, 3).

Yashwant also remembered that the film *Bombay* "exaggerated a little bit." Though the Ayodhya incident did not affect him, he recalled that he lived in a Muslim area in Calcutta:

> I used to play with Muslim friends, and Muslim maidservants used to come and work at my place . . . no problem at all . . . I never saw anything so drastic as killing, murdering, this and that or burning that was shown on TV or in the movie *Bombay.* (FG 1, 2)

He recalled an article at that time:

> It was so stupid, I felt; we were talking about Aurangzeb breaking all the temples at one point of time and then what would happen if the Hindus broke down one *masjid.* I said that it does not have any basis. What is history? We

were talking about history repeats itself and all, but I said these figurative meanings had no sense in this term when you don't talk about breaking down a *majid*. It doesn't make any sense in breaking down a Muslim *masjid* to portray yourself or your party to be something or other.

Meeta also recalled that she had read in the papers that "it was not Babar who actually built it; it was somebody else." She said that her "grandmother had gone to that place when the mosque was still there. She said that the mosque was there but that it was nothing, and just next to it a small wooden shed where *pooja* [worship] used to go on."

Dev, Meeta, and Yahswant flayed the role played by the media in reporting the issue.

Dev: I think more than the issue itself, the media killed it. It was media that was solely responsible for actually making a big thing out of it. Of course, it was a fire that was expected to rise, but I think media played a very bad role in it. It actually got people angry.

Meeta: Today the BJP is in a position. It started at that point of time and the media and the other political parties actually helped the BJP what it has become today. . . . Though we may be in the majority, we need some security, we need some voice.

The group attributed the rise of Hindu fundamentalism to the media coverage of the BJP and the Ayodhya question.

Yashwant: The birth [of the BJP] was from Ayodhya. The media had put itself . . . BJP is a saffron party and all. I was talking about the newspapers and TV in general.

Meeta in particular believed that the media's negative publicity helped the BJP, that the constant use of terms like "*Hindutva*" and "fundamentalism" to describe the BJP, the Bajrang Dal, the RSS and the Shiv Sena helped the BJP.

Yashwant recalled that the *Telegraph* was read in his family. His father "used to say that this was a Congress Party paper, and the *Statesman* was basically an anti-Congress paper."

International Events

The international events were not as readily recalled as the national events. Also, the young teenagers were not as forthcoming in the expression of their views. They were unanimous that the death of Princess Diana was certainly not an "international issue," whereas Mother Teresa's demise merited international media attention. Princess Diana did not have much importance for the boys in the group, but at least one of the three girls in the group was convinced that her work for landmines and also her beauty were enough to give her international attention and to elevate her to an international status. Mrs. Clinton came to attend her funeral, she argued, and heads of state gave her due recognition (FG 1, 3). Clearly, their vote was for Mother Teresa (three of the participants were from Calcutta, the city of the Mother). The boy from Delhi, however, voted for Baba Amte.

The Gulf War

Mention of the Gulf War and the recent NATO attacks on Belgrade demonstrated that the images of television were etched on the young people's memories. Sadam Hussain was not necessarily the villain of the piece for these young minds, who were high-school kids at the time of the Gulf War. The more recent NATO bombardments of Yugoslavia also were condemned outright; they were cynical about the media hype on the attacks.

This excerpt from the discussion illustrates the trend of the views and memories expressed. Memory and opinion are mixed up gloriously here. This also illustrates the politics of memory.

Dev:	The Gulf War reminds me of tanks burning and other stuff. Seeing every day the jets firing, the missiles launched, and the petrol on fire, the commodity prices going higher, and all those countries that were dependent for oil on these Gulf countries plus Indians coming back. It was a very bad thing. Saddam really acted like a maniac . . . for no reason killing his own people. (FG 1, 1)
Marie:	All I remember about the Gulf War was that Saddam Hussain could never be found. Looking for him . . . there were two or three Saddams [Laughter all round]. . . . That was very interesting. (FG 1, 5)
Meeta:	The only thing I remember is my dad telling me about the Gulf War, the water getting polluted, the birds and animals dying in large numbers. (FG 1, 3)
Nabo:	Even I remember the same thing . . . the birds flying, black water . . . its effects on nature . . . I remember.
Meeta:	I was in Class IX or X. In the Modern History class, they said that the U.S.A. had followed the policy of the policeman, a big-stick

	policy. Then I remember my father telling us [that] surely, Saddam has done something wrong, not having the right to go into Kuwait and start destroying everything he gets. U.S.A. is practicing the big-stick policy.
Yashwant:	I am a great follower of Hitler and I like him a lot . . . Saddam Hussain and his racist policy in Iraq. It was absolutely an internal [matter]. He had occupied Kuwait that was . . . the United Nations were against it. Fine. But I don't understand why we say that the Gulf War was between the U. S.A. and Iraq.
Dev:	U.S.A. has always done this. It's no more United Nations. It's just U.S. It is in fact a very strategic position . . . oil, the black gold.
Meeta:	U.S.A. has been following this policy. Not only in Kuwait, in South America, everywhere. Panama Canal.
Dev:	What China did in Taiwan.
Meeta:	Ya, the same thing.

On the reunification of Germany, Yashwant, an unabashed admirer of Hitler, remembered:

. . . people were happy that Germany is united, and West Germany will never next play [East] Germany. I remember my father, actually my grandfather, told me lots about this. He was already close to Subash Chandra Bose when he was going to Germany. So he was telling me about the Second World War all the time. . . . There was this West Germany and East Germany. Then my grandfather becomes nostalgic and says, "One day or the other, India and Pakistan are going to shake hands and become one India again." (FG 1, 2)

Meeta took up the discussion on German reunification and on Hitler. She said her father too was an admirer of Hitler:

He admires Hitler a lot. So when the German teams united, he was very happy. He said: if West Germany wins the World Cup . . . my father used to identify the whole East Bengal team with Hitler. They're the Hitler . . . [trails off]. (FG 1, 3)

Dev, a student of a German school in New Delhi, chimed in:

The day the Berlin Wall was brought down, there was a grand celebration. We had a great time, you know. In fact, the Germans announced a big campus for us. We had a great campus, but we didn't have a new building, we needed a new building for new courses coming up. . . . Today, if you go and see it, it is a magnificent piece of building with all those photos of Germany. We also got a few students from Germany under the student-exchange scheme. They used to come and they used to talk. Actually, German kids grew up faster than Asians. We asked them what they had. They said: We had the Berlin Wall. That's all. That was a great incident. (FG 1, 1)

The articulate young people who comprised the group were as forceful in recalling national and international events of the 1980s and 1990s as in expressing their opinions on political matters and on the role of the media in sensational reporting. They took clear positions on events, issues, and personalities, and expressed them in strong language. Memories and opinions were often confused in the discussions; they remembered politics as much as they politicized memory. For them, the memory of political events was no different from the politics of memory.

Media Memories of Three Generations

What is the nature of Indian memories of the violent events of childhood and early youth? What were the social and cultural conditions that influenced such memories and the role played by the media? Also, what is the relationship between such memories and knowledge, especially the knowledge of reality? What is the kind of knowledge provided by the media in relation to national and international events? How reliable, valid, and significant is such media-based knowledge?

These are some of the philosophical questions that need to be addressed in order to fully appreciate the significance of the research reported here. We were dealing with personal and subjective experiences of childhood and early youth, with particular attention to the mass media, as they are articulated in a focus-group setting. The discourse of such talk about media experiences deserves close cultural analysis.

Violent events taking place in India were recalled much more vividly and with much greater emotional involvement by the younger generation than the middle-aged or elderly generation. One could sense anger and even cynicism as the younger generation recalled the events of their childhood and the role played by the media in reporting violent events such as assassinations, wars, and Hindu–Muslim communal tensions. This could have been for several reasons. In the first place, it could have been because the media (especially television and the press) were more widespread and more accessible during the childhood of the younger generation than during the childhood of the middle and the elderly generations. The middle-aged cohort, for instance, had no access to television, and the cohort of the elderly had extremely limited access to radio and the press. Their main source of information was public meetings, theater, and the folk media. Second, the distance from the event (chronology) was not so remote. Third, it could have been because more violent events took place, or, more likely, were reported more widely during the childhood years of the younger cohort.

These three focus-group discussions, with nine men and six women of India, suggested that recollecting such media experiences in a small focus group is largely a cathartic exercise, though at times uncomfortable. Some experiences, especially national events, were more vividly and more accurately remembered than others that were geographically and chronologically distant. For instance, memories of the freedom movement, of the assassinations of Mahatma Gandhi, Indira Gandhi, and Rajiv Gandhi were more sharply etched in Indian memory than so-called international events like the Vietnam War, Watergate, the 1968 student revolution, or the death of Princess Diana.

In any case, what was it that made one event global, and another merely local or regional or national? A major factor was the amount of attention given to such events in the mass media—the agenda-setting function of the mass media. There was nothing intrinsic to an event that rendered it naturally local, regional, national, or global. For instance, the death of Princess Diana or that of Mother Teresa was given a global character because of the continuous live coverage for consecutive days by the transnational networks such as the BBC, CNN, and the transnational news agencies such as Reuters and AP. Further, they were already media celebrities long before their tragic deaths; the media, especially cable and satellite television, capitalized on this celebrity status. Thus the global character of an event or even a personality was dependent on the media, and in particular transnational media. A small earthquake, a sex scandal, or a minor racial skirmish in the United States or in Britain is reported as a global event; in contrast, national elections or workers' strikes in any Asian or African nation are not reported at all by the transnational news agencies. For events, personalities, and scandals taking place in any Asian or African country to qualify as global, they need to have a larger-than-life dimension, must affect or touch the richer countries in a dramatic manner, must be totally unexpected, and involve large populations and mass destruction. Also, of course, they must make for exciting television pictures.

It was evident then that global events were media "constructs" as much as were the focus-group respondents' memories of those events. The phenomenal expansion of the media, especially cable and satellite television during the last decade, has meant that many more events began to take on a global dimension than was the case earlier when few countries had access to more than a couple of terrestrial channels.

Besides being very selective, memories of childhood media events were affected by distance (both in terms of time and the extent of personal experience) from the events or the people who were remembered. The 70- to 75-year-olds, for instance, were required to remember events that took place sixty to seventy years earlier; whereas the 15- to 20-year-olds had to recall events that happened just a decade or so earlier. Chronological proximity to the event is a vital variable, but so is the cultural proximity in relation to the event remembered.

Besides the geography and the chronology of media memory, there is the question of the politics of memory. We do not talk about our memories of events that touch on questions of personal or collective guilt, what we might term "the politics of memory." The group of 70- to 75-year-old Pune Brahmins who took part in the focus-group discussion did not even once mention the struggle of the Dalits against Brahmin dominance. They did not, at any stage, refer even indirectly to the partition of India. It was also observed that the 15- to 20-year-olds did not feel very comfortable talking about the Mandal riots and the demolition of the Babri mosque.

Further, some memories were extremely vivid: participants could recall the exact dates, names, and media images of events. Other memories were very faint and muddled; even prompting did not jog the memory. Media images are, after all, ephemeral and fleeting in nature. Is this possibly related to why some memories are so unclear and hazy and often confused? Apparently, there is more to memory than the images and sound bites of the mass media. Such images and sound bites often get mixed up with the whispers and rumors in the family and the community, as revealed by the young generation's talk about the Ayodhya demolition and the aftermath.

A final question that needs to be raised regarding the nature and dynamic of memory in relation to the media is: What is the role of social and cultural events (rather than the media) in jogging the memories of different generations? Are memories influenced by the culture and the religion we belong to, and the times in which we live? Are there cultural differences, for instance, in the way we remember and recall the violent events of our childhood and early youth? The reports from the discussions of the three focus groups suggest that culture, religion, language, age, social class/caste, and (above all) personal experience of events, are vital variables that influence *what* we remember and even the very *way* we remember. There is what one might broadly term "the politics of memory," for we are most likely to remember that which is of intimate concern to us and to our community, and gloss over the unpleasant and the uncomfortable.

Bibliography

Barnhurst, Kevin G., and Ellen Wartella (1998). "Young Citizens, American TV Newscasts and the Collective Memory." *Critical Studies in Mass Communication* 15: 279–305.

Carlsson, Ulla, and Cecilia von Feilitzen, eds. (1998). *Children and Media Violence,* Vol. 1. Goteberg: UNESCO Clearinghouse on Children and Media Violence.

Hargrave, Andrea Millwood, ed. (1993). *Violence in Factual Television.* London: Broadcasting Standards Council, Annual Review.

Kumar, Keval J. (1999). "History of Broadcasting in India: A Political Economy Perspective." In *International Satellite Broadcasting in South Asia,* ed. Srinivas Melkote, Peter Shields, and Binod C. Agrawal. New York: University Press of America.

Kumar, Keval J. (2000). *Mass Communication in India,* 3rd rev. ed. Bombay: Jaico Paperbacks.

Menon, Ritu, and Kamla Bhasin (1998). *Borders and Boundaries: Women in India's Partition.* New Delhi: Kali for Women.

Ralph, Sue, Jo L. Brown, and Tim Lees, eds. (1999). *Youth and the Global Media.* Luton: University of Luton Press.

Schlesinger, Philip et al. (1992). *Women Viewing Violence.* London: BFI Publishing.

Uchida, Ryuzu (1999). "Memory and the Transformation of Social Experience in Modern Japan: Rethinking the Song 'Home.'" *Media, Culture and* Society 21: 205–219.

Reiko Sekiguchi

1. Historical Background of Media in Japan

After the so-called Unequal Treaties in 1854 and 1858, following three hundred years of isolation from other countries, Japan kept its independence only with difficulty. There was the constant threat that it might also suffer the same fate as other "Eastern" (Asian) countries whose territories were divided by "Western" (European and North American) powers, only to become their colonies. Japan had to choose either to submit itself to the same fate as the East, or, following the models of the West, to combine its forces to take other countries' territories.

Japan chose the latter. This meant that Japan, because it was a latecomer, had to take the land Western countries had already controlled and colonized. The year 1935, which is the beginning of our investigation for our oldest cohort, was the year in which the political relations with Western countries were becoming increasingly tense. In 1937 a war began in China and the conflict continued until it became part of World War II in 1941.

In Japan, something like a newspaper had begun as early as 1615. Experimenting with radio broadcasting began in 1922, and public-radio broadcasts began in 1925. Soon after, the Ministry of Communications began to censor the news programs, forbidding the broadcast of political discussions or lectures. People had to pay fees to listen to the radio, so the number of fee contracts showed how the demand for radio broadcasting was increasing. It was 2 million households in 1935, while the population was 80 million. This number increased to 6 million in 1941, when World War II started. In 1942 the newspapers, of which there had been several, were integrated into one under official wartime policy. Along with the newspapers, the numbers of the radio sets decreased as the war reached the mainland of Japan.

During the war, the reports on the radio and in the newspaper were strongly controlled by the Ministry of the Interior. After 1945 the responsibility for censorship was transferred to the Governmental Headquarters of the United States. All content was approved before the news was published. After July 1948, content was reviewed after its publication. Gradually, Japan reestablished itself as an independent country and there was eventually no more official censorship. However, in 1965, as a result of protests by the United States Embassy, some TV programs had to be stopped and some newspapers' chief editors had to resign due to the articles they published.

After the desperate efforts for recovery from the damage of the war, exports began to increase in 1960 and the economic condition continued to rise until 1973, when it slowed down due to the energy shortages triggered by the "oil shock." Therefore, the target years for the middle cohort, 1965–1975, were those in which Japan's economy was booming.

TV broadcasting began in 1953 (on NHK, the first Japanese TV station). Color television was introduced in 1957. In 1962, the fee contract with NHK, which was half governmental and the only TV station that was permitted to collect fees, had grown to represent 10 million households. In 1965, many customers moved from radio to TV, and radio-broadcasting companies had to consider seriously how to retain their listeners. In 1969, many TV stations were established. They were financed by commercial (advertising) fees and did not collect fees from customers. In 1972 the fee contract with NHK TV was 23.52 million, half of which were still black-and-white contracts. In 1975, TV stations surpassed the newspaper companies in total income from advertising.

For the youngest cohort, color TV was the norm. In 1988, one year before the target year of our investigation began, the reception contracts for satellite TV reached 1,145,000 households. In terms of Internet connectivity, the Ministry of Education made it a policy that starting in the year 2000, every student should learn computer skills in school, and all the schools should be connected to the Internet.

Difficulties were encountered in the process of organizing groups to be interviewed. We could not follow our plan for age-cohort composition, which was that each group would be comprised of six persons, three male and three female. The groups we could obtain for the older and middle generations were: three couples (one were brother and sister) for the oldest cohort, and two same-sex groups for the middle cohort. Only for the youngest generation could the research parameter for age and gender be met. These group organizations revealed, unintentionally, how the social structure of Japanese associations in private life varied by generation. The middle cohort had worked together in offices, but in private life males and females were seldom together, except as husband and wife.

The interviews of the oldest cohort were conducted in their homes in Tokushima City; for the middle cohort at their work places in Niigata City; and for the youngest cohort in their high school in Kumamoto City. These cities are all near each other and have populations between 270,000 and 670,000. For reasons that will be explained later in the chapter, a student who is a relative of the oldest cohort facilitated that interview.

2. Media Environment

First, we will assess the physical media environment each cohort experienced when they were roughly in their teens, as the physical condition defines their media contact at that time.

For the oldest cohort, the newspaper and radio were their main media access to news. All six interviewees mentioned something about the newspaper. They all mentioned by name the local newspaper *Tokushima Shimbun*. Although there were several national newspapers, none mentioned their names. Regardless, the total subscription number for the newspaper was relatively large, at least in middle-class families.

The newspaper was delivered at home, usually in the morning (Sadao)[1] and was thrown into the garden. Today newspapers are delivered in mailboxes or newspaper boxes that are especially set for that purpose, usually in front of the house. But at that time there was no particular place to which the newspaper was delivered; it seems to have been delivered to various locations: in the garden or between the sliding doors (Motoe). Morio did not think it was delivered to his home. Chieko also recalled that it was not delivered by a newspaperman, but by a mailman. She commented that "not many houses subscribed to newspapers at that time."

The size of the standard Japanese newspaper was and still is broadsheet (A2). The pages at that time were only two sheets (Yoshio). Motoe and Sadao thought they had been just one sheet. There were no advertisement flyers, which are now customarily inserted between the pages (Sadao).

Under the wartime economic situation and strong political control, the newspaper size was reduced to the minimum (Sadao). He showed it to have been about half the size of one page of the present newspaper. Because of its scarcity, paper came under government control and was distributed by the government. In offices, old documents that had been used once were unfolded and the backsides of the sheets were used (Sadao). The reason why, under such restrictions, the newspaper could get an allocation of the paper distribution was perhaps because the newspaper was a source of information, and an important instrument that could be used to drive people to nationalism.

Four people stated there was a radio set in the house. Chieko and Morio said their family did not have one in the house. "In our village, one or two families had a radio set. That was the situation." (Morio) "We were not civilized," he commented, though his family subscribed to a newspaper. This remark suggests that the radio set was expensive. Only rich people could afford it. At first Chieko said she did not have a radio set from 1935 to 1945, but later recalled that she had one when the war became serious. Morio did not remember that he listened to the radio. Chieko suggested it was because his siblings were all male and all left home to go to war. Only when the mainland began to be attacked by U.S. airplanes, and people's lives began to be threatened, did people equip themselves with a radio set. They needed to obtain emergency information about where the enemy planes were heading. All the lights were turned off so that the airplanes could not detect where inhabitants were. Even the tiny light of the radio set had to be covered in order not to reveal where a human being existed (Motoe). Women remained inland and the radio, though it was expensive, became an indispensable instrument that informed them and protected their lives. But for men who went to war, the radio was not available.

The radio set was like a large box, as Sadao showed the size with his hands and arms. In it there were several vacuum tubes (Sadao), which looked like electric bulbs in which electric coils could be seen through the transparent glass.

One thing that attracted our attention was the place the radio set occupied in the home. Chieko said her family had one on the shelf. Sadao and Motoe's family had one above the family Buddhist alters. Another said it was next to the Shinto shrine, which is high up on the wall. There was only one radio set in a house and it was placed in an important place, or in the central place for the family so that all the family members were able to hear it.

As the participants were asked about their news sources, it was revealed that there was one more important media: film. It was a powerful news source and also a source of entertainment. Motoe, Morio, Sadao,

Kimiko, and Motoo said there was a movie theater called Ananza at the square near the station, and they were taken there sometimes for entertainment. Before the film began, several short newsreels were shown. They were announcements from the *Dai Honnei* (the War-time Headquarters) (Motoe). On the newsreels they could see what soldiers were doing and how they were fighting and winning (Motoe).

For the middle cohort, the media-memories were derived from expanded media availability. All six interviewees of the middle cohort mentioned something about a newspaper, a radio set, and a TV set in the household.

In this cohort all six families subscribed to a newspaper: four to a national newspaper and two to a local one. They were delivered at home. Jiro said few people took a newspaper, so not all families subscribed to it. His family began to subscribe to it when he went to high school. There was a morning version and an evening version, but Ginko's family subscribed to only the morning version. She said she noticed later, when she grew up, that there were two versions and people usually subscribed to both; she commented that her area was not advanced. They did not even know there was a version for kids. None of the six subscribed to it.

A characteristic for this cohort was the introduction of the TV set at home. It very quickly proliferated all over Japan. They said their family bought a TV set at the time of the Olympics, in 1964, one year before the time period that we were investigating. "We should not miss the Olympics, people thought, and bought a TV set" (Jiro). Therefore all had a TV at the beginning of our target years.

The image of the TV they had between 1965 and 1975 was "black and white" (Jiro, Ginko). It was a box that had legs. There was a big round channel switcher that made noise when it was turned (Ikuko).

The quality of the broadcast was not good and there were often interruptions. Snowstorms or strong winds altered the direction of the antenna, and the TV did not function; the pictures could not be seen. Before they had a common antenna on the top of the mountain, the pictures were not clear; but even after that it became dysfunctional when it was windy or snowing (Jiro, Kazuo). They remembered the TV stopped very often. The TV was a great impact to this cohort; we discuss this later, but the reception was incredibly bad when we compare it to the present. Still, the set was in the living room where everybody could get together. There was only one TV set in each household.

The TV set became common for the family, but many of this age group's peers had a radio in their room. Jiro saw his older brother making a radio set for himself. He bought a radio set from his allowance. The radio became personalized after government policy changed and people no longer had to pay radio-user fees.

Movies were still a source of enjoyment for this cohort. Adult-education departments of local governments brought movies to places where people could easily get together, very often to the playground or the auditorium of a school. Jiro remembered viewing movies in the school gymnasium every two weeks and going to watch them with his mother.

All six interviewees of the youngest cohort had two to five radio sets and two to three TV sets in the house, even though the number of family members per household definitely decreased from the two older cohorts. The radio and the TV were personalized and were available to each member of the family. The young cohort treated access to television as a given.

All six families subscribed to a newspaper: three mentioned a national newspaper and three a local one. Although all families subscribed to a newspaper, they gave only one name. Therefore, in contrast to the TV and the radio, they shared the newspaper in a family.

We did not include the Internet in our investigation, but one of the youngest (Kunio) referenced it spontaneously. When he was asked about a piece of news, he mentioned he learned it from a website. This generation had access to the Internet. Taro, of the middle cohort, also mentioned that he was now publishing his own website.

3. Media Interaction

It is not the physical existence of media, but how people interact with it that influences the formation of personality and knowledge.

Most members of the oldest cohort remember the physical existence of a newspaper at home. Access to print media fostered a type of familiarity: it was a kid's role to bring the newspaper to the right place so that father or grandfather could read it. The paper was also used to wrap things, or was placed under the *tatami*[2] mattresses to keep the moisture away.

To have access is one thing and to read is another thing. As kids in their early teens, they did not read it because "they could not read it" (Kimiko, Motoe). Their literacy was at first not high enough to read a newspaper.

But even when their literacy became adequate, Kimiko said, "You ask when we read a newspaper. I don't think we read it during the daytime." This suggests that it was a custom to read a newspaper in the morning when it was delivered. But she was responsible for housework in the family home, and was not allowed to idle away time in the morning or during the daytime by reading it. Reading a newspaper was the privilege of a person of high status. Only a person of a leading position was allowed to read it. When asked to name who read the newspaper in the family, the answer revealed that adult male members, "fathers or grandfathers," were major users of this medium—mothers or grandmothers were not mentioned at all.

Yoshio said, "We were blamed, 'You are reading a newspaper when everybody is so busy!'" Sadao, who was in the army, also said, "There was a newspaper in the office. But if we read it, we were yelled at, 'You, insolent!'" These remarks impressed the young students who helped me in the interview. For them, reading a newspaper was a recommended and expected activity. This memory was the same for the youngest cohort. For the participants in the oldest cohort, in contrast, reading a newspaper invited criticism for spending too much time on a luxury. If they had time to read a newspaper, they were expected to perform manual work instead. A newspaper was a privilege in a family or in a social group.

The oldest generation remembered that they had two radio stations in their childhood, NHJ1 and NHK2. Selection of the stations, however, was in the hands of parents or grandparents. Kids were not allowed to touch the controls of the radio set, which was "on the high shelf." Control of the radio was also completely in the hands of a father or grandfather.

Therefore, for this generation the two main information sources, newspaper and radio, were completely in the hands of the elder male member of the family. Information came through according to their selection, or through their verbal interpretations.

The oldest cohort was asked how they currently regarded the news they had obtained in their youth.

Sadao:	I could not get any news.
Interviewer:	How was that so?
Sadao:	I did not see newspapers at all.
Sadao:	We could not read newspapers [in the army] at all. What the commanding officer said, that was the only news.
Interviewer:	Then only the news on the War of Japan?
Motoe:	Yes, it was only about the war. Further, it was only that we were winning.
(Interviewer laughs)	
Motoe:	Wasn't it?
Sadao:	Yes. That we were losing was not . . . [cannot hear].
Motoe:	That we were losing was not reported at all.

This characterizes the attitude of the older generation. They were strongly skeptical about the news they obtained in their youth. It was really hard to motivate the oldest cohort to agree to be interviewed on their news and media memories. It was very fortunate that one of my students had relatives of that age and they allowed us to interview them in the condition that only she, without me, was in the room. The discussion was videotaped and reviewing this tape, I noticed that it took the interviewer quite a long time, even in this intimate situation, to get them to speak up. The analyses of this will come later in this report. For some topics, this was the first time they spoke of it after more than fifty years of silence.

For the middle cohort, the introduction of the TV was a big event. All six interviewees had a TV set at home when the target years began. But all six remarked on impressions from the time before they had a TV set at home. They would gather at a place where a TV set was. They went to an electric shop or to a school to watch it. Ikuko's family had a TV set earlier than the other families in the neighborhood. She described, "The oldest image of TV was . . . around my kindergarten age, when I was five or six years old. A TV was not in every house at that time. We had one. Neighbors came to us to watch the Sumo tournament. We watched it all together."

If it is in somebody's house, it was in the living room where all the family could get together, and where people in the neighborhood could easily come in. It was "Honorable Lord TV" (Ikuko), whose voice and performance people should attentively watch and listen to. People shared the program. The control of the TV switch was in the hands of parents. As soon as the TV set arrived at every home, despite the technical difficulties with reception, it became a powerful source of entertainment.

To the question of who watched the TV longest, everybody answered right at once, "We, kids!" However, they did not remember that they were watching for a long time. Ginko said it was two or three hours, because she, as a kid, "was not interested in watching news." Others watched it for three or four hours at a time (Hisako, Ikuko).

Children's programs were aired in the late afternoon. "We played outside till it became dark, and came home and watched it. There were not so many animations at that time."

Taro explained, "The life pattern of everybody: father, mother, is different now. They do not have dinner together. But [at that time] everybody used to work during the daytime. Kids came home in the late afternoon and watched TV. Maybe they were even the first to switch the TV on. At dinner time, we ate dinner while watching TV." This explains the conditions under which control over the media was taken out of the parents' hands. Kids came home when it was getting dark. Mother was still busy preparing dinners. Father was still working. Kids sat in front of the TV, waiting for dinner to be ready. Kids' programs were the only ones available in early evening. The TV set with legs was in the living room, no longer on the shelf; the switch and the channels became completely at the mercy of children.

With the prevalence of the TV, the function of the radio changed. As mentioned before, a radio set was individualized. When asked about the radio, the interviewees at first responded that they did not have any memory of the radio at all. However, during the course of the interview session, memories came back:

Jiro: Ooooh, well, yes, in this occasion. The TV was not broadcasted late at night. Perhaps, well, at night they broadcasted a late-night program. I remember I listened to the late-night [radio] program. After the TV finished.

Ginko: I was in the dormitory. At that time I did not watch the TV, but listened to the radio.

When the TV was not available, they listened to the radio. Recollections of radio, which had only sound, were weak in contrast to memories of television. However, people could do something else, such as homework, while listening.

Television viewing did not allow multitasking. It attracted some people, though not many. But those who were attracted were almost obsessed with TV. For this generation, the radio no longer functioned as the news source it had been for the oldest cohort.

The radio industry, for its part, had to change its program policy because TV took listeners away. New types of programs were invented: request program, late-night broadcasting, and a so-called whispering mood program. The radio allowed listeners to join the program, reading letters from listeners that conveyed their personal experience, and broadcasting music according to listeners' request, as Ginko reported about the case of her classmate. It offered bilateral, though not yet simultaneous, communications between listeners and the radio. It began also to whisper to "a listener" (not to "listeners"), late at night, "What are you doing now?" And a personal talk began. It no longer used the word *minasan* (everybody or audience) as the old radio program had done, but it began to use the word *anata* (you, singular, in an intimate way). The voice on the radio began to use a colloquial way of talking, no longer in the formal Japanese language. A listener heard it as if it were talking to that person only. They enjoyed, in the late hours, the one-to-one conversational style of the night program. Some young people were obsessed with it. This medium was also out of the control of parents.

Radio was no longer listened to as an exclusive focus, without doing anything, or in a group. For this middle cohort it was individualized and personalized in possession, in the form of access, and also in the program content. However, they all said there was no impressive news that they gained from radio. Radio, being only auditory, did not make as strong an impression as TV, which is also visual.

Everyone in this cohort had access to a newspaper at home, but they read it for a limited amount of time. It was thought that a newspaper should be read in the morning and they were busy before they left for school or work. Access to the content began at elementary-school age and the first contents of interest were TV scheduling announcements (Itsue, Kiyoe, Kunio) and cartoons (Itsue). They began with these pages and often read the weather forecasts. For them, the newspaper was the quickest way to search for particular information like the weather forecast of the day.

The image of higher prestige and intelligence that the oldest cohort had associated with newspaper readers was continued in this middle cohort:

Taro: (laughing) I did not have a particular image about a newspa-
                per. But a person who read a newspaper was a great person. By
                great, I mean, well, well, it's OK, great. A person who read a
                newspaper was a great man. Don't you think there is such an
                image even now, as mentioned before? A person who watches
                TV is a slovenly person; a person who reads a book is a great
                person. Isn't he? Printed letters have such an image.

Taro: Ooooh, well, if I am forced to say, well, people read it with
                obligation. A newspaper has some such image. Obligation.

Kazuo: Generally speaking, it has an image of being hardboiled.

Because of this perception, Ginko said she was "terrible" when she said she read a newspaper for only fifteen minutes. Hisako felt "ashamed of it now" because she did not read it at that time. They gave an ungrudging praise, "You were wonderful," to Ikuko, for reading a newspaper for longer periods. Although they read the newspaper only for a limited time, they place great value on it. That's why parents continued to subscribe to a newspaper even though they did not read very much of it.

Junior and senior high schools supported the value of reading a newspaper, especially the editorial section on the first page, but what the cohort recalled actually reading was the local community page. "When I missed the news on the TV the evening before . . . I read the article" (Kunio). The TV was the first source of news, and the newspaper became a secondary source of news, when more detail was wanted.

Jiro indicated one of the matters that showed change from the previous cohort. He said that the person who read the newspaper most in the family was his mother. She read articles on cooking, home-making, and other domestic interests. Here we saw that the function of newspaper media, and also the position of women in the family, changed from the previous cohort. At that time women were allowed to read a newspaper and the editorial policy also changed from targeting only men, as in the previous cohort, to targeting women as well.

For the members of the youngest cohort, TV was a part of their natural environment. From their babyhood the "TV was on when I woke up in the morning, well, yes, when I got up, the TV was on" (Umeo). As a result, "when I was awake, I was watching the TV even while I was eating meals" (Ochie); "through elementary, junior high, senior high, all through the time, all day long, if I had time, I was watching it, I was watching all the programs" (Umeo). This type of access is typical of this generation. It was an environment, and at the same time it was a tool for kids to play with. They also played family computer games for extended lengths of time, so the TV was entertainment, games, and toys—everything for them. The TV set was in the living room, so they generally had unlimited access to it.

If there were some obstacles to their free access, it was when older siblings came home and wanted to see a different program. Some of the cohort reported fighting between the siblings for channel control, but this was solved when the family bought a second TV set. This generation did not have as many siblings as other cohorts. Also, they did not recall their parents being in control of the TV switch or the selection of channels.

Only Istue mentioned her parents controlling the TV: "What was impressive to me was that when I became a junior-high student, I could watch—became allowed to watch—the TV after nine o'clock at night, a drama program." In her family, she had to go to bed at 9 o'clock until she became 12 years old. This was probably not because of the limitation of TV access by her parents, but for the sake of her health as a small child.

Jiro, who is in the middle age cohort and now a father, demonstrated a reason for this change when he said, "I do not like TV, because it is taken by kids. Even if there is a program I want to watch, I cannot. I cannot watch a program in [a] series."

A new thing to this youngest cohort, a new technology, was the introduction of satellite TV. Said Kiyoe: "What remains strongest in my memories about the TV was . . . satellite broadcasting. My father and mother liked movies and so they contracted with it, then with it I began to have interest in movies." Parental involvement was necessary in the introduction of a new technology, perhaps because it is expensive.

For the youngest cohort, TV was an entertainment source. Because it had become their "natural" media environment, they obtained all their news from the TV (Kiyoes, Kunio, Umeo, and Itsue).

This cohort offered few remarks about the radio. Still, they had some access to the radio, though their usage was minimal compared to the TV. When asked about radio, they had difficulties in answering and had to squeeze out an answer such as:

Umeo: Well, radio, well, in the car I listened to it a little. I did not have much access to it.

Kunio: I seldom listened to it on purpose. If I did, on rare occasion, it was the weather forecast during the typhoon. That's all I listened to.

4. Prompted Events

Here we will assess what knowledge people had about ten prompted pieces of news that we presented to each cohort, with the addition of some pieces of news that emerged spontaneously.

Great effort and patience were required in order to get the oldest cohort to share memories of their youth. Sadao began to talk about his experience as a captive in Korea, life in his prison camp, and hard labor outdoors in Siberia in minus-forty degree temperatures. Yoshio, who was a student engaged in factory labor, experienced piles of granite falling down, and many of his classmates died. He, together with his teacher, dug out their dead bodies.

As for their memories of events that we consider global news, there were events that they all knew well and events that none of them knew at all. None could explain three events: the Spanish Revolution, Crystal Night in Germany, and the Salt March in India. These events were not associated with Japan. Only one or two people knew about King Edward VIII and Auschwitz. The persons who knew these were male. Almost all knew about the Berlin Olympics, the fall of Singapore, the start of World War II, Pearl Harbor, atomic bombs, and the end of World War II. Japan was involved in these events. They did not recall much about the Berlin Olympics in general, only that Hideko Maehata won the gold medal in swimming. They remembered only the part that was related to Japan. The events they recalled were discussed very hesitatingly at first. But once they began, they could say the names of people involved, the place names, and the dates the events occurred.

In general, what the cohort from this generation was willing to tell was all they have learned long since the war: the knowledge common to the next cohort and what they felt safe to tell. An example was a notion about atomic bombs in Hiroshima and Nagasaki. At first they describe them in the same way the middle cohort did, as "mushroom shaped." They each had their own memories of what they experienced as they lived through that moment. Until the interviewer urged, however, they did not put it into words. Even the fall of Singapore and Pearl Harbor, which should have given great joy at that time to the Japanese, were related only with hesitation. Later in the interview they remembered well how it was celebrated, with a lantern march and a flag march. It was a characteristic of this cohort that, after they said something optimistic about the media-related events of that time, they added a comment that contradicted it, such as, "all were false," "that was the time that Japan was still in good condition," "nothing against Germany was told at that time," and, "I am not sure."

Before there was television, the voice heard on the radio had a strong impact on people. People retained vivid memories of how the radio reported that the Japanese swimmer Maehata was going to win, or how the events at Pearl Harbor were reported, or how the announcement by the emperor of the end of the war sounded through the radio.

Another characteristic for this cohort was that, along with the media, person-to-person communication played a role. For example, in order to listen to the emperor announce the end of World War II, all the people had been told, by policemen or others, to get together at a house that had a radio set. Since the communication media were totally collapsed by end of the war, news came only from person to person. The news of the atomic bombs was such a case. It was called "new-type bombs" or "Pika-don," onomatopoeia of the flash and sound of the bomb. "The news came to women, who were at home, with advice that one should wear whitish colored clothes because the skin and flesh would be melted under the dark-colored patterns of clothes and the body would be collapsed" (Motoe). Men, who were in the army, did not know the news for some time. Sadao did not learn of the use of atomic bombs until the end of 1946. He did not even know the war had ended until October 1945. All the news had come to him from his commanding officer, and the commanding officer did not convey unfavorable news at all. As a result, Sadao was not able to believe any news at all. Therefore, when he was told to go to take a ship to return to Japan, he was surprised to have found the ship really heading for Japan.

Although there was some variance between accounts from people at the end of the war, the oldest cohort generally has a clearly defined common knowledge of the mediated events in their youth. They all recalled the

same events and they explained it in the same way, although we interviewed them separately in three groups. There were certain events about
which no one knew. We can guess that the news source was limited. Their
collective lack of information is evidenced by their inability to discuss various global-media events. However, they also seem to have submerged their
memories deep in their consciousness, and seemed to be afraid these memories might float to the surface. But once they began, they became vocal,
and memories came one after another. They could tell the events in detail:
the names, the dates, the scenes, and the sounds. But they expressed themselves very carefully.

For the middle cohort, however, the event-based knowledge was not
unanimous. Knowledge about man's landing on the moon, the international
students' rebellion, and the Oil Crisis was relatively common. Most of these
were explained with strong relevance to their own lives, therefore as spontaneous memories. Even if the news stories were meant to be pieces of global
news, they were recalled only when they strongly connected the events with
their own personal lives. The Oil Crisis was a good example; it was explained
only in light of the suffering that resulted from it: the price of gas had soared
up (Jiro); and bathroom tissue disappeared from stores (Ikuko). Student
rebellions occurred in many countries of the world, but what they recalled
was only that a relative experienced it in Japan (Ikuko), or that a Japanese
school the person wanted to study at was involved (Ginko). If the event
occurred in Japan, then the incidents remained firmly in their memory.

In contrast, if media-related events were not directly connected with a
person's own life, he/she did not show interest and did not remember
clearly, even though they were reported repeatedly. Watergate, the PLO,
and even the Vietnam War were not remembered much. As these were
long-lasting events that were the subject of broadcasts for years, these subjects remained in memory as sound, but the cohort did not remember the
contents well enough to explain them. They did not remember where they
heard the words.

The pieces of news they remembered varied by person, and they were
not always sure of which medium they obtained the news from; but it is
evident that TV was the most likely source. TV occupied their vision—one
cannot watch it while doing something else. They did not watch it unless
they were really interested in the content. That made a difference between
individuals' media impressions.

Another factor that keeps it in memory is repetition:

Taro: I saw it at that time perhaps, by the TV, I think. But it does not
                 mean that the matter stayed in my memory from that time,

> somehow, on various occasions, events of the past, well, in a
> special broadcasting program related to the event, then I seem
> to have re-confirmed it again; I have that impression.

This remark may be true. To establish news as knowledge, one needs repetition, or some kind of reinforcement. Therefore, the medium that conveyed the news became vague if there was little or no repetition. In Kazuo's case, this reinforcement was a recruitment exam taken in order to get a new position. He was forced to study news-media reports in order to get better marks in current or recent topics.

Another strong element in imbedding a scene into memory is color. Mars had an unusual color; it remained in the memory of people. Here again, the media by which it was conveyed was not remembered. The media was only guessed at with regard to the event or the situation. Because the newspapers were black and white, Ginko and Ikuko logically guessed that they noticed the color of Mars on TV. In this situation, the color gave a strong impression. Whether color works even now in this way, however, is in question, since everything is broadcast in color now.

All members of the youngest cohort seemed to know about some of the prompted events such as the O. J. Simpson trial. The case of Rodney King was a difficult one, but when Ochie began to explain, others recalled it. They could not recall it from the names, but the event itself was in their memory. They said they knew of Princess Diana's death and former President Clinton's private life in detail. Their knowledge of news events, again, was unanimous. However, whether the events were recalled well only because the events were recent ones deserves further investigation. They might fade from memory in the long run if some kind of reinforcement does not occur, or if the events are not a matter of their interest. Anyway, most of the interviewees knew almost all of these events, and they shared information.

The youngest cohort learned all of their news from the TV, even if they also heard of the events elsewhere. It may be a result of the fact that the TV was constantly on, like background music. Though there were several channels, the topics of news broadcasts were almost the same. As Umeo said, "I changed the channels. But that channel was also about that." Any news event that they all knew well had been learned from the TV.

With the prevalence of color TV and satellite TV, we noticed that such news as Princess Diana's death and former President Clinton's private life were no longer just an event in a "foreign" country, but a part of their life. For this generation, the international events became an everyday part of their own environment. They could experience understanding and sympathy with the matters of the world.

Because of TV reports of international events, young people had at least a vague knowledge of global political events such as the reunification of Germany, the economic crisis in Asia, the fall of the communist countries, and the installment of the euro as the new official European currency. Some of them also read the news in the newspaper. Newspapers were an additional news source for those who wanted to learn more details or digest the difficult or serious matters at a slow pace. A newspaper also worked as reinforcement for those who were are interested in an event. Some of the political topics, such as the meaning of the Berlin Wall, the fall of communist countries, and Nelson Mandela's liberation, were also dealt with in classrooms. This served as reinforcement, and news of these events were thus established as knowledge in their memory.

It became apparent that the age of a person was a factor in the settlement of the news or knowledge into memories. What they heard was retained as a memory of sounds, but not as content or meaning. When the case of Tiananmen Square (Beijing, China) happened, they were ten years old; Ochie and Kiyoe heard the TV news reporter repeatedly say, "I am now in front of the Tiananmen Gate." The phrase "Tiananmen Gate" remained in their memory, but they thought, "What happened with the Gate?"—until they later knew the meaning of the event. It was important to be old enough or mature enough to understand the content. If they did not understand the content, the contents were not established as memory or as knowledge unless some kind of reinforcement was added.

Another observation that is worth mentioning was that they picked up news of volcanic explosions and flooding due to the typhoons as spontaneous memory with strong impressions and interest. These occurred in their neighborhood and might have actually threatened their own lives. They referred to their personal experiences. These belong to a different category than the world news. Ochie remarked on news of the Gulf War: "Here we are in peace, but there . . . ," suggesting it was now a global matter of the other category, but it could be in the same personal category as the volcanic explosion and typhoon-caused flood. I will discuss this in the next section.

5. Three Generations and the Formation of Knowledge

In conclusion, I will review the three generations' media experiences, and briefly summarize how media worked in the formation of their knowledge.

For the oldest cohort, the main news source was the radio. During the early years that our investigation examined, the radio was not prevalent, but when the war began, it became the source for emergency information. However, all the communication media were completely collapsed by the end of World War II. At that time, personal communication worked together with the radio.

The radio and the newspaper were important news sources, but control of them was completely in the hands of the authority in the family or in the social group. News reported by radio and newspapers were tightly controlled. For the people in their formative years, information was doubly controlled, by the government and by the people in social authority.

This cohort eventually realized that much of the information they had obtained was not reliable. They also experienced the complete turnover of the social value system that coincided with the defeat in World War II. Those who were outspoken during the war were purged from any official position during the inspection of 1948 (78 publishing companies, 217 individuals in the field of publishing, and 335 authors). Not only in this official purge, but also in everyday life, it was very risky to speak out about the situation before the end of the war. Everything that existed before the war was regarded as obsolete and evil, and was renounced. Those in the oldest cohort had to repress what they had known, heard, thought, felt, and what they had believed. They remembered many matters from the years between 1935 and 1945, but those matters had been carefully sealed and were kept secret deep in their consciousness. The information they had obtained in their youth, therefore, was not formed into any common social knowledge by this generation. Also, this information did not contribute to the formation of knowledge for the following generations, because the oldest cohort suppressed their memories deep in themselves and were afraid to let these memories surface in their consciousness.

The middle cohort, in contrast, talked willingly of their media memories. For them, the main information media was the black-and-white TV. However, much of what they talked about spontaneously were matters dating before 1965, the first of our target years. The introduction of a new technology had a strong impact on them. All six remembered vividly how they shared TV programs with neighbors. At that time, TV was like an "Honorable Lord TV," who collected people around him and requested people to listen attentively to him.

Most families had a TV set by the time of the Tokyo Olympics. The year 1964 marked a special epoch for the history of media in Japan, because with the introduction of the TV in every family, the power relations between parents and children changed concerning the control of the media. When the children's programs began in the early evening, parents were still busy working. Children came home, switched on the TV for themselves, and sat in front of the TV by themselves for a considerable time until dinner was ready. The control of this medium became completely in the hands of children. Families began to eat dinner watching TV, and TV became the source of entertainment rather than the source of news.

In the late sixties there were educational discussions about television. Some believed that TV was an evil cultural influence from which children should be protected. Ultimately, these arguments did not overlap into the consideration of media literacy in Japan. These discussions faded to silence under the overwhelming power and popularity of the TV. There were several channels, yet the news content was basically identical. The variation in individual's news memories could be attributed to their recollection that the news was not their main purpose in watching the TV.

To the youngest cohort, the most important media was color TV. For them, the TV was no longer a medium but a part (and the most powerful part) of the environment into which they were born. The TV was on when they awoke and was constantly delivering some kind of information to them, although they may not have been conscious of the input. Even if they were not interested in the information, it was delivered as pictures with sound and stayed in their memory like the case of Tiananmen Gate.

Another thing that we noticed is that, with the prevalence of the TV, the world has become a part of their environment. They watched reports on President Clinton and Princess Diana, and they unanimously reported feeling close to these international figures. But they reserved a safe element of distance, to the extent that these events did not threaten to impact on their lives.

Here we saw that pieces of news were divided into two categories. The first may be called local or personal. The other may be just "non-local." There used to be categories of local, national, and world. The category "national" seems to have disappeared. Whether the incidents occurred in Japan or in other countries, they seemed to be regarded in the same way. They attended to local news with serious interest, but viewed the personal news as part of their environment or as an entertainment. National and international politics became something to which they attended only in response to the efforts or encouragement of other people, radio, or by reading newspapers.

We have seen how the media played a role in the formation of knowledge by three typical generations in Japan. In order for information to be assimilated as knowledge, some factors must be present. One requirement is competence—the content of the information must be understood. The remembered news events that occurred in the early half of our target years were not explained much. The events that occurred in the latter half were explained in detail, which was common to all three generations.

For information to be established as knowledge, the competency to understand the content, when people first get the information, plays a role. This was correlated by age in our cases, but this will also be applied to over-all intellectual ability, as in competency that may be obtained by education.

Another factor was reinforcement. This may have been achieved by repetition, or some other media or social opportunity to reconfirm the information. A related, crucial factor was the value system of the society. If people encountered pieces of information that seemed to be antagonistic toward the prevalent value system in their society, that information was less likely to be reinforced. Rather, it was often repressed and was not a basis on which to form knowledge.

Margarita Maass, Daniela Rivera, and Andres Hofman

1. General Introduction

The 20th century is characterized by the great development of mass culture all around the world. Mexico is not an exception. The process of social development in Mexico during the 20th century cannot be understood without considering the role played by the mass media. During this century, 40 newspapers were founded in Mexico City alone (Bohmann, 1994: 366); commercial radio broadcasting started in the early 1920s; television in 1951; and electronic media, though already in use during the 1960s, were developed and made available in the 1980s. Mexico is a country that inherited a culture made of plural cultures. At the beginning of the century there were about 10 million inhabitants; by the end, the population reached 100 million people. The waking of this century was also an era of tension, the consequence of a dictatorship that lasted almost three decades. During this time a small group of Mexico City dwellers completely ruled the country, over an agrarian population representing 80 percent of the country's inhabitants. This rural majority was mostly Indian and illiterate. Society was full of deep contradictions, which fostered the outbreak of a revolution during the first decades of the century. After this war finished, and until the 1940s, Mexico went through social and religious uprisings that forced the reorganizing of the country during the times of President Lázaro Cárdenas. After these years, a period of national peace started, which, as defined by Enrique Semo (1999: 27) was "a new social agreement" based on one hand on a new redistribution of property, and on the other, on taking Mexican crude oil away from foreign control. As of the end of the 20th century, Mexico has survived a long, 70-year period of presidential successions in a single-party political system, where authority overruled democracy.

At the beginning of the 20th century, two newspapers existed: El Imparcial (official) and El País (Catholic). Different kinds of journals, booklets, and loose flyers started to emerge with the purpose of spreading the news. Generally, newspapers indirectly informed about notable international events like revolutionary wars in other parts of the globe: Russia in 1905, Iran in 1907, China in 1911, again Russia in 1917, Germany and Hungary in 1918, and Turkey in 1919. In spite of this, newspapers were hard to find outside large cities because distribution was not easy. Therefore, since 1886, when the first industrialized newspaper, El Imparcial, emerged, the Mexican press of the 20th century started developing, and eventually came to be represented by today's newspapers. In this fast review of the Mexican press history, it is important to point out that though many newspapers work on an independent basis and are privately owned, they emerged "under official protection," and reflect official trends and specific political interests. There has always been strong control over the media by the government—initially over the press, but later on over radio and television. This "media–government" relationship was strengthened in the days of President Miguel Alemán, at the beginning of the 1940s, when the state held a monopoly over paper, and permits and concessions had to be granted. This general situation came to an end during President Zedillo's administration, except for television and radio concessions. The press did finally manage to be independent for some years: El Nacional (the official newspaper) was closed, thus reflecting an important symptom of modernization, democratization, and liberation that started at the beginning of the 1980s. The first broadcasting was heard in 1920. A year later, new, commercial-radio broadcasting projects started. Radio concessions began and this led to rapid growth in the number of radio stations. When radio arrived in Mexico, during the first decades of the century, the press already worked as a mass medium. During the 1920s, when religious rebellions were intensified, the Cristera War was the focus of mass media, which by then were the press and the radio. These two, both relevant media for spreading news, maintained their status of submission to state power. Government oversight, at greater or lesser levels of control, continued throughout the whole century. This fact had a decisive influence on the people's choice to consume or not to consume the media; and evidently, government control was part of the formation of the identity of people and their social practices within a structured context where cultural phenomena are produced, transmitted, and received. Before radio appeared in Mexico, two telephone companies already existed. Because of presidential decree, the companies' services were not interconnected until 1936. In 1940 there were 113 radio stations.

During the 1950s, commercial television came to Mexico. Since the beginning, station grants were established, and with them, conditions regarding submission to power. Starting with the sixties, radio, press, and television became tools for building political strength. An example of this could be seen during the Luis Echeverría administration, when a series of radio stations, as well as TV Channel 13 were confiscated. Subsequently, the Instituto Mexicano de la Radio, and later IMEVISION, were created and operated as a communications network controlled by the state. By 1963, there were already 455 radio and television stations that operated in the country. In 1965 radio holding companies emerged, such as Grupo Radio Centro, Grupo ACIR, and Grupo Radio Mil; and in 1968, the states of Baja California, Michoacán, and Chihuahua restricted the use of the radio. In this same year, two forms of tax payment for radio and TV grants were announced, which allocated either 25 percent of the income, or 49 percent of the stocks for the government. In 1985, satellites named Morelos I and II were put into orbit; and in 1986, fiber optics were put into use by the telephone industry. Following this, open competition to gain audiences began in 1990. The privatization of IMEVISION happened in 1993, as well as the emergence of TV Azteca and Channel 22 in Mexico City. By 1997, transmissions with the DTH (Direct to home) system began. Likewise, the Morelos and Intelsat satellites have been fundamental elements for the growth of radio and television in our country in these last years. Competition was stronger, and communication possibilities increased. The national development is still in process and at the same time, fiber optics in telephones has accelerated integration of the population into the globalized world through the Internet. In the final balance, we are still in the phase of rapid growth. In the decade after 1990, with the globalized world and Net technologies, the media continue to be increasing in scope and power. Practically all the population of the country has access to television and radio. There has been rapid growth of the world market for telecommunication services, and Mexico has participated in it. In spite of the fact that, by the turn of the century, we have an infant and juvenile majority population, and

40 percent functional illiteracy in the country, the young of this decade are living deep in the world of the media, cinema, radio, television, and, to a lesser degree, the press. The influence that these media had over individuals has produced, beyond any doubt, a society with a highly mediated cultural structure. Esteinou (2001) defines the media by the end of the 20th century as "the center of contemporary power," though we should add that this relationship (of media to power) is already in a very serious crisis. As the 20th century ended, Mexico was, little by little, acquiring confidence in the media. It is not until now that society has been learning the truth about real scenes of the past, like what really happened during the massacre of October 1968. Thus, the opportunity to speak of politics on the radio and on television occurred in our country only with the advent of the 21st century. This change is thanks to the fact that over many decades there have been voices that have dared to express themselves openly, even at the risk of being shut up.

2. Media Environment

Radio Generation

The oldest generation was born when the press had formally begun and when radio was born. The speed of life and of technological changes was, indeed, much slower than today. Daily life was quieter, less stressed. Participants in this group spoke much about this aspect:

Rebeca:	It seems to me that, between the years '35 and '45, it was the time when the influence of communication exploded.
Roberto:	It was then when cars actually began to cross Mexico . . . going to Acapulco was a two-day journey, to arrive . . . in those days you could watch how persons changed by the effect of communication . . . all those which were isolated in the Republic received the newspapers that [were] carried [by] the muleteers; but they were old newspapers . . . there were no telephones, telegraph or highways in many places . . . suddenly, communication began, and it began to change people's mentality.
Eduardo:	In those days, there was a characteristic on the radio that has regrettably been lost . . . one was free of excess advertising, all the contrary of what happens now.

This generation witnessed the birth of radio in Mexico. In spite of the fact that all of the members of the focus group were well off, and could have had a privileged access to the reception appliance, not all of the members reported they had immediate access to a radio.

Television Generation

Due to economic restrictions, it took more time for the lower classes in Mexico to acquire television sets for their homes. It was very common then for small neighborhood stores to set up a room with several chairs in front of a television set as if it were a cinema room, to entertain the neighbors. People had to pay a few cents to watch television—a cover charge—and on occasions, a minimum purchase was required. This was how lower- and lower-middle-class children of this generation could remain for hours watching television, especially during the weekend, while they enjoyed a lollipop or chewing gum they'd bought at that store. When they didn't have enough money, they would borrow it from the shopkeeper on the condition that they would pay it back on Sundays, the day in which children received their weekly money from their parents. Thus, there were socioeconomic impediments to watching television. As one person stated: "There was a kind of self-constraint for TV, because our budget would not allow us to pay 20 cents daily in order to go and sit there. My parents gave me 30 or 50 cents every Sunday to buy a candy."

When television finally arrived in poor households, it usually preceded the acquisition of a refrigerator and a washing machine; in one focus-group member's household, it arrived before the stove or refrigerator. It is possible that having a television set at home was a social status indicator. How else could we explain why many poor families bought televisions before refrigerators and other basic-need appliances? That first television set—the one that was always there, or the one that arrived afterwards—was recalled, without exception, as a great piece of furniture installed in a prominent place of the living room. All the family gathered to watch it, especially during the evenings and nights. But having a well-installed television at home was not enough. It was not easy to watch television due to the fact that reception technology was not sufficiently developed. Real epic battles resulted among family members regarding the rabbit-ear antennae or their substitutes—hooks for hanging clothes that were connected to all sorts of metal artifacts or wires. Also, early television watchers would beat on the television set with stronger or weaker force, according to the state of exasperation in the audience. This was, without any question, the most frequent method for adjusting reception. But the result was, almost always, that they ended up watching whatever the capricious technology of those times permitted, and not necessarily what the viewers wanted to see:

Gilberto:	The television sets were wonderful, mainly the epic of the rabbit antennae.
Román:	They were appliances that one had to beat.
Gilberto:	Exactly, it was a natural selection.
Rafael:	I remember how the vertical control would begin to blink out of control, so we stood up to fix it, you would get there, you'd move something, and it would be fixed, but when you'd go back to sit down, it would fuck up again, so then we'd say, "now it is your turn to fix it."

Digital Generation

For the digital generation, access to media in general, and TV in particular, was scarcely controlled. Probably, an important reason for this had to do with the absence of parents from the home:

Monserrat:	They never paid too much attention to us. Everybody was always working; so, we went to school, we were picked up, we got home and, in the afternoons, the only thing we wanted to do was watch TV, watch TV all day long.

For the members of this generation, there was a clear predominance of television in relation to other media like the radio. Except for one participant, none of them recalled a radio program or radio announcer. Radio was a medium for older people, for the parents.

There were specifically mentioned alternate activities, but they were carried out during weekends without totally suspending TV watching. On the other hand, these side activities were not completely disconnected from the use of the TV because it operated, in this case, as technical support for the videoplayer. In the case of video games, with the rise of Atari followed by Intelevision and Nintendo, time spent in front of the TV increased. As Monserrat said: "It was total alienation. I lived in front of the television." Home, as we had already said, was an environment of scarce restriction for the children of this generation, and therefore to the symbolic worlds that these presented.

3. Media Interaction

Radio Generation

Some very traditional families saw the radio as a hazardous appliance in their households, since they felt it was a bad influence:

Guadalupe: In my house, my dad did not want us to have radio. We had music and records, that was okay; but not radio, since he wanted to protect us from all news . . . everything related to the government was anathema . . . it was them who published the newspapers.

In spite of this, in a short time all the members of this group eventually had a radio at home. They recalled that moment with great excitement, the event that strongly determined their social and leisure practices:

Roberto: In my house we did not have any restrictions. . . . We had a radio appliance. . . . It was very exciting. . . . We always had a radio at home.

Eduardo: Actually, I did not read the news in the newspaper; but I learned about them by means of the radio . . . that was the main media.

The radio came to occupy a very important physical place in the house. The whole family would sit around the large appliance, which was generally located in the living room. The same thing happened with the press, to which the majority of the group had access.

All participants were very close to other media that were essential for them: recorded music, printed materials, and the movies. Among the group, all report that they were, and continue to be, avid readers, and that they went frequently to the cinema. The musical production of RCA (Record Corporation of America), as well as the films produced in Hollywood during the decade of 1930 to 1940, had a great influence in this generation, and this is reported by all members of the group:

Teodoro: I loved to read, as of this date, I still read a lot. . . . It was not rare that I read a complete book daily. . . . We read from Salgari, to Jules Verne, the *Paquines, Adelaido the Conqueror,* that sort of stories that really thrilled us.

Rebeca: I was fascinated by American movies. . . . I was a movie fan. . . .
               My mother, my brothers, and I went twice a week to the cin-
               ema . . . we had the Cinema Roma a block away from home.

It is important to remember that in these days, the speed of changes was
much slower than nowadays. Cultural experiences through mass media
were much less frequent and delivered to far fewer people, a fact that is in
contrast to today's way of life:

Guadalupe: Transformation of women, it seems to me, is due to a large
               extent to communication. . . . Women stopped thinking that
               they were human beings . . . communication broadened their
               horizons. . . . Earlier, men died at 40, 45 years of age, and their
               wives were dowagers at 40, and automatically they were
               dressed in black, with headdress and everything, ready to ded-
               icate to church chores only. . . . Now, at that age, they are as
               active and productive as young ladies of those times.
Gloria: In those days, women used to lose their personality. . . . They
               did not think neither of themselves nor of their future . . . they
               were totally devoted to their families. . . . They did not think of
               what they would do when they remained alone.

As Thompson (1998) says, symbolic forms are valued and evaluated,
approved and refuted constantly by the individuals who produce and
receive them. Likewise, the expressions of a social person are produced by
agents located in a specific sociohistoric context. There was a certain form
of individual thinking and acting and, at the same time, a collective identification, the one manifested in the group's games and activities.

Teodoro: We played to the war patrols, some were Nazis and others
               Allies. . . . It was an era that gave me many values, that gave
               me much safety feelings and, thanks to which I have been able
               to overcome many things of my life. . . . In the days when one
               was a teenager, you were easily impressed, and you almost
               wanted to do as they did [the actors in the movies].
Rebeca: We listened to many radio novels. I remember *Anita of
               Montemar, The Right to Be Born, Bird without a Nest, Chucho el
               Roto, Raffles,* and others with Arturo de Córdoba. . . . They were
               very appreciated because people gathered around the radio
               after supper to listen to the radio novel. . . . *The Insane Monk* . . .
               there was a heap of things.

In the home, the radio set facilitated in the family's "being-together rite." A place of interaction with an opportunity for shared symbolic content was generated.

Foreign actors and actresses were perceived as heroes; they were unreachable, but worthy of imitating. Mexican music conductors and singers, heard on the radio, were sensed to be emotionally much closer and are mentioned more frequently in the group's recollections. The reception process was not that of passive assimilation; but it molded the ways in which symbolic forms were received, understood, interpreted, and valued:

> Guadalupe: . . . . the great American actors, Gary Cooper, Robert Taylor, Errol Flynn, they were my top idols; but I saw Arturo de Córdoba in the *Cinema Monumental*. . . . I was fascinated by the American movies. I was enchanted by the great bands of Harry James, Jimmy Dorsey, Glen Miller. . . . It was an extraordinary era. . . . We fully lived the golden age of Mexican Songs . . . we lived it . . . Agustín Lara, Cri-Cri, Tío Polito . . .

Television Generation

The TV generation engaged in an ongoing struggle to watch television, developing strategies to undermine prohibitions imposed by parents. Especially in the poorest homes, they were restricted to a few hours during the weekdays, with more hours permitted on weekends. However, for one of the participants, there was no way of avoiding prohibitions because the television set was kept inside a cabinet with doors that were locked throughout the day. Her father, who had the keys, would open those doors every evening so that his children could watch television for one hour:

> Elsa: At seven o'clock my dad arrived and turned the radio on. . . . I would listen to *Count Bartok,* a radio soap opera about vampires . . . and when it finished, he would open the little doors and let us watch TV for an hour.

This situation did not occur solely in the poorest homes. Other sorts of prohibitions to watch television referred to specific programs: the two participants who grew up in middle-socioeconomic-level households would watch television many hours a day, every day, and without restrictions, except for the soap operas, which were banned by their parents. However, they connived to watch them through various subterfuges. The main one was visiting their grandparents:

Román: My parents did not let me watch soap operas, but my grand-
                mother did, so in the afternoons, when I was at my grandpar-
                ents' house, or when I was on vacations with them, I would
                stick to my grandmother, who would take marathonic soap-
                opera sessions while knitting.

With keen insight, their parents discovered that watching television
was a good method for keeping children (especially daughters) at home.
This was how teenage children, distracted but very much entertained, were
occupied during those long and irksome weekends:

Teresa: In my house we are five women and one man, my sisters were
                teenagers, my dad was very jealous and would not let them go
                out because then, entertainment of youth were parties. . . . So
                then I believe he thought this was a way of keeping them at
                home, watching television.

In any event, beyond the practical difficulties that children faced in
order to watch television, or the attributes that their parents gave to television, they managed to establish fixed routines to watch it. One of the cohort
had paid for watching, and routinely went to the store on Sundays to watch
specific programs, while another participant would watch certain cartoons
during the weekdays at given hours. Another would watch TV only for one
hour every weekday, at 7:30 P.M., and more hours during the weekend.

Access to the radio did not have restrictions. There was a radio in each
of the six households represented in this group. During the years they lived
without a television set at home, the poorest participants listened to children's radio programs at noon, and radio soap operas, live contests, and
live musical programs in the afternoon or at night. Those of middle and
upper-middle classes listened to the same radio programs at noon, but
watched television in the afternoon and at night. In the first case, the family
would gather around the radio; in the second case families would gather
around the television.

When participants of this generation became teenagers, these rites
changed in the sense that the "mediatic" experience was homogenized. All
of them had a television at home and used it during the afternoons and
nights, and all of them used radio to listen to music during daytime hours.
The poorest participants quickly abandoned radio soap operas, live musical programs, and radio contests. Another homogenizing aspect of the
radio experience was that men of all social distinctions, but not women, listened to soccer, boxing, and baseball events that were aired. Children that

originated from middle and upper-middle classes did not listen to radio soap operas. Neither did their parents, and the family never gathered around the radio. During their childhood, radio does not seem to have been very important. They could live without it.

Members from lower economic sectors did not recall the presence of printed materials at home. At the other levels, however, the morning newspaper and some other magazines were always there. They "devoured" the newspaper comic strips, especially on Sundays, and regularly read comic magazines. For the poor, on the other hand, comic magazines never existed.

> Román: I was a great comics consumer, and the greatest gift that my father would give me, whenever he would give me a gift, was when he would buy me four comics, and I was wealthy, that Sunday I was very rich, he would buy *Lágrimas y risas, Memín Pinguín, Los Supersabios,* and *Archi,* and that Sunday I was very wealthy.

Cinema definitely had a great impact on this cohort. However, its specific influence, as compared to that of television and other media, was not very clear. Nevertheless, some participants gave transcendental importance to films.

> Román: I believe that for all of us cinema was fundamental, maybe more than television.
>
> Gilberto: I believe that what really reached our souls were the movies, much more than TV, simply by the dimensions, by the huge screen maybe, it was something more serious . . . it was something you had to go and see, you had to go towards it, and pay to see it.

During the decade we targeted for these memories, all the members of this focus group were exposed to the abundant production of Mexican films: mainly *Cantinflas'* and Pedro Infante's, though also present was the Spanish cinema—*Rocío Dúrcal's* and *Raphael's.* However, American movies had more impact for them. They mentioned 17 theaters, many of which no longer exist. The memory of the first movies they watched is directly associated with the impact provoked by the movie houses:

> Lilly: I attended to the inauguration of Cinema Manacar, where they showed *The Sound of Music,* it was an immense cinema.

Elsa: The first cinema where I was taken, I must have been five years old, and they took me to Cinema Bucareli, to see *The Ten Commandments.*

Advertising and program headings from several television and radio programs were recalled in an almost generalized manner. This generation lived an altogether homogenous process in the usage of radio during their adolescence, since they used it exclusively to listen to music.

The TV program *Teatro Fantástico,* transmitted on Sunday afternoons, inspired children to invent games with their classmates. In both cases, children imitated the characters, making theatrical representations that combined the backgrounds and sets of the programs with improvisational drama created by interraction with their schoolmates:

RL: My friends and I commented, and played to repeat the programs of *Teatro Fantástico.* It is incredible how we drew ideas from there to play.

AR: Suddenly we were playing being bewitched and you'd say "Oh, Kalimán," in a serious moment in which you were about to ask a girl to be your girlfriend, you'd say to yourself, "Patience, *Solín,* serenity and patience, much patience."

Gilberto: When children played they believed they were those *Combat* series soldiers, they believed they were Sergeant Saunders and this is how the children in the neighborhoods, they played to represent the TV characters.

Watching a program enabled them to transfer the mediatic experience into a face-to-face interaction context. Impressions from content watched on the previous day, in one or more programs, could be commented on or imitated because everyone had seen it.

From a very early age, children were exposed to symbolic worlds that constituted bridges between local—familiar, intimate contexts—and symbolic products that originated in foreign countries. Media brought the outside world, its culture and its circumstances, into the home, and in the Spanish language. For this cohort, this occurred predominantly through cinema, television, and photos of printed materials. In newspapers, photographs, especially those in color, were more frequently recalled than were articles, and all of them related to foreign news. *Life* and *Look* magazines were real windows through which they started to observe the outside world.

Digital Generation

In contrast to the other two generations, this generation was born with the presence of the television in their house; therefore the integration of this medium into family life was an established norm. Nevertheless, this generation has witnessed obvious technological changes, and the modernization of this medium, such as the remote-control device. This generation also has witnessed the occupation of different household spaces by the television. Other generations experienced the arrival of the medium as an invasive presence that occupied a very important place in the house—the "public" area—that was accessible to all members of the family.

In the case of video games, with the arise of Atari followed by Intelevision and Nintendo, time spent in front of the appliance increased. As noted earlier, Monserrat stated, "It was total alienation. I lived in front of the television."

Home, as we previously indicated, was an environment with few restrictions for this generation of children, and therefore access to the symbolic worlds that media presented. However, there were certain types of programs, particularly soap operas, to which they did not have access. As opposed to soap operas, parents considered cartoons to be programs made for children, so they had free access to these.

4. Media Memories

Radio Generation

In spite of the fact that the 20th century was beginning, and that the process of globalization was in a preliminary phase of internationalization, in Mexico the press, radio, and movies were the linking media with the outside world. Few people traveled, even if they belonged to the upper classes (in the group we had an example of this). The development of a concept of international reality was, in the generation studied, totally determined by the news that arrived through the media. Close proximity to the United States promoted a strong cultural influence, mainly in the northern states of Mexico:

Rebeca: In 1932 I was sent as an intern to the United States. . . . I was there for four years. . . . I returned in 1936. . . . at the beginning of World War II it was very strange, because in Mexico we liked the German culture. . . . There was a tremendous amount of dead Englishmen, but no Germans. But when they changed, then the dead were the Germans. . . . There was in Mexico a German newspaper. . . . The idea people had before the War was that German products were the good-quality ones . . . Japanese stuff was cheap quality. . . . American products were regarded as today's Chinese products. . . . They had told us that Americans were the good guys, but we thought: how dare they kill that huge amount of persons. . . . It is that they are telling us lies . . . it is that what they say is not true.

Mass media, especially the press and the radio, were the most important channels for learning world events. All participants mentioned that their contact with foreign news was the cinema and radio news briefings, as well as the main newspapers. As it is shown here, individuals in this generation did not passively absorb symbolic forms. Due to the context in which they were received, they were given a creative and active sense; something that produces valuation and meaning in the reception process itself:

Guadalupe: From '35 to '45 was the time of my awakening . . . all my cousins and I went to a teacher's house to take our lessons.

Rebeca: :   To me, the Spanish War was very impressive . . . my father knew all about it . . . we got home to listen to the "Carta Blanca" news briefing.

In the mediatic international recollections of this generation, we see the "intertextual" sense expressed in the combination of events received by the media, with sideways-reinforced personal, historical, musical, or fiction events. A physical and symbolic mixture of environments is detected:

Gloria: In 1935 I began to go to school, since at the beginning there were no schools because Cárdenas had closed them; when the war began, and with the war [World War II] there were many things on the radio.

Guadalupe: I remember very well the Spanish War because I had many friends who were daughters of Spanish men. . . . I even believe that in the Site of Toledo was killed Edmundo Ruidias, the brother of a friend of mine.

Teodoro: I remember I arrived at the house of my Jewish uncle and aunt, and I read to them the news of the war. . . . They liked me to read for them. . . . If it hadn't been for this, I would not have learned about the war.

| Roberto: | Then, when Germans were removed from their houses, and the Japanese were sent to Perote. |

The reinforcement of war through cinema in the adult generation is very meaningful, for example, some participants mention:

Eduardo:	We watched the great stories of the atomic bomb, the end of the war, the beginning of the War of Abyssinia . . . all those stories were very vivid to me.
Rebeca:	We played to the war patrols, some were Nazis and others allies. . . . Then, when the incident of Squadron 201 happened, where the man who commanded the squadron was Antonio Cárdenas, who was from my land, it was a very impressive incident to me.
Roberto:	The way in which this generation understood and experienced everyday life definitely influenced the sense given to worldly news as "foreign."

All of them had lived through the Cristera War (religious chase) in Mexico. They experienced hiding in order to go to school; and Catholic families, who were a majority, were forbidden to attend mass. All felt the tense environment of government repression, which shocked this generation in their perception of the Spanish Civil War and World War II, for example:

| Roberto: | The religious chase we lived in full youth, when we had to go to school hiding. . . . We were recommended not to enter the school altogether, the school in Havre Street #34. . . . In the year 1935, I must have been in fourth grade of elementary . . . these were the same days of the beginning of the religious chase. . . . We had to carry our books under the sweater, with fear of being discovered. . . . there is another aspect that one must not forget . . . psychology in the war, in the battles, where everyone uses the best weapon they have . . . they move multitudes so tremendously, with such rapidity and such . . . let's take Hitler, how Hitler rose, by means of communication, by the speeches he said to those very impressive multitudes. |

Television Generation

For this cohort, most of the prompted news events were known thanks to color photographs. Television was the second source of media-related memories. However, news events that were spontaneously mentioned were originally known through television, printed materials, and face-to-face interaction in an almost equivalent proportion. As opposed to the youngest generation, spontaneous events that were mentioned here were mainly of foreign origin.

With respect to the induced ones, memories were overwhelmingly monographic, while spontaneous news was clearly intertextual. Concerning depth of memories, induced news events were superficial and somewhat detailed, but not profound. For spontaneously mentioned news events, on the other hand, memories were proportionally distributed between superficial, somewhat detailed, and profound. Therefore, knowledge of past news events is more specific in the spontaneous than in the induced-memory news. Finally, involvement in the construction of the memory pointed out a very low sensibility toward induced events, against a highly individual and collective involvement in spontaneously mentioned news events.

Digital Generation

In all five members of this focus group, memories of the news events were intertextual. This means that in the construction of memory, personal meaningful contexts converged, mixed with fragmented images from television and movies, among others. The depths of the memories were superficial, though more detailed in spectacular events such as the Gulf War, the death of Princess Diana, or President Clinton's personal life. The memories were vague, and at no time was there recall of a complete story on a given event.

The emotional involvement in the construction of memories was collective in a high degree. Perhaps this reflected a memory that, though intertextual, was deeply shared. This was not because there was coincidence in the face-to-face contexts in which these news events were lived, spoken, or discussed, but because of the coincidence in mediatic sources of information. This leads us to say that this generation shared a good amount of memory and a mediated knowledge about foreign information. We must mention other types of events that emerged throughout the session in a spontaneous way—most of these events occurred in Mexico. The media were the most important source of spontaneous memories; however, face-to-face contexts were also important, both in quantity and in quality. Once again, television was the predominant media source, followed by school.

We must emphasize the fact that the local news events were experienced in a direct way. They were represented in daily life, though television gave them a mediated character that referred to an immediate and daily experience context. The spontaneously mentioned news events had strong links to personal biographies. This was probably so because they were speaking about national news. However, it came to our attention that the depth of knowledge continued to be superficial, in spite of the fact that they referred to local events. Likewise, the degree of memory sharing was reduced; it was more of an individual memory, which was marked by a lesser degree of participation. Therefore, what was closer to their experience, though more vivid, was neither more nor better known.

For this cohort, intertextuality permeated the shared symbolic world and memories. Memories were told and structured in a narrative style similar to that of television. Basically they consisted of assembled fragments of senses, meanings, and images, with which they explained themselves and gave explanations about the reality in which they lived. This we called intertextuality of the memory: a narrative that was unified in a somewhat random and anarchic manner, with different texts that originated from different media and moments of the individual's biography. These texts put together different times and spaces with the sole purpose of generating a more or less coherent memory, loaded with sense—for those who remember—in two basic dimensions: narrative and meaning.

5. Conclusion

Radio Generation

Media have become mass media and have transformed notions of space. They have created images and visual texts that affect senses and create new "mediated" meanings. The symbolic forms conveyed by media have had direct consequences on the nature of the social relations. These forms transformed the interaction on mental landscapes, stages of life, and action, and therefore the conformation of our present and future biographies, and the ways in which we keep our memories. John B. Thompson (1998) adds to this idea; that in a shared physical space/locality, traditions have a primarily oral character, and depend for their existence on a continuous renovation process through oral history, and in face-to-face interaction contexts. But mass media have generated new forms of interaction in which symbolic content and information are exchanged between individuals who do not share the same time and space.

Through mass media, individuals appropriate meanings and symbolic contents through mediated forms of communication. Today, individuals incorporate and attribute similar meanings to distant events that take place outside of their communities, or the physical place in which they live. In this work we distinguished two general types of interaction. One is the face-to-face interaction form, which has an oral nature, and is located in shared space-time contexts. The other is the mediated interaction form that is generated by mass media. In this case, contexts are uprooted and experience becomes a process of displacement that makes possible the sharing of meanings and mediated symbolic systems. It is important to mention that an increase in the mediated interaction forms does not mean that the face-to-face interaction form disappears. For individuals, the appropriation of contents and symbolic meanings is an all-important selective process. This is the process by which they discriminate among and adapt symbolic materials and their meanings to their own history, in order to assume their sense of place in the world.

Television Generation

With the presence of television there has been a tremendous increase in symbolic forms available to the individual. Therefore, the individual has the possibility to access more events, situations, and mediatic products. Today, under these circumstances, the appropriation process has acquired a relevancy that it did not have before. At present, global media produces symbolic goods that confront, conciliate, and transform the meaning and uses of locality. This is why the concept of appropriation gives us the chance to explore the conditions by which individuals make local use of global products and meanings. Moreover, the transformation of interaction is linked to the meanings we give to our past.

Perception of the past will increasingly depend on a growing stock of mediatic symbolic forms. When building a retrospective story, one must appeal to memory, which is clearly selective and intertextual. These characteristics seem to be stressed when mass media operates as a central actor in this process. The selectivity of the memory is reinforced at the same time by intertextuality, a key element that makes possible the convergence of text fragments rooted in different times and spaces.

Remembrance and its narration—the moment of verbalization—is full of symbols and meanings that come from the most diverse sources. Mass media generates symbolic and physical environments. Before the rise of mass media, people belonged to world experiences circumscribed to face-to-face interactions. Print media introduces information systems that create placeless forms of relationships.

Digital Generation

With electronic mass media, the situation changed dramatically, since these media permit a more homogeneous and less segregated access to its content. This facilitates the sharing of symbolic forms. Mass media have a meaningful effect in the structuring of the social information systems. Media shapes these systems and at the same time, makes access to them possible according to their physical characteristics and the uses they generate. Joshua Meyrowitz (1985) mentions that each media promotes or restricts the possibility of sharing social information. In contrast to books, through which the reader lives a highly individualized experience, mass media (like television) tends to generalize access to symbolic forms. Therefore, the shared mediatic experience is generalized between groups that belong to different places, times, genders, ages, and socioeconomic levels, among others. We think that it is important to emphasize the trend and possibility of sharing information systems that is made possible by the media. The boundaries that delimited the experiences of persons or specific groups are progressively fading. Our hypothesis is that mass media generate communities of meaning, which are constituted by diverse groups of individuals that, without sharing the same place, time, or common information fields, share symbolic and personal experiences, memories, texts, and meanings. By using the term "communities," we are not referring to conventional communities, rather to para-communities that transcend local experiences, which are under conditions imposed by face-to-face interaction. The grounds of these communities are no longer the face-to-face interaction forms, but rather the shared media experiences.

Bibliography

Bohmann, Karin (1994). *Medios de comunicación y sistemas informativos en México* [Mass media and information in Mexico]. Mexico City: Alianza Editorial.

Esteinou Madrid, Francisco Javier (2001). "Medios de comunicación, crisis nacional y participación social." ["Mass media, national crisis, and social participation"] in *Communication Spaces No. 5* Mexico City: Uia.

Joshua Meyrowitz (1985). *No Sense of Place: The Impact of Electronic Media on Social Behavior.* New York: Oxford University Press.

Semo, Enrique and Eugenia Meyer (1999). "Cambios sociales" In *El mexicano y su siglo. Las trasnformaciones de un país y sus habitantes a lo largo de cien años.* ["Social changes" In *Mexicans and their century. The transformation of a country and its habitants during one hundred years*]. José Gutiérrez Vivó. Mexico City: Editorial Oceano.

Thompson, John B. (1998). *Ideology and Modern Culture*. Mexico City. Universidad Autónoma Metropolitana.

· S O U T H   A F R I C A ·

Ruth Teer-Tomaselli

The South African study was conducted in Durban. The South African experience was marked with less homogeneity than the other countries in this study. This was to be expected, given the enormous differences in social class, race, and language, which marked out the South African polity. All of these elements contributed to very different, and until recently, segregated life experiences and perceptions. The media, too, followed these internal divisions of race and language, with separate radio channels for each of the eleven linguistic communities, television channels that followed "targeted" audiences, and a highly differentiated and varied range of newspapers.

1. History and Demographics

Radio was introduced in 1924 as a commercial enterprise, and national broadcasting was taken over by the government in 1936, modelled on the British Broadcasting Corporation. Broadcasting began in English only, followed a few years later by Afrikaans. "Radio Bantu," the now-derogatory term for programming aimed at black South Africans during that time, was introduced in 1943, with just a few hours of broadcasting during each day.

The early 1960s saw an economic boom that resulted in the growth of Afrikaner capital, and the dominance of the Broederbond—a secret Afrikaner society in the areas of economics, politics, and culture. These tendencies were evident in the media. The VHF/FM (Very High Frequency/Frequency Modulation) network was introduced countrywide in 1960, allowing for a flexible yet ideologically controlled network of radio stations, all inside the umbrella of the South African Broadcasting Corporation (SABC), including a continuation of the public-service broadcasting (PSB) tradition of the English and Afrikaans radio stations.

In South Africa, the second-generational cohort is a non–television-viewing group, since television was introduced into the country only in 1976, ironically the same year as the Soweto uprising. Initially there was a single channel divided equally between English and Afrikaans programming, and four years later a second channel was introduced, with a third channel added in the early 1990s. At present, the SABC3 broadcasts in English, while SABC1 and SABC2 is scheduled in a predetermined mix of ten other languages. E-TV is a free-to-air commercial television station, and M-Net is a subscription channel with a two-hour window of unencrypted time. The home holding company of M-Net, MultiChoice, operates a 24-hour encrypted satellite bouquet of 23 channels, some of which are custom-made for the South African market, and many of which are internationally well known (e.g., Discovery, CCN). At a relatively high subscription price, little more than a million subscribers from a nation of more than 20 million households support this service. Thus, the great majority of people are dependent on four free-to-air television channels.

The SABC maintains its position as the dominant broadcaster with a bouquet of both public-service format and commercial radio stations. In addition, there were 13 private commercial stations at the time of writing, and some 63 licensed community radio stations, not all of which are broadcasting at the present time. Though small by North American or European standards, South Africa remains the largest and most influential media terrain in Africa, with Egypt the possible exception.

2. Media Environment of Each Cohort

In the 70- to 75-year-old cohort, media was an important part of their experience, though predictably, there was less availability of media to this cohort than to the other two age groups studied. Radio, and to a lesser extent newspapers and cinema, were the mainstream of the media, making up their world during the time period under discussion. Radios were part of the furniture of the household, fixed in one place, and used in common by the entire family. "My parents did have radio. They bought their second radio in a big elaborate cabinet with six valves set in it. It was a big stream radio with big glass bottles, which used to generate a lot of heat. There was no FM: there were crackles, bangs, squeaks and squawks. There was a tiny dial like this to tune in on. The range was minimal and we had these tremendous big aerials" (Joseph). Rural living frequently meant not having access to electricity, but ingenuity was able to overcome this difficulty:

Stuart: We lived on a farm, and we had a wind charger for the radio. In fact, I still have it, a big old square thing. When the war came, Mum and Dad used to listen to the radio, but I just listened to many tunes.

David: We had one these battery sets and we only listened to the news. We took it to the village to be recharged.

Newspapers appear to have been a less important source of information among the respondents, although many had access to them at home. For those who lived on farms, newspapers were associated with the town, and were bought only occasionally. In a pre-television age, radio provided a full-spectrum service, including "a lot of entertainment." While for some "news was the main thing" (Stuart), music, stories, and comedy were equally important. Respondents recall listening to the children's hour "in the afternoon when they told stories" (Phillip), and radio soap operas provided much entertainment, eliciting the same sort of following as current television series:

George: There was a serial called *The Sign of the Purple Fighter* and I was excited by the story. My grandmother, my mother, and father sat listening to this serial.

Hermanus: We listened to the Afrikaans serial *Soekmelksvlei*.

Cornelius: I didn't listen to radio programs until after I was married. I had friends who used to listen to these stories. My mother-in-law did, and she came visiting and then I had to listen to them too. I went to a friend's house across the road once, and a neighbor came over and she was crying. She said "so-and-so" has died—she was speaking of the nanny in the serial.

The final medium of importance was that of the cinema, or "bioscope," as it was known, which, at one shilling and sixpence, was cheap and accessible. News programs shown on newsreels were not advertised in advance, rather, "the manager put a notice up outside, something to the effect of 'Just arrived—Atrocities in Russia.' Then the bioscope would be filled with people just to see these movies, and . . . they played them twice" (Joyce). The idea of these showings being a public experience was very important, since this information was shared with the whole community, and not consumed in the privacy of individual homes. In a mediated sense, this came close to the Habermasian notion of a "public sphere" that generated information that was then discussed in peer groups (Habermas, 1994).

Some respondents mentioned that their access to such information was restricted. Responding to a discussion of anti-German war propaganda replete with graphic scenes of atrocities, Mary remarked that such scenes were probably "why I was not allowed to go to the cinema unless I was told I had to go. [When I went without permission], I was in trouble after that." It is worth remembering that during the period they were recalling, the respondents would have been restricted as "children," and would only have been allowed to visit the cinema during the day. This contrasts significantly with the last/youngest cohort in the studies, whose participants were teenagers in the late 1990s, and were afforded considerably more latitude in the media products they consumed.

Of the three age cohorts studied, those between 40 and 45 years of age—closest to my own age—appeared to be the most vague about world events during their adolescence. This may have something to do with the intense isolation of South Africa in those years (1965–1970). The inward-looking national approach is reflected in the memories, or lack of memories, of the participants.

The group consisted of eight respondents: five men and three women. All of the respondents came from middle-class, educated homes characterized by a high degree of media consumption. Three of the men served time in the military as conscripts, the other, Charles, immigrated to London for finishing school, in order to avoid military call-up. Some of the men served in active duty in the Caprivi Strip, a thin finger of South African territory between Namibia and Angola, which served as a cover for the South African military incursions into both these countries. While the entire group considered themselves to have come from "liberal" homes, most were frank about their lack of political awareness during their youth.

Television was introduced into South Africa in 1976; therefore in the period covered by this part of the research, radio was the only broadcast medium available to South Africans. Partly because the focus of the group was skewed towards a relatively well-educated, middle-class group of people, not strictly representative of South African society, most respondents recall newspapers as an integral part of their daily lives. Most of the respondents recalled receiving at least one daily newspaper, and one or two weekend newspapers. For many, there was some ritual around access to the newspaper: usually with the father of household reading it first, after which the wife and children would be allowed access:

Paul: I still remember the procedure. When the newspaper was delivered my father, if he was at home, would read it. If he wasn't, someone could look at it but it was available for him. He had a strong ritual of coming home, sitting down, and reading the newspaper. The fathers of a lot of my friends did the same kind of thing. You could look at it but you couldn't mess it up, and it had to be available. So you couldn't finish reading it. That I remember, because my mother would have been cooking and she wouldn't have been able to read it, she would probably read it later that evening.

This quote clearly illustrates the unstated, taken-for-granted gender roles of the period: mothers cooked and cleaned; fathers read the newspaper.

Newspapers were also seen as entertainment, not only a source of news. Mavis recalled the importance of the comics in the Sunday papers. Her family collected them, and at one time had a complete set covering six years.

In a society as divided as South Africa, language played a very important role. All the white respondents in the group spoke English as their home language, while the black respondents spoke Zulu, with English as a *lingua franca*. While people remembered the titles of Afrikaans newspapers, none of the group read Afrikaans newspapers, and indeed, there was an antipathy towards them, indicating the strongly polarized and frequently intolerant nature of the society at the time:

Paul: Both of my parents were from Afrikaans families, but Anglophile [they spoke English at home]. I was spoken to in English, and there was no local Afrikaans newspaper. My mother would listen to the radio in Afrikaans. We never even got a Sunday paper in Afrikaans. The Sunday papers, and particularly the Afrikaans papers, at that time were political or party organs. The Afrikaans papers were National Party. My parents were not NP supporters. My cousins and uncles and aunts had Afrikaans papers and I would have read them. It was clear to me from the start that the stance that they took was not "ours."

The choice of Afrikaans as the preferred radio language speaks to the intimacy of radio as a medium (McLeish, 1994), which was seen as more intimate than the "political" newspaper. Apart from newspapers, respondents recalled reading magazines. The locally produced South African magazines of the time were aimed mainly at a female readership. International magazines, notably *Time* and *Life,* were seen as rare opportunities to view the outside world.

Most respondents claimed to have relied more on radio than on any other medium, but newspapers, magazines, films in cinema, and recorded music also provoked discussion. For English-speaking South Africans of the time, three radio stations were important: Springbok Radio, a full-spectrum family oriented format; the rather staid English Service of the SABC; and the LM Radio, broadcast from Lorenco Marques (Mozambique), which was a music station and considered too racy for the national broadcaster to transmit.

When the discussion turned to specific programs on the radio, a surprising number of radio shows were mentioned by name, covering genres such as radio theater, quiz shows, comedy shows, news, and current-affairs programming. For this cohort, music was of overwhelming importance. The most remembered program was *Forces Favourites,* a music-request program dedicated to the armed forces, which was aired on Saturday afternoons. When asked which bands and musical groups were recalled, only two genres were mentioned: rock and roll, and folk songs. For both, the megastar international artists were named: the Beatles, the Rolling Stones, Bob Dylan, Joan Baez, and the Beach Boys, along with others.

The youngest cohort was the most ethnically and socially mixed, and had the most varied spectrum of experience among the three age groups surveyed. The nine respondents, four male and five female, were drawn from well-to-do private schools, middle-of-the-road, racially integrated state schools, while three girls lived in St. Monica's, a children's home housing girls from the lower-socioeconomic class in need of foster homes. All respondents had been brought up in the city, with no rural youth being sampled. These differences made for very interesting exchanges and different worldviews. Media consumption was quite different, corresponding directly to the socioeconomic position of the household. While some respondents reported newspapers coming into their households an average of two to five times per week, in the wealthier groups there were more than eight newspapers per week, plus a wide variety of magazines and specialist journals. The girls in St. Monica's home received several copies of two newspaper titles daily, courtesy of the publishers. Home, as opposed to school or college, was the site of most television watching. Despite the plethora of television channels that were available to wealthier homes, the majority of respondents claimed to listen to radio for longer periods than they watched television. The radio stations that were most listened to included: 5-FM, an SABC-owned, nationally broadcast commercial format; East Coast Radio, a commercial, all-music station with a similar play list, but which included more local music; Metro FM; and a clutch of small community-based radio stations, including those specializing in religious broadcasting. A number of respondents mentioned watching a great deal of television as children and younger teenagers, but watched less in their later teenage years. Access to the Internet was also varied, with five of the nine having home connections, while all had access at school.

3. Media Memories

70- to 75-Year-Old Cohort

As a result of the predominance of the war experience, most of the memories evoked in the discussion group centered on the war. The most important event not related to the war was the 1938 centenary of the Great Trek, a milestone in the history of South Africa. All of the respondents remembered the commemoration, often recounting personal experiences that took place around the same time. This incident illustrates the personal nature of recollected memories. Turning to the list of marker events, the war in Spain was seen in the light of its connection to the pact between dictators Franco and Mussolini, and the subsequent Italian annexure of Abyssinia. Reference to the Salt March in India led to minimal discussion. The Berlin Olympics elicited a slight, but stereotypical response, "A Negro, Jessie Owens, fought against this German chap," offered Cornelia. The Second World War was the most important theater of events for this age group: "the war was the main topic of conversation" (Stuart). Three of the men in the group eventually enlisted for active service for part of the war.

As was true of many events in the history of any country, the war did not evoke memories of uniformly patriotic fervor. For many Afrikaans-speaking South Africans, including some of the members of the focus group, it called back a past of ideological division. In the 1930s and 1940s, political loyalties of white South Africans were deeply divided, with some Afrikaans-speakers having overt sympathies with the Nazis. The most vehement of these joined a secret group, the *Ossewabrandwag* (loosely translated as the "burning flame of the ox wagon"), who perpetrated a number of acts of sabotage on key South African installations. Dawie recalled: My father was considering joining this business. They broadcast clandestinely. I think it was about 8 o'clock for about quarter of an hour on the radio. It was done in secret code or whatever."

This opened an opportunity for other group members to claim familiarity with this part of their joint history. Some of the stories seemed far-fetched, but whether they were literally true or not is immaterial; what is important is that this episode in history is closely tied to their own sense of identity, even 50 years after the recollected events took place.

When asked about the fall of Singapore, the response entailed a quite detailed exposition of the situation of an event in history that occurred half a century previously, and to which the South African connection was minimal. Although Joseph claimed to have heard the news on the radio, it is not clear whether the knowledge came from contemporary information, or was acquired subsequently.

Joseph:	I heard it on the radio. I remember the Chindits were a very active force. Sort of quite a secret army, a version of commandos.
Stuart:	Weren't those the werewolf men?
Joseph:	Yes, but they worked in Burma and all that area. Of course all this was subsequent to Pearl Harbor, which was ear-shattering news on the radio. The American Navy was devastated, and this is what led America to come into the war.
Moderator:	Let's just stick to Singapore.
Joseph:	Subsequent to that [Pearl Harbor], Japan seemed to rush through Asia, and Singapore was set up as a fortification to last forever. The only thing was no one had thought to face guns inland. When the Japs came, all these solidly mounted guns couldn't fire inland, and the Japs just walked in from the back. There are pictures [that were] made, documentation about the [Japanese] infiltration [into Allied territory] . . . but to offset this situation, a commando unit, the Chindits, were established to attack the Japanese. There were not many of them, but they were effective.

The interchange above illustrates the way in which the conversation meanders through various events that are related, at least in the minds of the respondents. Discussion of one situation tended to trigger recollections of another, and even if the precise causality between the two was not clear, in the perceptions of the group, they seemed inextricably linked.

The Japanese attack on Pearl Harbor was perceived to be a major turning point in the course of the war. The attack also rekindled old hurts and resentments, stirring long-held anti-American sentiments, as were evident in the following exchange:

Dawie: It was big news, to do with America. It was in the newspapers and everybody talked about it. It was a turning point because the Americans joined the war.

Joseph: Yes. The story was not allowed to die, it was very good propaganda to chivvy up America, to revenge Pearl Harbor.

George: I think until that time nobody knew whether America would go on the side of Britain and the Allies. They had this thing— bring buy, cash and carry. Any power or any navy could call at America and buy aircraft, whether they were German or British or Japanese or anybody, as long as they paid cash for it. A lot of people said that Churchill engineered Pearl Harbor to bring America into the war.

Generally, events during the war were discussed in terms that were not historically or entirely accurate, but rather reflected the perceptions and propaganda of the time. Nor was much of the discussion structured in terms of any specified media intervention; rather there was a realization about the confusion between contemporary memory and subsequent knowledge: "You get confused between what you've read until that time," commented Stuart, while Dawie reflected about the fall of Singapore that he "read about it afterwards. I didn't see it on movies at that time."

40- to 45-Year-Old Cohort

International news did not appear to be particularly important to most of the middle cohort. Unprompted, Gray remarked on the five-minute propaganda slot after the radio news each morning:

Gray: I do remember listening to it, and I do remember my father listening to it at the same time, and getting extremely angry with it. I remember wondering why he was so angry, but clearly I didn't understand it.

Jimmy: Personally it was the huge revulsion to what was called "current affairs," which when it come on, I would switch off the radio . . . because we know it was the government trying to justify the unjustifiable. Other than that on the radio news, I have no actual [spontaneous] memories.

Of the marker events, only the six-day war in Israel was recalled spontaneously. For the rest, the marker events were discussed only after they had been prompted. The 1968 Student Revolution in Paris was recalled because "it was linked to the idea of a youth culture in revolt . . . to things like Woodstock and Bob Dylan and so on" (Jimmy). The Cultural Revolution in China left only a "vague impression of oppression, or persecution," with Paul noting that he knew "nothing at the time, only in retrospect, [it was] something that had been analyzed and presented" subsequently. Memories of political events in Czechoslovakia and Hungary were equally vague and uninformed. Paul also remembered the Palestine Liberation Organization from a personal, rather than a mediated point of view: "I remember it because I was at boarding school. With lots of Jewish kids who were very disturbed about it. I remember being told that there was a war and listening to the radio with them."

The OPEC crisis and the rise of fuel prices in 1973 had a more immediate impact on the lives of the respondents. Gray recalled hearing the news on the radio, which "said that the oil had been cut off by the Arab States, that we all needed to use petrol very sparingly."

The music festival at Woodstock was remembered through the film that was made of the occasion. Lindiwe saw the movie with girlfriends; Paul saw it "more than once" and in terms of counter-culture "I would have identified very strong with that."

The Vietnam War was remembered more as a series of external influences than in terms of the actual course of hostilities. The conflict "was pretty closely linked up with the '68 student rebellions. . . . Alongside the Vietnam War, we were reading what people like Jane Fonda were saying about it. . . . It seemed to be linked with a general dissatisfaction with the old order and so on" (Jimmy). External events, particularly the Vietnam War, acted as "triggers" to move the discussion toward the respondent's own experiences, either as draftees, in the South African army, or as wives and girlfriends, a theme which will be developed later in this chapter.

The Watergate scandal once more indicated the level of indifference toward American politics by the respondents during their youth. Gray noted that he was "very confused for a long time. I didn't follow the story very carefully; I couldn't make sense of it. It seemed to me that Tricky-Dicky [Richard Nixon] organized a cover-up." Jimmy had a similar reaction: "I had a vague idea of the politics of it, and felt [that] Nixon was such an odious character himself." Charles reminded the group that television was only introduced into South Africa in 1976, and Nixon resigned to avoid being impeached.

Finally, the photographs of Mars drew much discussion about the entire U.S. space program—beginning with the Soviet launch of Sputnik and ending with the moonwalk—but the specifics of the Mars photographs seemed to have been lost in the debris of memory.

For this group, what happened within the country was of overwhelming significance: as teenagers, army draftees, and young students, they were at the forefront of the country's embryonic antiapartheid struggle, which expressed itself as an anti police sentiment. While they weren't very sure about the sociology and politics of those years, they recalled the occasional skirmishes and encounters with the police.

Very few memories of any news-related items were recalled spontaneously, and the moderator prompted almost all of the discussions around specific events, both domestic and international. The political situation in Zimbabwe (previously Rhodesia) was an important arena of consciousness. All of the respondents had some memory of Ian Smith, then prime minister of Rhodesia, declaring Unilateral Independence from Britain in 1965. At that stage, the respondents would have been very young, and had little personal political affiliation, recalling rather the opinions of their parents or communities in general: "Everyone kind of loved 'Smithy.' . . . Certainly, my parents had strong sympathy for him and I didn't really have any position" (Paul).

Sometimes, the memories were irrelevant to the larger issues, focusing on details of lesser importance: "My mother was so embarrassed that Ian Smith went to London in such a shabby suit. And his socks showed. The man deserved what he got. If he didn't even go to an international meeting dressed properly, how could he think of being treated seriously?" (Nancy).

However, others were more critical of Smith's position. Edward referred to Smith's infamous "never in a thousand years" comment regarding the possibility of black-led government taking control of Rhodesia.

Edward: I had read enough about the Third Reich to realize that when people make a mistake like that, they are in for a fall.

Gray: By that stage I was fairly well educated, and I kind of seemed to think that the Lanchester House Agreement [on independence] was an inappropriate solution.

It is not possible, from the hindsight of more than 30 years, to know now whether these were the contemporary (1970s) thoughts of the respondents, or whether they have been retrospectively projected through the lens of history. Jimmy seemed to sum up the unease of the group's musings when he said, "I think I tended to have many ambivalent feelings towards Smith, and the images of so-called quiet diplomacy, because Rhodesia was so crassly linked to our apartheid . . . that, you know, tended to link them together and created a difficulty." This sentiment was probably true of a number of issues faced by this group in relation to Namibia, Rhodesia/Zimbabwe, and Mozambique.

The 1974 Portuguese Revolution, and the subsequent coming to power of the colonial independence movement in Mozambique, Frelimo, was a watershed for many respondents. Charles recalls: "By that stage I was quite grown up, [and] to some extent I understood the political situation. It was the beginning of the rise of black consciousness and radicalism here [in South Africa]."

On the topic of the conflict on the Angolan-Namibian border, all respondents had some contribution to make.

15- to 20-Year-Old Cohort

The death and funeral in August 1997 of Diana, Princess of Wales, was singularly the most important international item recalled in detail by the youngest cohort. The topic evinced the most response, and the conversation flowed with very little intervention from the moderator. Several themes stand out in the discussions: the initial incredulity, followed by the subsequent confirmation through watching on television, listening to the radio; the empathy with the young princes; the visual spectacle of the funeral, and particularly the flowers; the sentimentality of the speeches, and unexpectedly, the connection made between Princess Diana and Mother Theresa of Calcutta, who died a few weeks later.

In a real sense, this was a Media Event (Dayan and Katz, 1994) par excellence: many of the respondents followed the story closely, watching television both on the day of the accident, and during the funeral the following Saturday. Respondents spontaneously related how they first found out about the death of the princess, without any prompting from the facilitator:

Janey: I remember, I was up early in the morning and my dad was watching the television. . . . I couldn't believe it. I just sat there watching as well. Then all of us [were] watching, we were just talking and nobody seemed to be in the right kind of mind.

Jacinta: It was a Sunday. My dad walked into my room and said, "Hey, Princess Diana is dead now." And I was like, "Yeah, alright, you are trying something again this morning." And then I went and watched TV, and I was, like, you can't believe it, that it actually happened. It was unreal.

Kumi: I just remember I was at my grandpa's house, and when I woke up early in the morning, because we actually had a prayer that day, and . . . my Grandma told me that Princess Diana had died. You know, I didn't believe her; I thought that she was joking. At first I didn't feel much. I was sad for her children and her husband, her husband no so much [laughter], but for her children, after everything she had done, and to be killed in such a tragic manner, but it didn't hit me as much until after the funeral. That was when the sadness came, when . . . I think I shed some tears.

In contrast to the positive role of Princess Diana, Monica Lewinsky and Bill Clinton were seen as sleazy, but not intrinsically wicked. Most respondents felt the entire situation received too much attention: "It was the biggest waste of time," said David. There was a feeling that it was wrong that Lewinsky should be getting publicity from her actions. Indignantly, Thokoza remarked, "Recently on television it was so ridiculous, they actually invited Monica Lewinsky for one of the Hollywood functions." This remark triggered a number of other examples of the excessive publicity given.

The third international story that made a significant impression on the respondents was the O.J. Simpson saga, which, although regarded as "very sensationalized" (Mark), appeared to be as compulsive as a soap opera: "I thought it was very interesting. I read every article," admitted Baree. Here again, a plethora of small details rather than a coherent narrative, dominated the discussions: the matching of the shoe size, cars outside the home, and the blood samples in the evidence that were switched. Sometimes the details became confused, as in the name of Simpson's wife:

Mark: His wife was Karen.
Sanjev: I think it was Tracy.
David: I have no idea, except she was a pretty blond.
Mark: Nicole, that's it!

In contrast to the events in America, what happened in the rest of the world was hazier. Although they were close to home, the wars played out in Africa were not recalled with any clarity or specificity: Jacinta mentioned that her father had fought on the border of Angola; Janey talked about the Mozambique War "when we were little," that is, in the 1980s; Baree added, " . . . and the Rwandan war. People hacking each other." Stereotyping, as in "people hacking each other," was also evident among a number of respondents. Recalling the war in Rwanda, Sanjev said, "I remember on the news they were showing us footage of all the people who were killed, like skulls and leg bones; it was a genocide." David asked, "Wasn't that Zaire or something?" "No, that was Rwanda," was the reply. Africa, north of the southern African region, seemed to be very far away to most respondents. Zimbabwe, however, elicited a more heartfelt response:

Sanjev: Something like that could happen here.
Mark: Yeah, especially the land crisis, people can come back and reclaim the land.
Moderator: Does the Zimbabwean crisis frighten you?
[Most respondents nod in assent]
Mark: I grew up in Zimbabwe, so it's happening where I used to live, so it can happen where we are now.

Recollections of happenings in Europe and Asia were hazy.

Baree: I remember like a wall in Germany or something.
Jacinta: The wall separated East Germany and West Germany.
Mark: And they broke it down.
David: Lots of wire and that sort of thing.
Jacinta: There's a piece of the wall in Cape Town.
Mark: Wasn't that the unification of Germany, or something like that?
David: Just like the First World War.
Jacinta: No, the Second World War.
Sanjev: When did they break it down?
Kumi: 1990.
Mark: I remember watching that on CNN.

In this interchange, a number of elements are evident: the lack of specific knowledge around world events, which are remembered only as a series of unconnected images from television ("I remember watching that on CNN" and, "lots of wire and that sort of thing"); the need to claw back the experience in terms of the respondents' own worldview ("There's a piece of the wall in Cape Town"); the incomplete, but nevertheless present attempts to relate television viewing to their knowledge of history ("Wasn't that the unification of Germany, or something like that?"); and the confusing of the sequencing of historical events over an entire century, from the First World War to the destruction of the Berlin Wall.

Turning to the events in South Africa, the class/race divisions were very evident, with the less well-to-do black and "colored" respondents showing a greater awareness of the recent history of the country. Bongi, who had lived in a poor, strife-torn area in the early 1990s, found the violence of those years very real. She recalled: "Also people were just killing, they were not worrying about who's getting or how many children were being hurt, they were just fighting one another. I saw it in the paper. I was scared. I enjoyed reading from a very young age. I started reading properly when I was in Grade One. I remember, one day my father bought the paper and I read it all, and I didn't want to go to school because I was scared. My father said, 'Don't worry, it won't happen around here.'"

Little, if anything, was remembered about the last white president, F.W. de Klerk. The release of Nelson Mandela happened shortly before most of the cohort was able to take a coherent interest in politics or social affairs. Janey recalled that she saw "pictures on television of people screaming and clapping. I didn't know who he was though." Kumi remembers "people saying on the television how many years he was in prison, and [the television coverage of the prison release] was really long." Others had more concrete memories:

Thokoza: I was watching when he was let out of prison, and de Klerk and Mandela were walking together at the mall.

Jacinta: I remember walking into a school building center, and there were a group of teachers standing there, watching the television.

Turning to the watershed 1994 elections, the same dichotomy along racial and class lines was evident. Respondents from the upper-class suburbs were confessional and ironic: "My parents though it would be the end of South Africa and everything would be destroyed," said Sanjev, the son of a middle-class Indian home. Baree, a white boy from similar socioeconomic circumstances, concurred: "We thought we'd get kicked out of our house. That some black people would live there and we'd be told to live in a township." This comment caused an embarrassed twitter of laughter from the rest of the group.

However, there was a degree of optimism in the recollections too. Thokoza reminisced, "I remember my parents and neighbors came over and sat for close to three hours in front of the television, having tea and talking about how they were going to vote. At first I didn't understand how important that voters' day was." All the respondents, despite their comparative youth at the time, remembered the actual election. Mark's comments are typical of the conversation: "Everyone was excited. There was this air of anticipation [even though] most of us knew who [was] going to win, but especially for the people who couldn't vote previously. My parents were also excited when they were watching the news in the morning and [they saw] all these people, especially in the rural areas. They were standing in long, long, lines, but they were also happy."

4. Media Use across Generations

At the outset of this chapter, the racially and linguistically divided nature of South African society was alluded to. From the group discussion within the three cohorts, it was clear that the divisions within the society were generational as well. Each of the cohorts was representative of very different stages in the country's historical development. The first cohort represented a period during which South Africa, like the majority of states in the third world, was in a position of semi-colonization. As part of a commonwealth with a nominal alliance to the British Empire, the country was at once part of the world system, but on the periphery, isolated by distance and different levels of wealth, as well as different levels of commitment to the Commonwealth ideals.

During the late 1960s and early 1970s, South Africa was at the height of apartheid, with all the desolation, militarism, and repression that the name implied. From a media point of view, the delayed introduction of television meant that unlike other middle cohorts in the wider study, this cohort still relied entirely on radio as its main source of entertainment, education, and information. A wide spectrum of genre formats was still broadcast, with respondents recalling their favorite quiz shows, narratives, dramas, and request programs in great detail. However, radio, for the most part, was state controlled, with no truly commercial stations (except for Lorenco Marques Radio). As a result, the cohort regarded radio news as propagandistic and suspect, and tended to use the radio mainly for entertainment and music.

The 1990s saw the country as part of the global world once more. Teenagers had access to 24-hour news coverage, and were exposed to the same concerns that occupied their contemporaries around the world. Yet, the socioeconomic unevenness of resources was felt even in the consumption of media, with the great majority of young people relying on radio and free-to-air television as their mainstay of news and entertainment. Few had home access to the Internet, and even fewer had access to satellite television. Therefore, radio, albeit highly differentiated and segmented radio broadcasting, remained preeminently important. Knowledge of current and historical events beyond the national borders was skimpy, and international megastars, whether they were Princess Diana or Monica Lewinsky, were more likely to catch their attention than were the details of wars and public policy.

Bibliography

Dayan, Daniel, and Elihu Katz (1992). *Media Events: The Live Broadcasting of History.* Cambridge, MA & London, England: Harvard University Press.

Habermas, Jürgen (1994). *The Structural Transformations of the Public Sphere.* Cambridge: MA & London, England: M.I.T. Press.

McLeish, R. (1994). *Radio Production: A Manual for Broadcasters.* 3ed. Oxford: Focal Press.

Matthew D. Payne, Jill Dianne Swenson, and Thomas W. Bohn

1. General Introduction

Media Context, Political Context, and Demographics

American media have always been mainly commercial. As soon as the newest medium arrived, it seemed that business was hungry to sink its teeth into the new innovation and find a way to turn it into a profit. Each of the generations represented by the U.S. cohorts in this study had their own form of media conglomeration, whether it was with the radio and television generations (GE, Westinghouse, RCA, AT&T, NBC, and CBS) or with today's information-age generation (Microsoft and AOL come to mind). As each new form of media came along, there was an initial and overwhelming explosion of services before the government came in to start regulation.

At the turn of the 20th century, the United States was at peace once again. But even though the first voices on radio were heard in 1906, it wasn't until the refinements in technology brought about during World War I that radio broadcasting was marketable. After WWI, the technology was taken up so quickly that the airwaves were soon saturated. The rush to build the radio market was finally regulated in 1927, when the Federal Radio Commission, the beginnings of today's Federal Communication Commission, was created. Luckily, the saturation helped keep radio alive through the Great Depression that started in 1929, and along with movies (just as popular, but not quite as widespread), radio was the voice that informed Americans about the events of World War II.

Born just before the Depression, the first cohort in this study was the generation that grew up during World War II. Movies, comic books, and radio shows provided virtual heroes and villains. Real-life heroes and villains were presented on the radio and through newsreels, this generation's primary source of information about the actions taking place during the war. The effects of this mediated information spurred some into action: after watching newsreels at the movies, some returned home eager to sign up for the war effort.

While World War II acted as fuel to the radio boom, it delayed the coming of the medium that would define the next generation. It wasn't until World War II came to a close and gave way to the baby boom that investors and businesses finally noticed television, which had been present in the United States since 1939. By 1948, saturation occurred in the television spectrum and, between 1948 and 1952, the FCC called for a freeze on new licenses.

The media events recalled by the middle cohort in this study played a formative role in this cohort's understanding of U.S. politics and history. After the boom and prosperity of the 1950s, the unprompted memories from the 1960s were of national and political tragedies, most of which were delivered through the television set: the assassinations of John F. Kennedy, Martin Luther King Jr., and Bobby Kennedy; the Vietnam War; and Kent State. Many of these media events, including Watergate, generated tremendous disillusionment. These recollections are described as integral to that era's identity and social location.

Television was king through the economic downturn of the 1970s and 1980s. But with the economic upturn starting in the early 1990s came the information age, during which this study's youngest cohort developed. Soon, people all over the United States were plugged into the multimedia world. For this generation, the oversaturation of information didn't create a single media "moment" as much as it did a media spectacle stretched out over time.

From the above media context came the eighteen participants of the U.S. focus groups. Each subject of every cohort (70- to 75-year-olds; 40- to 45-year-olds; and 15- to 20-year-olds) now resides within the Ithaca area, a suburban college community within the Finger Lakes Region of upstate

New York. "Hometown" listings in the below tables reflect the location and type of community within which each subject experienced their earliest/formative media experiences. "Media Equipment" reflects the media appliances/material present within the member's childhood environment. All are of middle-class background; all are Caucasian. As mentioned in Volkmer's introduction, because the focus groups are not homogenous, the diversity is found at the individual level, rather than the demographic level.

One last, interesting demographic note: some focus-group participants were both consumers and producers of media in their lifeworlds. Many of the group members talked about family photographs, films, and videos as part of their personal biography. Many had experienced taking photos, shooting video, or filming at family events. Some had careers in media production. One male in the 70- to 75-year-old group had worked as a publicist for a major television network, and a female in this group wrote occasionally for the local daily newspaper. In the 40- to 45-year-old group, one of the males managed a college radio station and one of the females taught photography at a local college.

2. Media Environment

For the oldest cohort, the sounds of radio ruled their day. One individual told us, "I'm a sound person. I don't know about this nonsense about pictures. . . . News was news! Now it's chewing gum for the eyeballs." Movies and the accompanying newsreels were another common experience. They also grew up with magazines, comic books, dime novels, and flipbooks. They remembered stereoscopes and photographs. There was a lot of discussion about the many media "firsts" they experienced in their childhood, such as the first radio, phonograph, and telephone in their households; the first radio broadcast of a baseball game; the first photograph and movie cameras; and as they grew older and had their own households, the first television sets. These "firsts" extended the reach of their social experiences, allowing their lifeworld to be expanded by material and memories coming to them through their mediaworld.[1] Their descriptions of childhood media environments are explicitly social, often public, and in the moment, rather than recorded for later replay or for private consumption. The family radio was situated honorably in the center of the household, and going to movies was a "weekly ritual" performed in public.

For the 40- to 45-year-old generation, media were less public and became more private. While television functioned as the radio did in the generation before (as a family-time activity), music now became very important. Acquiring his or her own personal stereo system marked this cohort as distinctive from the previous one.

Most homes had one room with a television set in it. Programs are similarly remembered: Saturday-morning cartoons, Sunday-evening Disney movies, and *The Ed Sullivan Show*. Musically, the Beatles, Motown, and rock and roll played a significant role in their mediaworlds. Books, newspapers, and magazines were common to this 40- to 45-year-old group when they were young. As in the previous generation, magazines and newspapers were dependent on the parents and what they subscribed to. All families had radios, usually attached to their stereos. Most also had books. Movies were also prevalent.

As with the previous generation, the 15- to 20-year-old cohort grew up watching television: *Full House, Family Ties, Family Matters*, and game shows like *Family Feud* and *Wheel of Fortune*. Each household subscribed to a newspaper and some magazines, most frequently *Newsweek*. This group is the first to actually subscribe to magazines separate from their parents. One had a subscription to *Ski* magazine.

What made this cohort unique from the others was that they grew up in households in which there was access to a variety of electronic media: TV, radio, VCRs, stereos, CD players, and, most important, computers. Each had computers in the house, some of them as early as when they were two years old. Most of them also have had their own Internet connection. This generation had an abundance of media all around them, at home and in schools. Many describe media being used as common background noise; whereas in earlier generations, there was more focus on individual media. Whether watching television shows, listening to unique music, or surfing the Net for the topics they found interesting, this generation was able to pull exactly what they wished from a multitude of media. Ice-skating fans watched skating coverage on television and surfed the Net for skating highlights. Enthusiasts of space exploration watched sci-fi movies and searched for pictures of Mars on the Internet.

3. Media Interaction

Like other focus groups from the other countries in this study, there were similarities in the way the Americans were "colonized" by their media. The U.S. focus groups showed distinct patterns in memory; in fact, there was more similarity in the way fellow generations from each country memorized media than there was between the different generations within

America. As mentioned above, the youngest generation of Americans, Mexicans, and Australians, for instance, all seem to be masters of information gathering.

However, even with the colonization similarity, the U.S. groups differed from other countries in the way that they remembered "international" events. On the whole, it seemed that if an event didn't have anything to do with Americans, it was not memorized. This may be because the bulk of international media material that comes to foreign countries is from the United States; and in the U.S., what others would consider international is mostly national. Thus, even though our generational groups are being colonized with the rest of the world, their memories are lacking in the area of international media events.

Not only do the individuals in the oldest cohort group vividly remember the media that surrounded them, but also how the media were used. Their memories of specific radio programs included a specific listening context. It was a family experience where they sat in silence together as a family to listen to a particular program at a particular time each week. The radio was never on to produce background noise. One explained that the radio "was turned on to listen to a specific thing."

For people living in more rural areas, using media involved a trip to another person's house. For one participant's family, everyone went over to a grandfather's house on Saturday nights to listen to radio programs such as the *Grand Ole Opry, The Shadow,* and *Dr. Christian.* When his father finally bought his first radio, this same participant described his father's transformation into a "news freak." When his father listened to news correspondents, it was as if nobody in the room was allowed to breath. When parents were using the media, the rules were followed closely.

For a different participant, it was often the same night, but a different program. On Saturday nights she remembers listening to Canadian hockey radio broadcasts, "Eight people and no one said a word." Other rituals surrounded the radio: her father smoked, she remembered, while listening to the games. During her lunch hour as a girl in school she remembers rushing home to catch the soap operas and rushing back to school when the program was over.

For the 70- to 75-year-old cohort, the greatest amount of time has elapsed between event and recollection. They have been eyewitness to more events in the media, and as media format and content changed, they are the generation with the greatest longitudinal effects of mass-media exposure. And yet, because more time has elapsed, more sedimentation of memory has occurred. The media served as the means to extend the potential reach of socially appropriated knowledge. This cohort was reflective, reflexive, evaluative, deliberative, and judgmental in their dynamic discussion of media and memories.

The key to the middle (40- to 45-year-old) group's dynamic was the talk about "owning" media. They talked about their first transistor radio and stereo as personal property. They also talked about the sense of being a media consumer and buying specific content, as in one's selection of music, movies, and magazines. This stood in contrast to the other two groups: the youngest cohort seemed to regard media (both in terms of the conduit and the content) as personal property; and the oldest cohort articulated a much stronger sense of media as public, common, collective, and shared.

For this generation, media consumption pitted them against their parents. A few recalled parental restrictions regarding media consumption: one participant's parent wouldn't allow their daughters to watch *Batman* because of its violence. Others remembered parents who disapproved of their choices in music. Parental limits on media exposure were depicted as denying access to socially acquired knowledge. Music, for some, provided an avenue for adolescent rebellion and a challenge to adult authority: one fought with his parents about his rock and roll music. For the most part, however, parental control of media consumption did not work, according to these individuals' self-reports.

There were, however, times where the family came together in harmony to share media. Different families had different rituals, as did individuals. One participant's family went to the movies on Saturday afternoons and watched TV on Sunday evenings. Her family often took in a film as a Thanksgiving Day ritual. Another remembers his household being devoted to *CBS News.*

Memories about particular TV programs, rock-music groups, and movies were easily elicited from this group. One person's recollection would sometimes spur another to affirm or dispute the memory of a particular media event. This group talked about collective media experiences in a way that made each telling an individual one. They made the connections between the common media event as socially acquired knowledge, and the specifics of their personally acquired experience of the media phenomenon. Also, there was little commonality between the participants' interactions with media, except that each had a unique way to interact with the media.

For the youngest generation, memories about growing up with media generated discussion about the transmission of family history and how media can be the glue between generations. One participant mentioned letters that her grandfather wrote during WWII, and another remembered a photo of his paternal grandfather at a young age in front of his house. One participant told how she'd recently found a news clipping at home that included her father: "He was at some demonstration." She then talked with her father and he told her about his experiences demonstrating in the 1960s. Family videos were more common than home movies, although photographs continued to chronicle family histories for this generational group.

In terms of mass media, participants recalled rituals of watching family-friendly shows—*Family Ties* and *Family Matters*—because parents wanted them to spend time together. Several participants said that their parents regulated television viewing in their early years, although the rules usually didn't work and didn't last. One participant, if he misbehaved or got a poor report card, had parents who would say, "You can't watch TV for a week," but that "pretty much ended by middle school." One exception where parental control was achieved was when one participant was allowed to watch only *Sesame Street* and *Mister Rogers' Neighborhood*. "Other kids got to watch *Full House*, but not me."

Many of the participants spoke of having media present as "background noise." One participant's mother would have the TV tuned to the news when he woke up. Another's family never really sat down and watched the news together; people would float in and out of the TV room as they pleased. Music was now portable: some listened to CDs in the car, and at home played MP3s on the computer. The ease with which media could be accessed could bring a family together and also cause conflict: one participant and his brothers would fight for access to the computer. However, "whenever we'd rent a video, the family would all sit down together to watch it."

Regardless of cohort, participants talked about experiencing and consuming all kinds of new media phenomena and remarked on the rapid tempo of change in media technology. This was especially true of the youngest generation. The media infrastructure of the 15- to 20-year-old cohort was oriented toward connecting and interacting. Participants described media experiences as a form of social activity. Connecting through media bridged the generations in a variety of ways, such as e-mail between grandchildren and grandparents, and teens and baby boomers bonding with classic rock music. Yet, connecting through contemporary media was not necessarily a collective experience. Unlike the 70- to 75-year-olds' collective-type memories, the connections created through contemporary media were not collective and catalytic for a mass audience. Interactivity with media also seemed to shift in focus from the 70- to 75-year-old group members' mutual remembrances of media events as socially interactive, to the 40- to 45-year-old group members recollections of common media events by telling their own eyewitness narratives, to the

15- to 20-year-old group members personal and private memories of media events that permeated multiple social structures: family, school, and organized social and leisure activities.

For the 70- to 75-year-old group participants, memories about growing up with media also generated discussion about the many media-technology "firsts." Lifeworlds and mediaworlds sometimes overlapped, and when they did they were public rather than private experiences. For the 40- to 45-year-old group, participants' lifeworlds and mediaworlds increasingly overlapped by weaving mass media and personal consumption together in everyday life and unproblematic practices. They made the connections between the common media event as socially acquired knowledge and the specifics of their personally acquired experience of the media phenomenon. For the 15- to 20-year-old group, lifeworlds and mediaworlds were synonymous. The everyday experience of one's lifeworld was saturated with media. They had their own personal computers, CDs, VCRs, TVs, telephones, and sound systems in their own rooms, unlike the previous generations, which involved more public, social, and family media.

Like the eldest cohort, these individuals remember many "firsts" as they also recalled experiencing new media. Akin to the 40- to 45-year-old generation, this younger group took personal ownership of media for granted. Patterns in memories, however, suggested strong comparisons between the generational groups. The overlap between lifeworld and mediaworld for the 15- to 20-year-old generation means their personally acquired experience is often socially acquired knowledge: information that was gained through personal media consumption. In other words, using the computer or watching a video was "real." It was no less real and no more mediated than riding a bike or eating lunch. This cohort did not divorce reality from mediated reality in their discourse.

4. Media Memories

At a visceral level, movie newsreels conveyed central cultural values for the oldest cohort. "I didn't have brothers or sisters, but through the news clips, I felt the horror of the war," a female participant said. Too young to join the war, much less fully comprehend the political struggles, this group absorbed the images and ideas of World War II that were presented by the media as a reference point for their lives.

But even with the radio and newsreels saturating the public with views of World War II, some participants didn't fully comprehend media events

until later in their lives. One participant said she was too young to understand what was happening during World War II and did not feel very
involved. Another also said he "simply missed Pearl Harbor." He didn't
realize how important it was until later in life.

It is interesting to note that this group remembered many of the same
media events in the same way, and not just the events of the war. For example, they all recalled the same impact of the radio broadcast of Orson
Welles's *War of the Worlds:* the others echoed one's recollection that "people
in my hometown were terrified." Everyone in the group unanimously
affirmed the memory of the Hindenburg disaster, that the radio "rebroad-
cast it so many times." Rarely did only one person remember a media
event; generally they all remembered the media event or none of them did,
as was the case with the Salt March in India.

Those who grew up in a more rural setting believed their lack of exposure to media as children set them apart from the others, not just in the
group but in the larger culture. "I was a little removed from that because I
lived in the country," one explained about her lack of WWII media memories. The participants with a rural background attributed their lack of
media exposure to its inaccessibility and/or unavailability.

The senior group dynamics proved to be the liveliest. Participants
sparked one another's responses and reactions with little need for moderators. They asked each other questions, jogging one another's memories and
recollections. While their contributions revealed their specific social locations, the descriptions of media memories resonated as common and
shared among the group's members. Their recollections were vivid and
specific and the conversation was animated. Of the three cohort groups,
this one offered the most evaluative and reflective statements regarding
media memories.

Their spontaneous recollections of media events had two common traits.
First, they recalled where they were when a media event occurred, linking
the socially appropriated with the personally experienced knowledge of the
media event. For example, one participant's memory of VE Day exemplifies
this convergence, as she recalled the famous Times Square photograph of a
sailor kissing a woman alongside her own experience: "I was in Times
Square with my boyfriend!" Second, they recalled what other people said
about a media event and how it affected their social world. Media events
from their childhood were experienced directly, but within a social context
for reception. Angus recalled the very sad moment when he learned of the
death of Franklin D. Roosevelt. Others within the group expressed sympathy
as well. "I thought, 'What are we going to do now?'" was one participant's
recollection of hearing on the radio that FDR had died.

The depth of the senior group's knowledge of national events was so great that they covered most of the prompts before we could get to them. However, many international probes were used on this cohort, and most drew little or no response. When asked about the Salt Marches of India the response was, "That's news to me!" Of the few prompts that garnered any sort of response, the abdication of Edward VIII and the liberation of concentration camps at Auschwitz stood out. In fact, unless connected to the United States in some way, international events did not generate much discussion of memories.

The moderators did not ask the question, "Where were you when . . . ?" However, the middle-cohort group's discussions of media events repeatedly offered this specificity of time and place. For each of the media events, their memories were of particular moments in time. As they described media events, they mentioned the sensibility of suspended time, and that afterward, the world was different because of the media event. "We interrupt this broadcast . . ." invoked a sense of doom and gloom even today, according to several in this group.

Various individuals' contributions to the group discussion created a dynamic of "witnessing." Their recollections were almost a confessional form of self-disclosure. Telling about their media memories was a way of revealing their social identity and life narrative. Their stories assumed the shared nature of the mediated experience and explored the personal experience of the event. In short, these media events served as life-markers in their biographies.

As expected, the events surrounding the Vietnam War left a lasting impression on this cohort, and elicited some of the first unprompted memories. The war itself, as well as the Kent State tragedy, was remembered collectively. The other strong collective memories consisted of the three assassinations that shocked the U.S. in the 1960s: President John F. Kennedy, Dr. Martin Luther King Jr., and Robert Kennedy.

On a more personal level, individual participants remembered the Invasion of Prague. Several also remembered the Beatles' appearance on *The Ed Sullivan Show*. A few also remember the fear surrounding the Bay of Pigs incident, and the showdown between the United States and Cuba that came extremely close to nuclear war. Other personal memories from the group included the 1964 World's Fair, Motown music, and the 1972 Pittsburgh Pirate's baseball season.

Most of the media events were uncovered in the unprompted discussion, however some prompts were still made. Watergate garnered the most response, as it tied in with the whole era of disillusionment. A strong response also came from recalling the mission to land the first man on the moon, which had Americans glued to their TV sets.

As with the previous generation, very few international events left any impression on this group. When the OPEC crisis was mentioned, there was a small response, due in part to the fact that it affected America negatively. Once again, if a foreign event didn't involve the U.S., nobody seemed to recall it.

Of the three generations, the youngest group provided the least amount of dialogue and dynamic interaction. The volume of their speaking voices was quite low and the moderators used multiple probes to elicit specific memories. Their group discussion did not bounce back and forth among participants, but rather between individuals and the moderators. Contributions from participants were idiosyncratic and distinctive from each other.

This group did not offer many evaluative, deliberative, or reflective answers to the moderators' probes. This may have been in part due to their limited years of life experience and the lack of material upon which to reflect, but it is doubtful this could fully account for the lack of critical engagement with the questions about memories and media. The sedimentation of childhood media memories may not have occurred yet or may occur differently for this cohort. It was as if very little socially appropriated knowledge "stuck" unless there was a personal connection besides the shared social experience of an event.

Their general unresponsiveness may also have been indicative of a generational style in discourse. Their lack of interactive discussion about media was somewhat surprising, since this age cohort was historically distinctive in having had more types of media and more media content available and accessible to children than at any previous time in U.S. history. One participant hinted at her lack of network TV exposure, because of parental restrictions, as a lack of access to shared media experiences and social inclusion. For the most part, however, participants responded to moderators' probes like Rorschach pictures: they said whatever came to mind and summed it up quickly before waiting for the next question by the two moderators.

For this generational cohort, unsolicited media events included President Clinton's sex scandal, Michael Jordan's retirement, O.J. Simpson's murder trial, different hurricanes and disasters, and a rash of local child abductions. However, it was the Gulf War that seemed the most spontaneously salient media memory for this group. They saw an abundance of news coverage about the Gulf War on TV and most talked about it with family and adults.

Each remembered where they were when they first learned about U.S. involvement in the Gulf War. One was on a trip to New York City with his father and he sat for hours watching the coverage in a hotel room. Another remembers first hearing about it at her grandmother's house. One participant learned when she got home from school one afternoon and the family television set was on. What is most interesting about their recollections of the Gulf War is that they are not about a particular event or a moment; rather the Gulf War represented a period of sustained attention to news media.

As with the Gulf War, the O.J. Simpson trial and verdict wasn't a single media "moment" but a media spectacle stretched out over time. One participant mentioned the "Bronco chase" and others discussed the never-ending news about the trial. A few talked about the moment when the verdict in the trial was announced. "Jane Earl went running through the halls screaming!" exclaimed one participant in his recollection of learning in school of the trial's outcome.

Princess Diana's death elicited spontaneous emotions from the three girls in the group. One said, "Maybe it touched me more because I lived in England for a while, but I was sad. I was very sad. I thought she was a great lady." Another thought it was terrible and pointed the finger at the media: "She was harassed to death." She also recalled that Diana's death received more coverage than Mother Teresa's.

The most recent "media moment" that was spontaneously elicited was the plane crash of John F. Kennedy Jr. Group members nodded as one participant described a sense of "time suspended." He was at a friend's house for dinner and instead of the friend's mother preparing dinner as planned, everyone sat down together to watch the news coverage. "We didn't do what we usually would do." The death of JFK Jr. was one of a handful of media events during which participants reported a sense of time being suspended. The start of the Gulf War, the school shootings in Columbine, and the jury's verdict in the O.J. Simpson trial were mentioned in terms similar to the recent plane crash.

There are many historical events that took place before their time that they know about primarily through media, such as the Holocaust, Hiroshima, JFK's assassination, the Vietnam War, Martin Luther King and the Civil Rights Movement, anti–Vietnam War protests, and the integration of southern U.S. schools by busing.

Few unprompted international media events surfaced, with the exception of the Gulf War (once again—U.S. involvement). When prompted, only one international event was remembered, and by only one participant: she remembered the Berlin Wall coming down. "I was there—really close to it.

We watched the [German] news on TV there," she said. She admits her mother tried to explain the significance of the Berlin Wall to her, but she didn't have the context at that age. "We know more about it now," another said. Audrey explained: "I think it has more of an impact as we get older and begin to understand what is going on."

The three groups differed in their discussion of media events. How formative these events actually were can be tied in with how the event was perceived: as a life "marker" or as a phase. For the 70- to 75-year-old cohort, their discussion of media events identified key moments in history, the sense of time suspended, and the idea that the world was changed as a result of the event. For the 40- to 45-year-old cohort, the discussion focused on mediated events that made history, suspended time, and the idea that the world was tragic. For the 15- to 20-year-old cohort, the media events they spontaneously recalled were not particular moments but long-running spectacles of questionable historical note.

There were differences across the three generational groups in the dynamics of their discussions with the moderators about media memories. This pattern moved from communal to individual to privatized memories, respectively, from the oldest to the youngest groups. There was more socially appropriated memory, as opposed to personally experienced memory, respectively, from youngest to middle to oldest cohort. At times in the oldest cohort, when media events were brought up, instead of someone exclaiming, "I remember," they said, "I was there!" The fact that people experienced more memories personally may have led to so many common threads of memory among the eldest cohort.

For the 40- to 45-year-old cohort, memories about particular TV programs, rock-music groups, and movies created a dynamic of reflecting on their media memories as a way of revealing their social identity and life narrative. Biographical memories about media events exemplified Heidegger's notion of "participation in the common destiny" (1962, p. 384) The 15- to 20-year-old group provided the least amount of dynamic interaction, and the most multiple probes used by the moderators. What accounts for the lack of critical engagement with questions about memories and media? Schutz (1962) provides a phenomenological template for teasing apart the processes of sedimentation of memories from all the other factors. Perhaps there is another explanation: Overabundance of media lead to privatized recollections. There are so many media and so much information available that there is often little room or time for commonly experienced media events. Especially in the age of the Internet, people use the media for their own devices, reading the stories they want to read and looking up the information they yearn to know. More information becomes less important because common events are diluted in the privatized and personalized consumption patterns of teens' modern life.

Media memories moved from collective to narcissistic to idiosyncratic, respectively, as we moved from the oldest to the youngest groups. For the youngest cohort group, memories were formative, but idiosyncratically so. What was recalled had personal relevance, and was biographical rather than a milestone in world history. Despite all of this possible overexposure to mass media, however, these individuals talked about what mattered personally to them. This generational group seemed to pick and choose freely from the wide array of media events; and they seemed to tell us that they decided what events had left a lasting impression.

5. Conclusion: Mannheim's "Problem of Generations"

While American media memories seemed to consist mostly of national events, the consumers of those media were still "colonized" in a similar way as in other generations. As mentioned in the above paragraphs, the way each generation was colonized by their media differed in the dynamics of their discussion and how each generation remembered media events.

When we looked further into this phenomenon of the youngest cohort's lack of a real collective experience, we looked at Mannheim's concept of "entelechy."[2] Mannheim noted that it is not every generation that creates original collective impulses and formative principles. He also noted that it is not every member of a generation, but specific generational units that produce a generational entelechy. Mannheim's argument that "[c]rucial group experiences can act as 'crystallizing agents' towards entelechys" (1952: 310) suggests that we reflect upon the findings from these three groups. According to Mannheim, the determining factor was the tempo of social change. When it speeds up so that fast traditional patterns of experience can't be used, there is a new generational style or a new entelechy. The quicker the tempo, the more likely an entelechy will appear. Too quick a tempo may lead to destruction, according to Mannheim.

The 70- to 75-year-old group, born just before the Depression, was raised during World War II with a worldview of national honor, fighting the good war, evil villains, and red, white, and blue heroes. For the 40- to 45-year-old group, the en masse experiences of rock and roll music, assassinations of national heroes, the Vietnam War, and clashes between police and protestors served as crystallizing media events. Their recollections exemplified Husserl's theme of lidatic abstraction: vivid and distinctive memories.

For the youngest group, the 15- to 20-year-olds, the results were intriguing. It appeared that no pattern emerged; there seemed to be no defining generational experience such as the Kennedy assassination or VJ Day represented for the other two cohorts. It's as if this is a "Teflon" generation regarding media events and memory. There have been many spectacles and media events in their lifetime already, nothing "stuck" unless it was of personal and private relevance. However, as this study took place before the tragedies of 9/11, we were not able to gauge the effect the media events of that time had on the participants of this study. The authors, however, would wager a guess that those media events would indeed be the entelechy for the youngest generation. Further study, as always, is needed.

Bibliography

Heidegger, Martin (1962). *Being and Time.* San Francisco: Harper.

Husserl, Edmund (1968). *The Idea of Phenomenology.* Trans. William P. Alston and George Nakhnikian. The Hague: Martinus Nijhoff.

Mannheim, Karl (1952). *Essays on the Sociology of Knowledge.* London: Routledge and Kegan Paul.

Schutz, Alfred. (1962). *[Concept of commonsense knowledge] Collected Papers I: The Problem of Social Reality.* The Hague: Martinus Nijhoff.

PART II

Comparative Analysis across Generations and Cultures

· PERCEPTIONS AND MEMORIES OF THE MEDIA CONTEXT ·

Christina Slade

While the focus of this volume is on the fashion in which memories of global events are filtered through the media, and the implications of that process for our understanding of globalization, globalization over the twentieth century has been in part determined by the increasing global availability of the equipment of the media, and the increasing convergence of the content provided through that equipment. This chapter focuses on the striking similarities in memories of the media context—memories of the machinery, the hardware, and media-specific types of content—across the cohorts from the nine countries. We focused on the ways that hardware was perceived and is now remembered by those we interviewed, and not so much on what hardware and what content was available. The theoretical framework thus draws on sociological theories, such as the account of *habitus* due to Bourdieu (1993, 1998), on historical studies such as Lynn Spigel's (1992) landmark study of U.S. attitudes toward television, and such studies as that of Silverstone, Hirsch, and Morley (1992) on the processes of the adoption of technology into the home.

This article is divided into two parts. We begin with the issues of the machinery of the new media. Our cohorts were, respectively and successively, the first generation to have radio, the first generation to have television, and the first generation to have the Internet. In each of the countries and in each cohort, participants recalled a great deal about the hardware of the new media as it was introduced. On its introduction, the new medium was a large family purchase taking pride of place in the common spaces: the apparatus itself often had an iconic status, and sometimes was treated as a quasi-religious object. As the apparatus became less expensive and more readily available, the apparatus would yield its place in the common rooms to the newer media, retreat to the bedroom, and be adapted to portable forms.

Second, we talk of the issues of content: what sort of content is remembered in a form specific to the medium and what consequences did the introduction of new media have to the sorts of content remembered? It has often been remarked that the obvious consequences of the new media of technology and its entry into that most private place, the home, was a change in the of control of information (Meyrowitz, 1985). Before the rise of the mass media and its entry into the home, the access to information for children, servants, women, or other subordinate classes could be controlled. The television, even more than the newspaper, broke through that web of control. The second section of this paper raises questions about the extent to which the ways of learning about content have altered the ways and types of events remembered.

Part 1: "Sacred Relics"

The term "sacred relic" comes from the younger Austrian cohort, who are in the process of discussing an earthquake in their hometown:

Paul:	I can remember the earthquake as well. . . . When there was a thunderstorm and lightning, father unplugged everything immediately and took away the antenna.
Andrea:	Everything, yes!
Paul:	And out the plugs, this was a complete drama . . . about the TV set and the radio, as if they were sacred relics, I never was able to understand that.
Markus:	Yes, it was the same in our house [laughing]. Father pulled out the plug of the TV set . . . the house might burn down.
Paul:	But the TV set is rescued.
	(Austrian discussions, cohort 2, page 8, lines 444–453)

For the younger generation, the iconic quasi-religious status the television and the radio had for their parents was absurd. Yet that status is nearly universal. The television, and before that the radio, were seen as miraculous, and thus worthy of the sanctity attributed to them. In some cases the radio or television was treated as a religious object. The Japanese cohort explained that the new radio and then the television were placed in the niche where previously there had been the shrine. In other cases, more familiar in the West, the new technologies of communication were regarded as being in conflict with established religion; in the extreme cases, the work of the devil, and at the very least in competition for the souls of the young. The middle Mexican cohort, for instance, was forbidden to watch television in Holy Week (*Semana Santa,* the week before Easter), and during other religious festivals as it was seen as inappropriate.

The ambivalent attitudes toward the new machinery may be attributed to the fact that the new communication technologies are, at least when first introduced, expensive; but the attitude toward new televisions, radios, and computers are more complex than would be simply explained by attitudes toward a valuable piece of equipment. The sense of reverence for machinery that delivered media was different from the worship of cars, for instance. Cars, while expensive and high status, do not bring new ideas directly into the home, as did the new communication technologies. The excitement and reverence for the apparatus that delivered a new medium of communication, just like the fear and distaste for the apparatus, was a consequence of that fact. Both reactions were a result of the expansion of the world images they bring into the home, a space where formerly a *pater familias* was master. The newspaper could enter a home and not inform children or many women: for they could not read well enough to access the information. The radio altered the master's control—anyone who can speak and hear can understand. The television further undermined that control, requiring only sight. The computer took the process further. The older generation was unable to control, and currently, it often cannot even use the new equipment. The young are far more computer literate than their parents.

The comparative data from the project offers a rich field of study of attitudes toward the equipment, the hardware of communication, and the content that it conveys. We begin by comparing how the new media of communication entered the home, in the countries studied. Silverstone, Hirsch, and Morley (1992) offer a useful categorization of the processes of adoption of technology, particularly tailored to the phenomena surrounding the acquisition of the television. They distinguish:

- Appropriation (taking it into the home)
- Conversion (into social capital)
- Objectification (the placing of technology into the family spaces) and
- Incorporation (integration into family life) (Green, 2001: 44, based on Silverstone, Hirsch and Morley, 1992)

Appropriation

The appropriation stage for each medium is characterized by the iconic nature of new communication technology. For the older cohort, there were significant differences between the stages at which radios were acquired by the families in different countries. In India, for instance, where there were few private radios, listening to the radio "used to be a social experience," (Cohort 1, India), with rarely fewer than ten people listening at any one time. One Czech participant said, "in our village, our priest had a radio, so we were listening to football and ice hockey matches there. . . . All boys went. . . ." (Cohort 1, Czech)

The machinery itself, the particular pieces of equipment, was important when it was first acquired:

Anna: I can remember such a big box, you had to put wires [cables] together, first you heard *wauwauuuwaaauuwwaauuu* and then there was something to hear. It was very exciting for us children. (Cohort 1, Austria)

An Australian talked with reverence of the first radio:

When my mother died we had a big AWA radio that was like a gothic window, it was that shape and about that high and um that was sitting in the sitting room . . . um . . . on the mantelpiece it was narrow enough to fit. (H, Cohort 1, Australia)

The Austrians compared the status of different types of equipment:

Beate: Not an ordinary wireless, we had one of those modern shiny radios. (Cohort 1, Austria)

Maria: For the first ten years we had a wireless in the kitchen and later my mother was given a radio in a box and that one was always making funny noises. (Cohort 1, Austria).

Television sets had the same importance when they were first introduced. Buying a television was a major capital expenditure and not all were able to buy private sets. As one Mexican participant explained:

> Around 1961–62 there was a fever to buy televisions. In the poorer areas of the city of Mexico there were not many televisions, just about one per block, and so all the kids went to watch there. . . . In Xochomilco, there was the house of a person, like a small store, and behind there was a room with the televisions and cushions, so that all the kids sat around like in a small auditorium, and they paid 20 centavos, and the lady there sold sweets too. . . . In my case I could only go on Sundays because my parents only gave me 20 centavos a week. (Cohort 2, Mexico)

For the younger generation, the same sense of excitement could be heard with the first computer:

Christa: Yes, I still remember our first computer. A very old one. I was so excited and watched my brother all the time while he was doing things . . . until I took over. . . . Life was beautiful. (Cohort 3, Austria)

Among the Mexican youth, one made a similar comment about DVDs:

> I remember perfectly when the compacts arrived; our first compact was sacred and no one could touch it . . . the one of *Onda Vaselina* [*Grease*].

However, in general the young had greater access to both old and new communications technology and were correspondingly less reverent in their attitudes:

Adam: I've got TVs, radio, newspapers, newsletters, and Internet. I don't usually read the newspapers . . . I can't be bothered. I watch the news sometimes.
Interviewer: On television?
Adam: Yeah.
Interviewer: And do you ever use the Internet for news?
Adam: Yeah, or research. (Cohort 3, Australia)

While ownership of a home computer was not universal in the group, the issue of ownership appeared to be less iconic across the board. Kids, at least those from the middle-class cohorts of these focus groups, simply expected access to a computer and to the Internet.

Conversion into Social Capital

After the initial process and decision making in the acquisition of the hardware for the new technology, there is a process during which it is converted into social capital. Ownership of the new machinery gives social status: those informants who had been the first to own a radio, a television, or a color television talked of the social success. Everyone came over to see, to listen to the radio, or to watch the television, or, among the younger informants, to play the new game or watch the DVD. So for instance we find:

Ric: We had the first television in the street.
Interviewer: So what happened?
Ric: Every child in the street came to live. (Cohort 2, Australia)

Ownership of the hardware of the new technology was in itself, quite independent of what content is available, a signifier of social status.

One essential aspect of the early conversion process was the strict controls to which the new technology was subject. While newspapers were readily available for the older generation, the radio was subject to very strict parental control, control that the middle generation longed to circumvent. One Australian said:

Hilda: I wasn't able to listen to that [*Dad and Dave*] but I could because we happened to have a radio in the car, and in those days you didn't ever lock your motorcars and this was a particular radio which was not integrated and so you could just turn the knob without having to turn the key in the ignition and I used to sneak out and hide under the dashboard. (Cohort 1, Australia)

For the Mexican cohort, the first televisions were also exciting additions to the household and carefully regulated. So we found one informant saying:

Yes, we had a tele and I remember it perfectly as if I had just seen it. It was a large oak-colored piece of furniture, and it had doors that opened and there was the television, along with spaces for putting ornaments. But it had a key. My mother worked and we were six sisters . . . and [when the work was finished] they would open the little doors and let us watch television for one hour. (Cohort 2, Mexico)

In the Indian cohort, control in one family was so regimented it was almost militaristic:

Shoba: I don't think I had so much freedom to listen to radio or watch TV. There were a lot of restrictions. Timing, what to watch and what not to watch. My father was more like a military officer; everything had to be done at that particular time. (Cohort 2, India)

This regimen of control was altered markedly for the youngest cohorts. There is no evidence of control of the radio, and little evidence of the strict control of the Internet for the youngest participants. They appeared to have very ready access to television, but most commented that parents attempted to exercise control. As one Mexican youngster put it:

"To see or not to see TV was a reward or a punishment" (Cohort 3, Mexico).

However, there was generally no control of the television among the younger cohort; as another Mexican puts it:

"Everyone was working, always, then you go to school then they come to get you, you come back in the evening, then, the only thing you want to do is watch tele, you watch tele all day" (Cohort 3, Mexico).

Where control was most notable was in cases in which the events covered by media were particularly powerful. An Indian in the younger cohort commented on the family reaction to the death of Rajiv Gandhi:

Meeta: I remember I was sleeping at the time. My mother came and told me that Rajiv Gandhi is dead. She had seen some people in a sort of procession. I remember for one whole week all TV programs were stopped. I remember the cremation. Another thing I remember that my father had a magazine . . . that magazine my father showed to my mother. But we were not allowed to see that magazine. My father had kept it in the *almirah* [cupboard]. We were very curious what was in that magazine. One day my mother was away, I opened the *almirah*. It said: "Children should not be shown this magazine." Because there were lots of violent scenes. Many pictures were there, but I guess it did not affect me much because I was already hooked into Hindi movies.

With the death of Gandhi, normal programs were evidently stopped, possibly in the way normal programs on U.S. television were replaced by news of events in the wake of September 11, 2001. Control was exercised not just over television, but also over magazines. It was not the medium, but its content that disturbed the parents. This was true of others of the younger Indian cohort. Yashwant also associated the news of Rajiv Gandhi's assassination with the same magazine, *Outlook*, and was similarly forbidden access:

My father and mother never used to show it to me, and hid it somewhere. My brother and I said we had to see what was in the magazine. My mother and father go out and we climb up to the cupboard and take it out somehow. I realize I just conked off. My brother asked me what happened. I said, "*Kuch nahi hua*" [Nothing at all has happened]. Then I started crying. Then I realized something bad must have happened. I knew about human bombs, because I had always read about suicide bombers of Japan, but this human bomb and the state in which it left the bomber and the bombed was not expected by me.

In the former Eastern Block, such as Czechoslovakia, where Western content was jammed, and control of the media was in the hands of the Communist Party until the Velvet Revolution of 1989, the case was slightly different: the radio was considered "white noise," and the sharpest memories of the television news were during the period of the Prague Spring, in 1968, when the government-owned channel covered the events day by day. In such an atmosphere, the role of parents as controllers of the media was far less notable.

Objectification: From Communal Object to Possession

The newer technologies were shared, but as the technology became familiar and cheaper it became a possession. In the early stages, the radio or television was central to life in the household and was a focus of communal activity. From the senior generation, we found remarks such as this one:

Georgie:　　Some of the younger ones used to watch the radio. [laughter] We did. We sat and watched it. We weren't allowed to speak. When I was a child we weren't allowed to speak. And . . . um . . . at boarding school, we went to the physics lab and we had a hot-water bottle and a rug and we wrapped ourselves up with this and we listened to the Lux radio play in the physics lab. And that was great, that was, you know, every Saturday, every Sunday night, and that is where the word "soap" came from, of course. (Cohort 1, Australia)

These remarks are echoed in the Mexican cohort.

We listened a lot to soaps [*radionovelas*]. I remember *Anita De Monte Mar, El derecho de nacer, Ave sin nido, Rafles,* and another about Arturo of Cordoba. We liked them a lot, because we would all sit around after lunch to listen to the soap. (Cohort 1, Mexico)

The Sundays we spent by the radio were wonderful. I can remember sitting around the radio to hear them, just as the senora says. (Cohort 1, Mexico)

In the U.S. group, it was the Canadian-hockey radio broadcasts that were communal events: "Eight people and no one said a word."

The iconic object, the radio, or later the television, was incorporated into family life, and was at the center of the communal spaces and communal activities. In India, the television remained a communal object for longer than it did in the West:

John: Wherever there was a TV, maybe three or four families would gather together. . . . There was a distinction between the males and the rest of the family . . . they were more interested in the news items, whereas the female folk, they were more interested in the serials. (Cohort 2, India)

Consequently, the messages it carried were, in the words of Keval Kumar, "mediated by significant others. The terms and conditions of [the Indian] media exposure were determined by the elders of the family, specifically by the male elders."

As the object became less valued however, there was a further process, in which there was more than one radio or television in the household, and individual members take ownership. This process was described by Jill Swenson and Matthew Payne, describing the U.S. data: "Whereas the 40- to 45-year-old cohort would talk about possessing the media, this [older] cohort's discourse emphasized experiencing the media."

The U.S. cohort did report watching family shows on television together: "family-friendly shows—*Family Ties* and *Family Matters*—because parents wanted them to spend time together." However, personal owner-ship was important, and 40- to 45-year-olds in the States now possess an intimidating range of media hardware.

The move from the communal to personal possession was accompa-nied by a move in the location of the radio or television set, from the com-munal areas in which they were shrines or centers of family attention, to private spaces throughout the house. For instance, by the 1960s and 1970s, radios in Australia were "trannies"—transistor radios, which each child owned. Now, many kids have their own TV. The process has accelerated—over the last two years, we have come to expect that middle-class children will own a laptop computer and have Internet access. As Theo Hug puts it, referring to the Austrian cohort: "For the younger generation, having their own equipment seems to be more important than access to the equipment of the family or siblings. . . . In the 15–20 cohort 'my TV' means that I own it and decide what to do with it."

This process—personal ownership of the apparatus that delivers the mes-sage—does not imply a downgrading of the importance of the content or messages that are supplied by the media. To some extent the reverse is true. As each child was able to acquire his or her own tranny in the seventies, and music, rather than news or family entertainment became the preferred listen-ing, the music (and the channel chosen) came increasingly to define the iden-tity of the young. This is, in part, a consequence of the fact that, as broadcast-ing on the radio became relatively cheap, it was possible for a radio station to be designed for a niche market, and hence serve an "identity" function. The same is true of cable television. In the U.S., for instance, viewers of the Discovery channel tend to be a different demographic from Comedy Central viewers. By its nature, however, the Internet has been a niche-based operation since the beginning. And while there was still generally a single Internet-con-nected computer in a household at the time of the survey, the pace of change is such that in Australian homes, it is currently not unusual for there to be more than one connected computer in a middle-class suburban home.

Incorporation: Integration into Family Life

New technologies were in shared spaces: the sitting or drawing room for the early radios, the lounge and later the kitchen for television, and the recreation room for computers. The older technologies migrated to private spaces: first the playroom or the study, then the bedroom. The role of the technology in family life was then altered. What was once a shared communal experience, of listening to the radio or watching the television, became an isolated and private activity. Nowadays, many homes have a television set in the kitchen and each bedroom, and locate events in terms of where they were watching. Thus, one of the youngest subjects identified his reaction to the death of Princess Diana by locating the machinery and where he and it were:

John: I was sitting on that lounge, right there [laughter] on this seat and I was sitting down watching. . . . I was flicking through, and I saw, um. (Cohort 3, Australia)

In many cases, television was reported as having been on all the time, in different spaces across the house. What made a certain memory of watching television significant was the space in which it is watched. For some of the youngest cohort, television is still available in the kitchen or dining area, and news is watched communally, at times over dinner. For others in the youngest cohort, their warmest memories of watching television were in bed in their parents' bedroom, at times with the mother or father there. Certain ritual events are still watched on television or listened to communally: sports games, for instance. Among Indians, we found the cricket matches being listened to communally; in the U.S., sports bars show big games. Some soaps, and reality shows such as *Big Brother* are also enjoyed as communal viewing experiences.

What is evident is that the rhythm of family life is now set to the rhythms of the mass media. Some turn on the television as they wake; others the radio; still others prefer to read a newspaper. However, the morning is typically a time for information and news. The evening pattern is set to a background of various types of entertainment offered either by television, including cable television offering home movies, by DVD or video rental, or by the Internet.

Computing, in part because of the way the technology is arranged, was slightly different. Using a computer is not normally a communal event, since it tends to be one or at most two working together on the machine. However, in another sense, interactivity has meant that several members of a family or group can contribute to one final document. Responsibility for homework for instance, can now be shared. The growth of Internet communities and the pattern of some of the young, of intense involvement in on-line chat groups, means that the home community is no longer even centrally the genetic family.

Part 2: The Mediated Space: Technology and Personhood

In the older generation, memories were tied to a specific medium and to its technology. Informants shared memories of particular events as portrayed in specific papers: "The image on the front page of *The Advertiser*" or a particular concert that several heard on the radio. Media events were, when remembered, very explicit and highly detailed. Informants remembered the dates of attacks in World War II or the setting of newsreels, for instance. The Mexican cohort, even though from a neutral country in World War II, talked of the crucial images of the atomic explosion in Japan in 1945, and knew of the events in detail:

> We saw the great stories of the Atomic bomb, of the beginning of the war in Abyssinia. (Cohort 1, Mexico)

While the older cohorts from different countries shared certain memories, it was noticeable that each group saw those events from their own national perspective. Each group shared with his or her compatriots a very cohesive common culture. Undoubtedly the strength and force of wartime memories is one reason for this. As one German participant said, they remembered what had happened precisely because the memories were not mediated.

The middle cohort's memories were much less explicit, less detailed, and drawn from a far wider range of sources. They remembered information through a range of different technologies: news, magazines, television, and radio. Most were aware of the 1968 revolutions and student events in Paris, Prague, Sydney, Tokyo, Mexico, or Woodstock. But while some recalled the image of the shooting at Kent State in a magazine, and others mentioned television coverage of events in Paris, others talked of student protests in Japan. The 40- to 45-year-old cohort had a regional perspective:

> Uday: I did hear about the Woodstock festival. There was a similar festival in Bangalore at the time. (Cohort 2, India)

Although there were few single outstanding images, there was a common core to which many referred—the image of the naked child running away from napalm in Vietnam, for instance. One Mexican said:

> I had an issue of *Life*, dedicated to the year 1968, from which I remember the famous photos of Prague Spring, the May revolution in Paris, the assassination of Robert Kennedy, others on the famine in Biafra. (Cohort 2, Mexico)

Those images were clearly the product of international magazines and had become part of an international repertoire. What was notable was that the location of the events was clear in reporting by the cohort—they knew where the reported events had occurred.

The younger cohort was awash in media product, and they were typically unsure about the source of their knowledge. News was repeated so often across the media that it only penetrated after a media blitz. As a result, they have a surprising collective knowledge of the global soap operas of President Clinton's sex life, O.J.'s trial, and Princess Diana's death. Those notably private, if globalized, events were the common culture. In the middle-class groups we dealt with, there was a considerable overlap in views: the young saw the world, as it were, from a joint perspective. Typical of this was the attitude toward the mistress of Prince Charles, Camilla, in the wake of the death of Princess Diana. A young Mexican girl, in a country where the British monarchy has no natural connections, came out with a remark that could have been heard anywhere in the British Commonwealth:

I hated Charles, no, Charles and Camilla . . . the old thing [Camilla] is horrible. (Cohort 3, Mexico)

There were, however, notable differences. While Australian and Mexican youth remembered the reunification of Germany in terms of the concert held when the Wall came down, for the Czech cohort the fall of the Wall was the iconic image of much more force. That image, together with the lines of abandoned Trabant cars left by East Germans fleeing through Czechoslovakia in the summer of 1989, represented their own Velvet Revolution. For them, the death of Lady Diana was represented by a poignant song by Elton John.

We have suggested that in the older generations, the media memories were specific to a technology, while younger generations were awash in media product. As media become more enveloping, the source became less important. There were a number of consequences stemming from this. The older generation, especially, was very well aware of the controls that operated on information, particularly during the war years. In all of the countries we discussed, this generation mentioned not only that there was censorship, but also that either at the time or later they were aware of censorship. One Japanese member even said that the media had let them down in not telling the truth.

Consequently, mediated messages were seen as messages that could be distorted and not reliable guides to truth about the world. Very often, for this generation, access to information was independent of access to media.

Given the very close links between access to information and social power, this had the consequence that social identity was not reliant on access to the media. Identity in the war years depended on social role: and social role in turn dictated access to information.

The middle generation was skeptical of mediated knowledge but had a great many more sources of mediated information. Their attitude toward the media was cynical, but at the same time teenage identity was defined through music. There was a sense that certain media events belonged to the youth, whether Woodstock or footage of the Vietnam War, and that the older generations might not be able to see the meaning. At that stage, control of information within the home had been relaxed, at least in middle-class families with access to the media. A controlling *pater familias* or moralizing mother figure would be hard pressed to stop the young from finding out about the world. Radio, television, and youth magazines created identity styles for the young that had little to do with those of their parents. This is particularly true for the Vietnam generation in the U.S. and Australia, but is reflected in other comments of the Mexican and the South African cohorts. Access to the media was thus essential for the identity of this cohort. Those whose parents would not permit access to the media bemoaned their fate: they were left out of groups at school and ostracized.

For the youngest generation, this trajectory has continued. Information is power, and the media are the source. For the young, access to the media and ownership of the technology was and is central to identity. Control of the information flowing into the house is very difficult—once the Internet is accessible, the whole world is available. The continuing search for an effective means of blocking websites considered unsuitable for the young is evidence of just how effectively the parental controls have been usurped by new technology. The prime site for expression of identity is debate about the media—and evaluations of mediated characters, whether it is Homer Simpson ("cool") or Camilla Parker Bowles.

The young continue to find it difficult to assess the reliability of mediated information. When messages that they receive are repeated endlessly, sheer repetition seems to guarantee that they are true. Yet the young are at the same time cynical about the media. They displayed a high level of visual literacy and know how easily an image can be digitally altered, or a truth transformed. The mediated character of their experience was correspondingly reflected in their attitudes toward events reported in the media. They did not orient events in terms of location. Rather, they saw the world in terms of events that happened at the same time, such as "the week that Ayrton Senna was killed" or "just after the World Cup final." The ready access to distant places that characterizes cyberspace has been translated into the personal geographic world maps that young people use. Distance is unimportant as long as events are simultaneous.

Conclusion

There are striking similarities in the way the younger and older cohorts have accommodated the new forms of communication, and have seen the equipment and the world through the eyes of the media to which they had access. However, there has been a distinctive shift from the older to the younger generation in the role that the media play in forming social identity, and in the way their vision of the world is structured. We speculate that the fundamental change from the older to the younger generation is in the way that space and time are conceived. For the older generation, time is seen as if on a timeline—specialized. Their geographical model of the world was the Mercator projection, and they projected their understanding of events gleaned from the newspapers, newsreels, and radio, onto that grid. Their focus and perspective was that of their own nation-state, filtered by the empires of which they were or had been part. Those empires, the British, Spanish, Hapsburg, and Japanese, were global in scope; so their view of the world was global. But each country had its own national perspective.

For the middle generation, the process of globalization had moved away from the political empires to the cultural empires of the mediated world. To a certain degree this implies regionalization: the Mexican cohort was intensely interested in Latin America; the Czechs, in the Eastern bloc; the Indians, in the subcontinent; and the South Africans, in Africa. To a certain degree, the "Americanization" of culture in the Western world was also obvious. But the striking fact is that events recalled by this cohort had begun to break loose from temporal and spatial ordering. Was J.F.K. shot before or after man landed on the moon? They found it difficult to remember and often described such media events as if they were unconnected to a timeline of events.

The younger generation takes this perspective further. Philosophers often contrast a timeline with another series that was based on perception: before, later than, or simultaneous with. The young use this second scale, in which simultaneity, not order, is of the essence. They do not see the world in terms of events laid out on a map, but in terms of the time of the media events, and their own location when they found out about them. Princess Diana's accident in Paris was a paradigmatic case. When the young recalled it, they talked of where they were and what else was happening. One Mexican girl said:

I remember it perfectly. . . . I was in Europe and it was obviously a super shock, and then I remember it so well, Diana and then Versace. (Cohort 3 Mexico)

For her, the event was defined by what else happened and where she was when she was informed.

This way of thinking, influenced by the media in much the way that McLuhan (1964, 1967) predicted, is not restricted to the young. The focus of our media memories of 9/11 is not the World Trade Center, a particular building in downtown Manhattan. It is rather a media event that juxtaposes the World Trade Center, the Pentagon, and a field in Pennsylvania, together with our location when the event was conveyed to us. Each person will talk, if asked, about where he or she was and what he or she was doing when they found out. Rather than a singular event, located in space and time, 9/11 is an all-enveloping haze of media coverage—that endlessly repeated image of the plane crashing into the second building. Our perception of our environment has become, as McLuhan warned it would be, thoroughly imbued with the medium.

Bibliography

Bourdieu, Pierre. (1993). *The Field of Cultural Production: Essays on Art and Literature.* Cambridge: Polity Press.

Bourdieu, Pierre. (1998). *On Television.* Translated from the French by Priscilla Parkhurst Ferguson. New York: New Press.

Green, Lelia. (2001). *Technoculture.* Sydney: Allen & Unwin.

McLuhan, Marshall. (1964). *Understanding Media: The Extensions of Man.* London: Routledge & Kegan Paul.

McLuhan, Marshall, and Q. Fiore (1967). *The Medium Is the Message.* Harmondsworth, Eng.: Penguin Books.

Meyrowitz, Joshua. (1985). *No Sense of Place: The Impact of Electronic Media on Social Behavior.* New York: Oxford.

Silverstone, Roger, Eric Hirsch, and David Morley eds. (1992). "Information and Communication Technologies in the Moral Economy of the Household." In *Consuming Technologies: Media and Information in Domestic Spaces,* ed. Silverstone, Hirsch, and Morley, 15–31. London: Routledge.

Spigel, Lynn. (1992). *Make Room for TV: Television and the Family Ideal in Postwar America.* Chicago: University of Chicago Press.

Keval J. Kumar, Theo Hug, and Gebhard Rusch

The process of remembering the past is extremely selective, and often deliberate and self-conscious. Some memories tumble out of one's consciousness, as if they were on the tip of one's tongue; other memories take longer to be formulated and to surface into one's conscious mind. The former are what one might term "spontaneous" unprompted memories. The latter require more work, and prompting frequently assists in jogging the memory, hence the term "prompted" memories. But there is more to remembering than being prompted or unprompted: several other social, cultural, and political factors are at work. There is also the question of class/caste, one's social position, and whether the remembering is done in the privacy of one's home, or in a peer group, or in public. In the GMG research project, the articulation of one's memories of childhood experiences of the media was made in the context of focus groups of the same generation. A lot depends on the occasion and the situation and to whom one is recollecting the past. Also, there are other factors of importance, such as cognitive and social constraints, the distance from the event one is trying to remember (what may be termed the "chronology of memory"), the location of remembering as well as the location of the event remembered ("geography of memory"), and above all, what one chooses to recollect in the presence of others ("politics of memory").

Cognitive Aspects of Memory and Remembering

The most common understanding of the term "memory" is concerned with the management of content, once implemented, that has been stored and is waiting for retrieval (in a more or less original or authentic version). This picture, however, only holds for the functioning of information storage and retrieval that is performed by electronic devices, like a hard disk or other computer memory. But this manner of processing does not hold for human memory, as so many experiments (in the line of Ebbinghaus, Bartlett, Miller, and others) have demonstrated. The technical part—laying down traces or "engrams" that may be activated again later, and then recalled to our conscious mind and imagining, is only part of the story. Therefore, the term "memory" is somewhat misleading. Memory, as Humberto Maturana (1977) put it, is an explanatory concept helping to cope with the observed stability (e.g., recurrence) and change (e.g., learning) of behavior, which are taken to be caused by stable or changed cognitive structures or processes. "Memory" serves to explain the capacities of stability and change, which are integral parts of a cognitive system's reactivity. It designates the structure and dynamics of cognitive "wet ware," rather than a stock of fixed, formatted information. What we take to be the content of our memories— as it appears to us when recalling past events or experiences—does not seem to be engraved as such into neuronal networks and stored somewhere in the brain, readymade and waiting to be called to consciousness. Instead, what appears to us as memory is only produced by *remembering.* What we do actually deal with, not only in the case of media memories, is the private or collective "process of remembering" and its results. Memory, as change of reactivity, is the necessary prerequisite for remembering; but, in a complicated way, what we take to be (the content of) our memory is much more the result of remembering.

This process includes (1) the triggered *activation of cognitive structures,* the apparently spontaneous emergence of transparent or complex images, insights, ideas, visions, fantasies, and sensory impressions, etc.; as well as, (2) the conscious or unconscious, mental or verbal *elaboration* (Rusch, 1991). We may get an impression of these elaborations by following the streams of consciousness, which may take off from thoughts, images, or observations, adding some conceptual associations and sensory impressions, bridging the blanks with inferences (based on general world knowledge) and plausible ad hoc solutions (in the light of present requirements), and keeping the emerging pictures coherent with our own self-concepts and the assumed expectations of our social partners. Finally, our construction leads us to believe that we only elaborated on events that really happened. This occurs because our own elaboration is so convincing, coherent, and compatible with personal, situational, and social constraints. Processes of remembering, therefore, appear to shape and frame cognitive activity that originated from experiences, which changed the reactivity of the subject. This, however, may reinforce or—depending on the impact of the elaborative process of remembering itself—inhibit, disguise, change, or even displace the reactive response from which a process of remembering once took off.

In shaping our memories, the processes of remembering make use of and establish mental models (Johnson-Laird, 1983) of the past: (auto-)biographical models, models of social episodes, and historical models. As a consequence, our memories become more and more virtual in the course of time: elaborated elaborations of elaborations.

The impact of media on reshaping our memories can hardly be overestimated (cf. e.g., McKenzie, 1994; Vitouch & Tinchon, 1996). Media offer behavioral, auditory, and visual concepts; verbal, graphical, and pictorial instruments to designate, symbolize, or represent experienced and/or mediated events. Decades and epochs, global events and the whole universe may condense to one significant term or phrase, painting, photo, slogan, or statement: "renaissance," "WW2," "Hiroshima exploding," "astronauts on the moon," and "9/11." Reports, background information, headlines, and (above all) pictures, do offer strong and suggestive tools that keep our memories stable, communicable, and socially compatible. At the same time, these tools are used to innovate, update, modernize, and sometimes radically change the instruments we apply in memory construction.

Social Aspects of Remembering

The social dimension must not be considered as an additional set of constraints. Instead, it deeply impregnates even cognitive and affective processes—for instance, communication, language, and social codes—as demonstrated by the expression of emotions. Obviously, social aspects play a major role in the processes of *collective remembering* (Middleton and Edwards, 1990).

Communicating these "rememberings" to others, however, calls some sociolinguistic forces to action: the process of verbalizing images is grammatically driven by the need to select the words and sentences that can meaningfully depict what is remembered. Verbalization imputes tenses and time structures. Verbalization enforces the closure of grammatical and semantic blanks or slots in order to keep sentences coherent and comprehensible. Verbalization employs story schemata or grammars to construct complex events from chains of sentences and sequences of episodes: all under the regime of lexical repertoires, grammatical and semantic knowledge, general world knowledge, coherence conditions, and so on. The whole process is governed by communicative parameters and conventions such as conversational rules (Grice, 1957, 1969), and driving forces (in German: Zugzwänge); cf. Gülich, 1980). Finally, the social status of the involved partners and their relations to each other play important roles, too. The processes of *collective elaboration of memories* also have to serve communicative and social aims. The partners have to keep their own identities stable and comprehensible; they are under pressure to care for a kind of consensus with their relevant others. In order to keep themselves members of their group or community, they have to be attractive as social partners and have to be socially calculable, reliable, and behaviorally consistent (Festinger, 1957).

What we have to talk about here is the *conversational elaboration of memories* as we have it, not only in our focus groups but also in everyday life. It is common practice to elaborate on memories conversationally (cf. Rusch, 1996). This also complicates the issue because it becomes more and more difficult to distinguish personal verbalizations of memories from personal comments on other's elaborations and from elaborations of elaborations, etc. Collective remembering appears to be a mix of personal elaborations, associative memories, (explicit or implicit) evaluations, and meta-statements. It does not, however, suffer from this fuzziness, but rather gains its character exactly from this kind of *socially distributed contribution* to a consensual construction of the past. Moreover, "what is recalled and commemorated extends beyond the sum of the participants' individual perspectives: it becomes the basis of future reminiscence. In the contest between varying accounts of shared experiences, people reinterpret and discover features of the past that become the context and content for what they will jointly recall and commemorate on future occasions" (Middleton and Edwards, 1990: 7).

So, we have to take into account processes of negotiating about socially acceptable constructions of the past (memories, histories). This holds for the family memories of the last holidays as well as for the scholars who continually work on and renew our histories, which we take to explicate or stand for our past (Rusch, 1987).

In sum, the following four social dimensions need to be considered:
1. The situation in which the events were experienced for the first time as well as the social situations of sharing one's experiences with others. It is the social situation that somehow marks the importance of an event. For example, in Cohort 3 of the Austrian discussions, one of the participants

stressed the role of the parents in her reception process. With reference to the fall of the Berlin Wall, she said:

Nora: One was happy together with them, the parents were happy and all the people were happy, and then you knew that this was important and you were happy together with them. I still know it was something extraordinary. (Cohort 3, page 6, line 241 f)

In other cases it was obvious that peer-group or classroom situations had similar meanings.

2. The socioeconomic status of the participants. A glance at the tables included in the chapters of this book shows that in the GMG project we aimed at middle-class focus-group participants in order to get comparable data. Even if we disregard the problem of socioeconomic grouping in general (e.g., diverse models of three, five, or seven main groups like in Mexico), we have to be aware of various divides such as religious, cultural, or digital as well as environmental and lifestyle differences.

3. The social contexts of the focus-group discussions. Some of the participants were friends or even relatives; others were strangers who came together for one or two hours for a group discussion. The group dynamic influenced interpretation of the research context. For instance, some participants tried to be especially good and informative while others mainly had fun in discovering common experiences. So the research situation may have been more of a talking, discussing, or even an interviewing situation. Furthermore, the social contexts are important in the sense of collective memory process with elements of confirmation and reinforcement. The following excerpt offers an example of "the social practice of commemoration" (Middleton and Edwards, 1990: 8):

Beatrix: Yes, the story with Diana . . . she still is admired in London, also on pictures. In school we have talked about it and also have seen a film. You have heard a lot. (Cohort 3, page 9, line 397 ff)

Christa: Although there was much more fuss about Diana than about Mother Theresa. Although I cannot understand that, because Mother Theresa was at least as important, even more important. (Cohort 3, page 9, line 399 ff)

Anton: Yes, the difference is, that Mother Theresa simply died, and in the case of Diana it was an accident. (Cohort 3, page 9, line 402 f)

Christa: OK, yes, that is true, all the circumstances, because about Diana you heard all the time, all the time . . . on the radio, on TV, in the newspapers . . . during the first year after her death. In the case of Mother Theresa it's just one year ago she died and that's it. (Cohort 3, page 9, line 404 ff)

Nora: Yes, that's gone without a trace. (Cohort 3, page 9, line 407)

Christa: Yes, and that is something I don't understand. (Cohort 3, page 9, line 408)

4. The research context is a social context, too, which is relevant for what is remembered in the focus-group discussions and also for the interpretation and analysis of the documents in our research group. On the one hand, we can talk of a social practice of commemoration as well: when the participants of the Global Media Research Group discussed the status of events in order to get a list of prompted global media events, at the same time avoiding a kind of "Commonwealth bias." On the other hand, the qualitative orientation allows flexible attributions, for example with reference to types and relevance of marker tags of meaning. Part of the social process of understanding occurs when the researchers talk of media as markers, events as markers, media events as markers, social situations as markers of the importance of the events, and processes of labeling or remediation processes as markers. In this sense, the focus groups are a means of putting on stage (*inszenieren*, in German) a collective process of remembering. Participants, in one way or another, have to adjust to that task. The elders did so much better than the young. Maybe they were much more acquainted with situations like these, and knew the game of collective remembering much better than the young.

There are other considerations that influence the process of remembering while in the research setting of a focus group. Some of these include: (1) the formality of a group setting where the discussion is recorded on tape for the purpose of research; (2) the competition among the participants (who remembers most/best); (3) the collective elaboration of events (for instance, through continued prompting; answers provoke memories that drive people to further answers, which in turn lead to reinforcement or inhibition); (4) the social pressure to be politically correct and to act according to one's status; (5) the nonspontaneous nature of the discussions; and (6) the fact that the focus-group discussion is a planned social event for invited participants who may be relatives, acquaintances, or strangers.

Further, the very act of remembering is an important marker. That which we remember, we usually take to be important, personally or socially. Memory may thus be a kind of treasure, box in which are stored all kinds of pleasant and unpleasant experiences.

Memory is a thus a multifaceted, constructed phenomenon. In demarcation of "storage and retrieval" models, we think that the individual memory is always incorporated in a group memory. We refer to collective frameworks when remembering events. There is no chance of recalling something outside of common frames and concepts.

Jan and Aleida Assman (1994) point out the difference between communicative memory and cultural memory, both being parts of the collective memory. In comparison to the cultural memory, the communicative memory is a short-term memory, which is held alive by living groups (e.g., recent past, about 80 years). The cultural memory is held alive by rituals, monuments, symbolic representations, and so on (everyday memory vs. festive memory).

Schuman and Scott, following Mannheim and Halbwachs, use the term "collective memories" to "describe memories of a shared past that are retained by members of a group, large or small, that experienced it" (Schuman and Scott, 1989: 361 f). They distinguish between two meanings of "collective memories":

> On the one hand, when large parts of the population appear to remember a common object, this can be thought of as a form of collective memory. . . . On the other hand, when a large part of the Vietnam generation remembers the Vietnam period as one of distrust and division, this is a collective memory in the more general sense of being collectively created and collectively held, and it probably has more general import for future actions by members of that generation. . . . Collective memories in this second sense of widely shared images of a past event need not be personally experienced and thus begin to be difficult to distinguish from Durkheim's ([1901] 1938) conception of traditional beliefs as a form of "collective representation" (see also Bloch, 1925). The difference may lie less in the content of the memory than in the degree of personal feeling that is apt to accompany events lived through, as against events learned about second-hand." (Schuman and Scott, 1989: 378 f)

Collective memory should be conceived of as the result of *collective memory construction*, that is, verbalization, communication, elaboration, and negotiation. Therefore, we always have to consider which group or collective is at work, what are the interests, the sentiments, etc.

To be precise: as a cognitive function, there are no collective, team, group, or generational memories. Individuals only have their own memories, but they are able to collectively elaborate on them. They may detect that they share some memories with others and that their memories differ in many respects from others. They may feel the obligation to come to a consensus about some memories, and they may tolerate certain differences with regard to others. Thus, all social memory depends on communication.

Cultural memory, then, turns out as "manifestations of communicative memories" (Assmans' term). Sharing pasts does not at all mean sharing memories; but sharing elaborated and negotiated memories does always mean, to the participants, that they share (because of the collective construction) the same past.

Taking part in the elaboration of collective memories may also, at least to some extent, substitute for authentic experience or eyewitness images. There is important evidence that memories may be faked by persuasive communication. Social pressure, together with some uncertainty, can drive people to believe absolutely fictitious stories about their biography or the historical past (Loftus, 2001).

Even though strictly fictitious stories about one's biography are not the rule, we can easily see that the distinction between fact and fiction is often flexible and commonly placed in a spectrum of more or less plausible and "useful" claims. Therefore, memory plays "tricks" sometimes, or to put it more precisely: we let the memory play tricks with what we remember, and also the way we remember.

Chronology of Memory: The Time Factor

A crucial factor in the act of recollection of the past is "time," the distance from the event recalled. The three age cohorts taking part in the focus groups were asked to recall the national and international events of their childhood and early youth. The first generation of the 20th century (the 70- to 75-year-olds) talked about their memories of events and experiences that took place in the 1930s and 1940s, more than 50 years earlier. In the same way, the second generation (the 40- to 45-year-olds), in each country where the focus groups were conducted, was attempting to recall the events of the 1970s and 1980s, 30 to 40 years earlier. But for the third generation (the 15- to 20-year-olds) the memories went back just 10 to 15 years.

It is true that all three generations were recalling the events of childhood and early youth, but the distance from the events varied from generation to generation. How did distance or chronology influence memory, not so much what was remembered but the nature of memory: how childhood events were remembered. Obviously, the greater the distance from the event recalled, the less vivid and exact it is likely to be, though vividness does not necessarily correlate with accuracy.

On the other hand, at least in some discussions (in Austria, for instance), the two older generations had more vivid memories. Maybe this paradox can be explained by the especially relevant contexts for certain experiences, and a reiterated processes of stabilization. Furthermore, we have to be aware of the fact that long-term memories become dominant with age because of physiological reasons.

All memories are, in essence, social constructions of the past, no matter how recent or remote. Memories are, after all, a re-telling, from different perspectives, of personal history/biography. They are, in other words, a reconstruction of subjective reality, a personal looking back at what was or what could have been. Here is where nostalgia creeps in. The more distant and remote in time, and the more pleasurable the event in the imagination, the greater is the nostalgia with which it is recalled. The 70- to 75-year-olds of Pune (India), for instance, talked with a lot of nostalgia about the "good old days." No such nostalgia was even hinted at by the other age cohorts of India.

With Karl Mannheim's distinction between the perspectives of different "generational units" in mind (Mannheim, 1951), we can take a look at the self-knowledge of a generation in the sense of similar experiences of events and the shared feelings of the time (being in the world) on the one hand; and the self-demarcation of other generations:

Bernd: The negative phenomena, which are complained about today, are traced back to the lost old standards, which were thrown overboard. (Cohort 1, page 15, line 809–811)

The process of collective elaboration of memories itself seems to create such "generational units." There is a certain kind of connectivity among those who share some knowledge or experiences. They are able to connect with one another and to understand each other. In the media age, then, generations do not only appear as sociodemographic units (as contemporaries, for instance), but as groups of people who share knowledge, preferences, habits, beliefs, experiences, and memories. Media generations, then, are widening because more and more people of different age groups and from different ethnic and cultural contexts share the same or similar media experiences; they know the same mediated events as they are reported worldwide, presented, and repeated, put on the Internet, or stored on tape, CD, DVD, etc. Transpresence and omnipresence of media events, therefore, are the prerequisites of a global, transcultural, and transgenerational media community.

In contrast, how did the Germans and Austrians recall the Nazi past?[1] Or how did the Australians recall their colonial past? What was the major emotion associated with such memories of a past that most wanted to forget about, and to wipe out from both private and public memory? Guilt? Embarrassment? Shame? Indifference? Catharsis? How did the first generation of Indians remember the horrors of the Partition? Hardly anyone in the first-generation focus group even mentioned the Partition. In this context, it is worth noting that the Brahmins of Pune did not even once recall the great struggles of the Dalits against upper-class oppression.

There are also ambivalent descriptions similar to the following:

Bernd: The positive and the negative aspects of the police state. (Cohort 1, page 10, line 553)

As mentioned above, the application of the term "generation" may be different with respect to the omnipresence and transpresence of media. The concept of generation becomes either obsolete or continually widened as more media products (like music, entertaining film, and news and documentary material) become available to (or are unavoidably presented to) members of different age groups over longer periods of time. After World War II— just to fix a date from when the media started to boom—this trend is noticeable in the case of the modern audiovisual and digital media. The more the sharing of experiences, memories, knowledge, preferences, values, and mentalities is bound to media use (print, radio, cinema, TV, Internet), the more all of the participants may be perceived as one media generation. The more distribution the same media offers (not to say the same content), from local to global, the more the involved recipients become potential members of one united global group, and a singular media generation.

This tendency, however, still seems to be counterbalanced by different ethnicities, mentalities, political and cultural backgrounds that determine what people understand of what media offer to them. The differences occur with the interpretation, appreciation, and evaluation of media events and the related memories. Many people around the world may know that certain events took place, but that might be the only thing they have in common. They do not need to share the evaluations, neither the political interpretations nor the personal involvements and consequences. This is where another aspect comes in. Virtual "communities," such as those formed through global media by the Internet generation, may similarly come together along their own super-cultural values or standards (e.g., the Human Rights Convention). But they can only do so when these standards, too, are mediated and communicated, and when all these people run through similar education processes. Obviously, it is not the media alone that creates one global media generation.

Mapping Memory: The Geography of Remembering

If the chronology of memory deals with questions of time—the remote past, the less remote past, and the recent past—the "geography" of memory is concerned with questions of space and location. It is a vital factor in the act of remembering. It refers to the location of the event that is recalled as well as to the location of the act of recollection. The 15- to 20-year-olds in India, Austria, Australia, Brazil, Germany, Japan, Mexico, and the United States recalled the deaths of Princess Diana and Mother Teresa, which occurred in Paris and in Calcutta respectively. For most of them, these were two news events, no matter how personally shocked or moved they were at these events that were located in distant Paris and Calcutta. The round-the-clock intimate style of media reporting on the events ensured that geographical distance was somehow closed or reduced. It is interesting that in most of the focus-group discussions, the participants invariably spoke about where they were at the time they first got the shocking news. This was especially so with the Austrian and American groups:

Beatrix: Yes, the cases of Diana und Mother Theresa, I was shocked a little bit, because I've heard of it when I was on vacation . . . at first I couldn't believe it. Then I read it in the newspaper and I thought: Is that possible overnight? I was totally shocked, because so many famous people died at once. [general agreement] (Cohort 3, page 9, line 391 ff)

The second-generation Indian focus group was conducted in Bahrain, not India. Did this location of the focus group make a difference to the nature of their memory? Certainly, the Indian events they remembered would have been the same, but would their "involvement" with the mediated information be different, perhaps more intense, since they were so far from home?

The Memory of Politics and the "Politics" of Memory

It is significant that the majority of national and international events recalled by the three generations in different countries were essentially political events, rather than cultural or social happenings. Of course, this could have been influenced by the way the coordinators framed the questions, and the kind of events that were listed. It could also be because we were looking for media events, and it is known that the media give prominence to political events rather than to cultural ones. News is for the most part concerned with reporting events rather than issues and processes.

Furthermore, sports events were also recalled in many focus groups. For example, in Austria, kids were allowed to see important sports programs at prime time when they normally had to go to bed (i.e., the importance of the Winter Olympic Games for the second generation in Austria). Also, we must not forget the importance of listening to music programs or taking part in musical events like Woodstock for the second generation, or the music of bands like Deep Purple, Nazareth, or Ike and Tina Turner performing in Tyrol (Austria).

There is an initial cognitive preference for attention to, and remembering of, events. An event is something that is significantly different, exceptional, unusual, new, or strange. It often has (or, evolutionarily, had) existential importance. It is emotionally emphasized. News is the very concept of such experiences.

There is a definite process of selection at work in the act of remembering. Participants in focus groups talked about their memories, but were careful to not divulge all, especially those elements or aspects of events that did not fit in with their personal politics or beliefs or convictions. For instance, when the discussion among the 15- to 20-year-olds of Pune/India turned to the question of the demolition of the mosque at Ayodhya by Hindu extremists, it was evident that this issue gave rise to some uneasiness. The participants (two Hindus, a Sikh, and a Christian) had to reveal their political affiliations, and some of them did so quite frankly; others did not. What we choose to remember and the way we express our memories are influenced by our politics (or ideology). It is thus the "politics" of memory at work when some events of the past are talked about freely and often colored by a vivid imagination. Memory plays tricks in the act of remembering: we remember some events rather than others, and while some memories are clear, others are confused and mixed up. Indeed, there are some events that we cannot remember, and others that we do not want to talk about. They make us feel uncomfortable, especially in the presence of strangers. Self-disclosure is, after all, not a very pleasant experience in a focus-group setting. But once self-disclosure has taken place, the participants do experience a catharsis, what one might term "the healing power of memory." This was the feeling one got when the Indian focus groups talked about their memories of Ayodhya, the Emergency, and the Partition.

There is yet another sense in which we can talk about the politics of memory. Nation-states propagate their own official histories of the past, which generally glorify the role of the nation concerned. National memory of the past is thus subject to being politicized in favor of one perspective or the other. Thus, the BJP (which is the dominant coalition partner in the ruling Indian government) has sought to rewrite school textbooks and propagate, through the media, a "Hindu nationalist" perspective of Indian history that belittles the role of Gandhi and other leaders of the National Congress. This is an attempt to play politics with national history, and especially with the history of the Freedom Movement in India. Political parties in other countries also play similar games in attempts to redefine (and therefore to distort) the national memory of the past. In the focus-group discussions conducted among a select group of three generations in different countries, there was little evidence of any attempt to challenge official versions of national history. Nor was there much evidence of an attempt to challenge media versions of national and global events. This could have been because of the kind of questions raised in the discussions, or more likely because of the focus on recollection of the media experiences of childhood, especially as they related to an arbitrarily selected number of national and global events.

Bibliography

Assman, Jan and Aleida Assman (1994). "Das Gestern im Heute: Medien und Soziales Gedächtnis." (Yesterday Today: Media and Social Memory) In *Die Wirklichkeit der Medien: Eine Einführung in die Kommunikationswissenschaft*, ed. K. Merten, S.J. Schmidt, and S. Weischenberg, 114–140. Opladen: Westdeutscher Verlag.

Bartlett, Frederic C. (1932). *Remembering*. Cambridge: Cambridge University Press.

Bloch, Marc. (1925). "Mémories Collective, Tradition et Coutume," [Collective Memories : Tradition and Practice]. *Revue de Synthèse Historique* 40: 73–83.

Durkheim, Emile. [1901] (1938). *The Rules of Sociological Method*. New York: Free Press.

Ebbinghaus, Hermann. (1971; Orig. 1885). *Über das Gedächtnis. Ein Beitrag zur experimentellen Psychology. (On Memory: Contributions to Experimental Psychology)*. Darmstadt: Wiss. Buchgemeinschaft.

Festinger, Leon. (1957). *A Theory of Cognitive Dissonance*. Standford: Stanford University Press.

Grice, Herbert P. (1957). "Meaning." *The Philosophical Review* 66: 377–388.

Grice, Herbert P. (1969). Utterer's Meaning and Intentions." *The Philosophical Review* 78: 147–177.

Gülich, Elisabeth. (1980). "Konventionelle Muster und Kommunikative Funktionen von Alltagserzählungen." (Conventional Patterns and Communicative Functions of Everyday Narratives) In *Erzählen im Alltag.* ed. K. Ehlich, 335–384. Frankfurt: Suhrkamp.

Halbwachs, Maurice. (1980). *The Collective Memory.* New York: Harper & Row (french original: *La mémoire collective*). Paris: Presses universitaires de France, 1950).

Johnson-Laird, Phillip N. (1983). *Mental Models.* Cambridge: Harvard University Press.

Loftus, Elizabeth. (2001). "Changing Beliefs about Implausible Autobiographical Events: A Little Plausibility Goes a Long Way." *Journal of Experimental Psychology* 7, No. 1: 51–59. See also http://faculty.washington.edu/eloftus/Articles/mazzloft.htm [12–20–02].

Mannheim, Karl. (1951). "The Problem of Generations." In *Mannheim, K.: Essays on the Sociology of Knowledge.* 276–322. London: Routledge & Kegan.

Maturana, Humberto R. (1977). *Biologie der Kognition.* Paderborn: FEoLL.

McKenzie, Wark. (1994). *Virtual Geography: Living with Global Media Events.* Bloomington: Indiana University Press.

Middleton, David and Derek. Edwards, eds. (1990). *Collective Remembering.* London: Sage.

Miller, Georg A. (1956). "The Magical Number Seven, Plus or Minus Two: Some Limits on Our Capacity for Processing Information." In Psychological Review 63, 81–97.

Rusch, Gebhard. (1987). *Erkenntnis, Wissenschaft, Geschichte: Von einem Konstruktivistischen Standpunkt. (Knowing, Science, History: From a Constructivist Point of View).* Frankfurt: Suhrkamp.

Rusch, Gebhard. (1991). "Erinnerungen aus der Gegenwart (Memories from the Present)." In *Gedächtnis. Probleme und Perspektiven der Interdisziplinären Gedächtnisforschung,* ed. S.J. Schmidt, 267–292. Frankfurt: Suhrkamp.

Rusch, Gebhard. (1996). "Erzählen: Wie wir Welt Erzeugen. Eine Konstruktivistische Perspektive." In *Strukturen Erzählen,* ed. H.J. Wimmer, 326–361. Wien: Edition Praesens.

Schuman, Howard and Jacqueline Scott (1989). "Generations and Collective Memories." *American Sociological Review* 54: 359–381.

Vitouch, Peter and, Hans-Jörg. Tinchon eds. (1996). *Cognitive Maps und Medien: Formen Mentaler Repräsentation bei der Medienwahrnehmung. (Cognitive Maps and Media: Patterns of Mental Representation in Media Reception)* Frankfurt: Lang.

Winter, Jay. (2002). *The Generation of Memory: Reflections on the "Memory Boom" in Contemporary Historical Studies.* URL: http://www.ghi-dc.org/bulletin27F00/b27winterframe.html [12–20–02].

MEMORY AND MARKERS: COLLECTIVE MEMORY AND NEWSWORTHINESS

Ruth Teer-Tomaselli

The project set out to discover, through a comparative methodology, what media events are recalled by three different age cohorts in nine different countries. The present chapter considers not only *what* was remembered by the various cohorts in different countries, but more specifically, attempts to understand *why* these events were remembered, and the manner in which the events were recalled.

The analysis is concerned both with individual memory, and crucially, collective memory, the theorization of which gives greater emphasis to the social context than to autobiographical, personal memory. The approach to individuated memory is dealt with under the heading of "lifeworlds." However, before considering that position, it is useful to take a short detour around the notion of collective memory. The approach taken throughout the project is deeply phenomenological, employing research methodologies that are inimical to those of positivist perspectives.

Collective Memory[1]

The human memory is constantly bombarded with images and information. Based on the sheer magnitude of processing and storage that takes place, it is reasonable to infer that the procedure involves something slightly more complex than isolated bio-cognitive functions. Out of this inference and other academic quandaries, scholars began to consider the social aspect of memory processing (Connerton, 1989). Indeed cognitive psychologists today can acknowledge, without undermining their precepts or principles, that "the memories of people in different cultures will vary because their mental maps are different" (Connerton, 1989: 28). These mental maps are constructed through human experience that is inherently situational and communal. Everything we remember, no matter how personal, exists in relationship to ideas, values, or feelings. Any individual memory is dependent on collectively constructed words, language, images, people, and locations. The scripts of our memories are written and revised based on external sources, often of a mediated kind. Thus, our personal and collective histories do not appear on a blank page.

The personal was situated within the collective for the first time by French sociologist Maurice Halbwachs (1950, 1980; Coser, 1992). Halbwachs argued that individuals acquire, localize, and recall their memories only through membership of social groups—particularly kinship, religious, and class affiliations (Connerton, 1989). Indeed, practical experience demonstrates that the bulk of our memories are prompted by questions or comments made by friends, family, colleagues, or others around us. Halbwachs suggested "we appeal to our memory in order to reply to questions which others put to us, or which we imagine that they could ask us, and, in order to reply to them, we envisage ourselves as forming part of the same group or groups as they do" (Connerton, 1989: 36). Therefore, in Halbwachs's theoretical construction, the individual memory is entirely dependent on the collective; "it is to the degree that our individual thought places itself in [the social framework] and participates in this memory that it is capable of the act of recollection" (Coser, 1992: 38). This collective situation builds on the foundation established in our discussion of identity, particularly in the description of social-identity theory. This links to Erikson's emphasis on peers and the research findings that a connection to peers is one of the primary motivators for young people selecting a fictional program.

Halbwachs's fervent rejection of the individual as the unit of analysis marks his dramatic departure from the standard psychological approach to memory. He contended that psychology divides the bonds that attach individuals to their social context; while experience teaches that memory is constructed within the very same social context (Coser, 1992). While Halbwachs acknowledged that in the individual "we observe dreams, the functioning of memory and the disorders of aphasia [such as amnesia and other memory-inhibiting disorders]" (Coser, 1992: 167), he opposed the way psychologists "exteriorise" internal states of consciousness (Coser, 1992). He wrote:

> Indeed, from the moment that a recollection reproduces a collective perception, it can itself only be collective; it would be impossible for the individual to represent himself anew, using only his forces, that which he could not represent to himself previously—unless he has recourse to the thought of his group. (Coser, 1992: 169)

This is where academic advancement would force a contemporary Halbwachs to revise his point, for psychology has made inroads into connecting an individual's memories to his or her context. Although the bulk of psychologists continue to speak of memories as fairly insular units, some have knowingly or unwittingly built upon Halbwachs's assertion that the individual and collective are not two separate elements, but rather "two points of view from which society can simultaneously consider the same objects" (Coser, 1992: 175).

All collective memories are partial—and hide as much as they reveal. In this way, they act as much as Roland Barthes (1972) suggested how mythologies act. No one memory brings forth everything that is known about a particular event, person, or issue. Nor does a single memory depend on a single source: rather it is an amalgam of several sources, often confused and almost always interrelated. From a methodological point of view this is of primary importance, since it is impossible to say with any certainty that a particular event was remembered with reference to a particular mediated experience. Memories of the Vietnam War or the first walk on the moon are mosaics of contemporary news programs, print newspapers, as well as subsequent narrative films, historical retrospectives, and discussions among friends, colleagues, and family. Further, one set of events "triggers" half-baked memories of other seemingly unrelated events. For South African respondents, the Vietnam War was interesting precisely because it allowed a space to talk about the South African border wars of the 1980s; for Indian respondents, discussions of Princess Diana's death evoked a discussion of the death of Mother Theresa of Calcutta. In this way, memory finds parallels between the sociopolitical and private lives of different interpretative communities, and utilizes them in ways that satisfy the needs of particular groups.

Marker Events

One of the underlying assumptions in the project was that, given a common list of "prompted" events chosen from a particular timeframe across the international arena, different country-specific groups would remember different topographies of situations, happenings, and people. Incidents that are held to be critical in the life of a nation are what Claude Levi-Strauss (1966) referred to as "hot moments"; they are historical conjunctures through which a nation or a cultural group takes stock of its own significance. Barbie Zelizer uses the phrase "critical incidents" in a similar fashion. When employed discursively, the term "critical incidents" refers to those moments in which people air, challenge, and negotiate their own standards of action. "In this view, collective memories pivot on discussions of some kind of critical incident. . . . Critical incidents uphold the importance of discourse and narrative in shaping the community over time" (Zelizer, 1992: 4).

The example explored by Barbara Zelizer (1992) is the collective memory of American journalists in the events surrounding the death of President John Kennedy in 1963, an event that, although outside any of the demarcated time periods studied in the present project, nevertheless evoked spontaneous memories among the respondents in a number of country studies. Zelizer holds that the Kennedy assassination was a "critical incident" in the American psyche largely because of the mediated nature of recording and commemoration: "it was a turning point in the evolution of American journalistic practice not only because it called for the rapid relay of information during a time of crisis, but also because it legitimated televised journalism as a mediator of national public experience" (Zelizer, 1992: 4). For an entire generation of Americans, and many people worldwide as well, the Kennedy assassination evokes memories of specific iconic images, which have become etched in the collective consciousness not only in terms of their contemporary distribution in 1963, but also by frequent reiteration in the four decades since then: "these moments—captured by the media in various forms—have been replayed as marketers of the nation's collective memory each time the story of Kennedy's death is counted" (Zelizer, 1992: 24). Ever since, journalists have used the event as a benchmark in discussions of appropriate journalistic practice, and it has evolved into a critical indictment against which journalists test their own standards of action (Zelizer, 1992: 19).

Newsworthiness and Media Recollection

In a seminal article on the structuring and selection of news, John Galtung and Mari Ruge (1973) identified twelve common factors affecting the selection of news items.[2] Five of these factors also play a major part in the memorability of news items, both in the period immediately after the events and the months, indeed years, afterward: the size and impact of the event; the negativity as well as the ongoing or continuous nature of the event; and those items that deal with elite personages and countries; and finally, and most crucially, proximity, both geographic and more particularly cultural. In this chapter, I will use these four categories as the organizing principles around which specific media events are remembered by specific generations, in order to begin to tease out some of the dynamics of what constitutes significant "markers" for each generation.

Size, Continuity, and Negativity as Markers of Impact

Bigger is better. The bigger an event, the more likely it will be reported, and the more prominence it will be given (Galtung and Ruge, 1973). The most widely and intensely remembered event across all the groups in the first cohorts were the Japanese attack on Pearl Harbor and the dropping of the atom bombs on Japanese cities, heralding the end of the Second World War in the Pacific. Only the German and Czech groups claimed low, or subsequent, knowledge of these two events, which can be explained in terms of the strict censorship of news in those countries during the war. The sheer immensity of these events, as well as the central significance in the lives of those affected by them, were sufficient to make them extremely memorable.

The continuity of a running story also contributes to both its newsworthiness and the likelihood of it being remembered. Many of the prompted events used in this research were less events, that is, specific once-off happenings, than they were processes—drawn out over a period of time and reported and reflected upon in the media as sagas. The Vietnam War, for instance, played out over a period of years, even though it is remembered as a series of specific, iconic happenings and images. Even those "stories" with beginnings and endings often lent themselves to sequels and expansions. The fall of Singapore from Allied into Japanese control took just days to effect, but the results unfolded for months after that. Respondents in South Africa, joined in interest to the defeated and humiliated British and Australian troops by their shared membership of the Commonwealth, speak in detail about the events leading up to the capitulation, as well as the repatriation of the women and children who had been evacuated in the face of occupation. Thus every "story" has a prequel and a sequel, and in recalling the story it is often these "peripheral" matters that appear to be more personal, more significant, and therefore more memorable.

Most of the events recalled did not refer to single news items, but were ongoing stories, frequently taking many months to come to fruition. A pertinent example was the O.J. Simpson trial, regarded as a "saga," and as compulsive "as a soap opera" (South Africa, Cohort 3). At every stage in the proceedings there were turns and twists, and no sense of a clear narrative with a set structure. Again, what was remembered by all cohorts across countries were a plethora of small details, minutiae—the matching of the shoe size, cars outside the home, the blood samples that were switched— rather than a coherent narrative. Sometimes the details became confused, as in the name of Simpson's wife:

M:	His wife was Karen.
S:	I think it was Tracy.
D:	I have no idea, except she was a pretty blond.
M:	Nicole, that's it.

Negativity

The more negative the consequences of the event, the more probable that it will become a news item. This news value is so axiomatic that the Glasgow Media Group (1976) named its groundbreaking study of television news coverage *Bad News*. Negative news fits the frequency criterion better than positive news does. In the choice of events and processes to be reported, there is a basic asymmetry between the positive, which is difficult and takes time to come to fruition (achievement is a long-term process), and the negative, which is much easier and takes less time. Galtung and Ruge (1973) provide the example of the comparison between the time it takes to socialize an adult and the time it takes to kill him.

Positive news is reported when an event culminates or something is inaugurated. Negative news is also more easily consensual and unambiguous in the sense that it is easier to agree about what is negative than what is positive. Positive news is more clearly defined by ideological factors.

A second reason for the ubiquity of negative news is that it tends to be more unexpected, or less predictable, than positive news. Negative events have the "advantage" of rarity. This presupposes a society in which progress is regarded as the norm, and changes for the better are regarded as "trivial" and therefore underreported. "The test of this theory would be in a culture with regress as the norm, and in that case one would predict an over-reporting of positive news" (Galtung and Ruge, 1973, p. 59, emphasis in the original). In a society in which "reform" is punted, any movement in that direction, no matter how trivial, is over-reported.

Some theorists have argued that news is more consonant with at least some of the dominant pre-images and expectations of our time. This theory presupposes a relatively high level of social anxiety that provides a matrix in which negative news in more easily embedded than positive news. This is a contentious argument and one that can be directly argued against in the South African situation, in which the level of social insecurity is consciously fought against by the presentation of positive news.

Contemporary and Subsequent Memory

Newsworthy events are broadcast and printed when they happen, but they are also recycled in the media, and hence in the public imagination, for years afterward. In reading through the transcripts of the various focus groups, it is apparent that it is not always possible to distinguish between contemporary memory and subsequent reconstructions of particular events. In some cases, it was clear that knowledge of particular events only came about months or even years after the original happening. This "coming into memory" is related to a number of other issues that will be raised in this chapter, notably, discussions with friends and family, and living in a country that is emerging from political or sociocultural isolation (for example, the isolation of the United States, Germany, Austria, and Czechoslovakia during the period of the first cohort; and the insularity of South Africa in the period of the second cohort). Frequently, however, it is simply a matter of respondents growing up and being more aware of the sociopolitical facts around them. The Prague Spring, remembered with great clarity by the Central European groups, was totally unrecalled by groups in countries farther away. A South African respondent summed it up by saying, "A couple of years later I only began to realize the dynamics of what was going on. I only really got a handle on the thing after I left University," referring to a period long after the contemporary events (South Africa, Cohort 2).

Similarly, in India, respondents recalled Watergate, "but not much, but then I had followed it up later on the BBC, when . . . they had carried a series of shows on TV . . . [about how Nixon] was trying to bug all information of all opposition members, and then finally how he had been asked to resign. This I followed up much later, but not when it did" (India, Cohort 2). Occasionally, a particular set of events is remembered in terms of the contemporaneous information available to respondents, but later reiteration serves to expand the depth or appreciation of that knowledge. The same Indian respondent vividly recalled the landing of the first man on the moon, which he first heard about on radio: "One of the events I can recollect strongly is the first man on the moon. Apollo. The person, the whole event, I still recollect because of the broken communication and when he landed on the moon the first time and what he said, all those things do come back to my mind. When subsequently, of course, in the early eighties, when we had television in Bangalore, we could see some of the international events" (India, Cohort 2).

The reiteration and circulation of events long afterward, often in circumstances very different form the original context, is a primary way in which memories are either evoked or reinvented. A U.S. respondent from the youngest cohort learned of the war in Kosovo through Internet research for school assignments. This inspired her to become involved in local fundraisers to benefit the war victims (USA, Cohort 3).

Elite Persons, Elite Nations

The category of "elite persons," people who attract the most public and media attention, as a criterion of newsworthiness is also borrowed from Galtung and Ruge (1973). Herbert Gans (1980) has referred to such persons as "knowns," and it is an established pattern in news bulletins to solicit the opinions of such people on a wide variety of affairs, often not even linked to their area of expertise. This is related to Galtung and Ruge's (1973) category of "personification." Actions that can be seen as being associated with particular individuals are more likely to be reported than occurrences with a more generalized or impersonal agency. Further, personification is more in keeping with the techniques of news reporting, since it is easier to photograph or quote a person than a structure. One interview will provide a person-centered story; several are required for in-depth analysis. The latter take more time to prepare—reserved for "magazine" and "discussion" programs. This opens the question of which is preeminent—the need for personification, or the need for structured news techniques. More crucially for the question of memory, personification is the outcome of cultural idealism, which is in keeping with the myth that every person's progress is the outcome of an act of free will. Structural factors are minimized, while persons as instruments of their own or other people's destiny is emphasized. Thus personification in news reporting fulfills the need for identification, with famous people serving as the objects of both positive and negative identification through a combination of projection and empathy. Furthermore, personification fulfills the parameters of the frequency factor, constantly recycled through reportage, speculation, and endless gossip.

In all the cohorts, there are examples of historical events and processes that are associated with specific people, rather than seen as the unfolding of sociopolitical developments. Watergate was remembered in terms of "Tricky Dicky," the moniker given to President Richard Nixon; the Palestine Liberation Organization is personified by Yasser Arafat; the end of apartheid by the release of Nelson Mandela.

Frequently, these memories coalesce around a specific traumatic event in the life of the person. Perhaps the most famous "media memory" event of all time is the assassination and funeral of the late U.S. president John F. Kennedy (Dayan and Katz, 1994; Zelizer, 1992). For the German cohort, memories of the Second World War were associated with the attempted assassination of Adolf Hitler; all of the youngest cohorts, regardless of country, recalled Mother Theresa and Princess Diana of Wales as much for their deaths as for their lives (see later in this chapter for more on both examples). The Indian cohorts recalled successively: the assassination of Mahatma Gandhi in 1948 (three years beyond the study period); Indira Gandhi in 1984, shot by her own Sikh bodyguards outside her residence in Delhi (see India chapter); and the assassination of her son, Rajiv Gandhi in 1991 by a suicide bomber near Madras in Tamilnadu: "I remember I was sleeping at the time. My mother came and told me that Rajiv Gandhi is dead. She had seen some people in a sort of procession. I remember for one whole week all TV programs were stopped. I remember the cremation." Another young respondent recalled: "A gentleman, a lady screamed: 'Rajiv is dead, Rajiv is dead.' My dad was shocked; my mom was shocked. Of course we were also shocked. But we were shocked the next morning. It just gave a shock" (India, Cohort 3). (See chapter on India in this volume.)

The ubiquitous nature of elite persons is also true of elite nations. Elite nations can be regarded as those with the strongest economies and the greatest ability to influence the security, trade, and cultural agendas of other countries. In media terms, an elite nation can be classified as a nation that produces large amounts of media productions in a language that is accessible to large numbers of people beyond their borders. Beginning with the debates around the New World Information and Communication Order (NWICO), considerable academic and political attention has been paid to the channeling of news and information through a few dominant news agencies (e.g., Boyd-Barrett and Rantanen, 1998 for survey).[3]

Tracking the export trends of "cultural goods"—including radio and television, cinema and photography, printed matter and literature, music and the visual arts—UNESCO calculated that 68 percent of the world share emanated from the "developed" countries (which represent 23 percent of the world's population); while 32, originated from the developing countries, representing 77 percent of the population (UNESCO, 1995: 27).

Of all the countries in the world, the United States has occupied the preeminent position in this respect: it has been the dominant world power and leading proponent and organizer of a neoliberal global order. "Among the great powers . . . the United States is the country in which market domination of the media has been most extensive and complete." (Herman and McChesney, 1997: 137). In recent years, noteworthy portions of U.S. media corporations either have been sold to buyers from other countries, or have acquired stakes in companies from across the globe. Thus, according to Herbert Schiller (1992: 14–15), it is no longer appropriate to speak of U.S. cultural imperialism, as much as one would speak of transnational-corporation cultural imperialism with a heavy American accent. While it is true that globalizing cultural processes are not entirely dominated by one country, the United States of America, or even by the "West" or the "North," and that "contributions to world literature, world music and world art are emerging from Bombay, Rio de Janeiro, Ouagadougou or Seoul, as they are from New York, London, Liverpool or Paris" (UNESCO, 1995: 27), the so-called developed countries continue increasingly to be hegemonic in the spread of cultural artifacts, media, and mediated personalities, and English increasingly is becoming the language of global cultural currency. Furthermore, the level of globalization becomes more apparent as we progress through the various age cohorts.

Elite persons who emanate from elite nations are therefore twice as likely to be remembered. Not unexpectedly, most of these iconic personalities recalled by respondents from countries other than their own originated from the "developed countries." Examples of such global personification can be found in the memories associated with O.J. Simpson, Bill Clinton and Monica Lewinsky, Princess Diana, and Mother Theresa. Speaking of O.J. Simpson, respondents in the South African group showed a strong awareness of the power of the media, and the media's obsession with celebrity: "The reason was because he [O.J. Simpson] was world famous. I don't think anyone was really interested in the murder; rather it was that a world-famous person could have committed a murder. It was kind of sensationalist. It is ironic, however, that the whole thing was to determine if he committed a crime in cold blood. We don't even remember the man who was with her [the wife], we can't even remember what her name was, but there was this whole big thing about this famous man" (South Africa, Cohort 3).

Proximity

The most important influence on what is remembered is that of cultural proximity. Galtung and Ruge (1973) note that ethnocentrism is evident in all news broadcasts, with particular attention being paid to the familiar. This is true too of media memories, where every country study, regardless of cohort, reported that the best-remembered and most significant media events were those that occurred within the country in which they lived. The first Indian cohort, for instance, displayed a deep and detailed knowledge of Indian political events. The discussions of the civil disobedience, the Hindu-Moslem animosities, and the assassination of Mahatma Gandhi, were all characterized by an intensely nationalist, sectarian, and regional fervor. The second Indian cohort similarly remembered in detail the Indo-Pakistani revolts, while even the youngest cohort, who would have been around ten years old at the time, recalled in detail (if not with total accuracy) the assassination of Rajiv Gandhi, discussed later in this chapter. Conversely, in groups in other countries, the Salt March was not even recalled.

Similarly, the first German cohort spontaneously talked about the attempted assassination of Hitler by Graf Stauffenberg and his group on July 20, 1944, the only cohort to remark on this historical event. Conversely, the Indian cohort recalled nothing of happenings in Europe during the Second World War: nothing of the war in Spain, Kristallnacht, or the Nazi concentration camps, while little was known of the abdication of Edward VIII and the Berlin Olympics.

Events in faraway places are recalled more easily when they exhibit a distinct sense of local relevance, an observation that is backed up by Galtung and Ruge's (1973) remarks that a foreign event is more likely to be reported when it is seen to have relevant implications for a domestic audience. Thus, even when events were recalled outside the immediate national area, they were frequently recalled in terms of factors that are associated with the audience's own country. In India, where the recall of international events by the first cohort was particularly low, one respondent remembered the Berlin Olympics simply from an obscure Indian connection, recounting the way in which Hitler shook the hand of an Indian athlete, while in Japan, the only memories of the event related to a Japanese gold medal swimmer. The youngest cohort in India recalled the release of Nelson Mandela in terms of "a kind of party feeling in Calcutta," while another respondent in the same cohort remembered that India was the first to invite South Africa to play a cricket test, and that a road in Calcutta was named after Mandela.

Edward VIII was remembered by the South African respondents not for abdicating the British throne, but for his previous tour of South Africa (Cohort 1). The middle South African cohort were unaware of world-changing events happening in Eastern Europe expect for a few decontextualized details recalled only in terms of their own experiences: "I remember my aunt coming in to say that the Russians have invaded Hungary and this might be a Third World War. Next morning my cousins and I went to see if there were tanks in the streets of Johannesburg" (South Africa, Cohort 2). This example also illustrates the importance of families, and the lifeworld memories of respondents, both of which will be discussed later in this chapter.

"Being there" was always an important prompt to remembering, and cuts across the distinction of mediated and lifeworld memories. While one would expect the German cohort to recall the demolition of the Berlin Wall, a U.S. respondent living in Berlin at the time experienced the same sense of immediateness. Although only seven years of age, she recalled watching the events and celebration live on German television (USA, Cohort 3). Similarly, the only South African respondent to be familiar with the Tiananmen Square episode in China was traveling through Hong Kong with her parents at the time, and picked it up on a television broadcast there.

Closed and Open Societies

Ethnocentrism is particularly apparent in "closed" societies, a situation that can arise from purposeful isolation, forced by the state, or a cultural exclusiveness and introversion imposed from within the society itself. At its most extreme, closed societies enforce strict censorship, both in terms of what may not be heard or seen, and ideologically, in terms of the prevailing ethos of what is "permissible." Beginning with the outbreak of World War II, Japan's media were tightly controlled, initially by the Ministry of the Interior, a task that was transferred to the General Headquarters of the U. S. Forces in Japan, which imposed prior censorship until 1948, and post-censorship after that, a practice that continued sporadically until the mid-1960s. The first German and Austrian cohorts are further examples of closed societies. Newspapers published official news sanctioned by the state, while it was forbidden to modify radios in order to receive shortwave broadcasts from foreign countries, what was called "illegal listening" or *Schwarzhören*. Nevertheless, many Germans, including the families of some of the respondents, did tune into these clandestine news bulletins. Ironically, a similar situation was described by South African respondents, some of whom recall fathers listening to secret broadcasts of the underground pro-Nazi sympathizers in a country committed to the Allied cause.

South Africa in the mid-60s and '70s could also be regarded as a closed society, the result of political insularity from within, and the political and cultural boycott of antiapartheid movements from without. The second South African cohort were singularly unaware of international events at the time of their happening, and only became interested in world affairs much later in life: "To have been in Durban in the early seventies, and to be white was really to be middle class and to be utterly insulated from everything" opined one; while another concurred: "The thing in Stilfontein during that time, because it was a mining town, there was an insularity."

Propaganda

Closely related to the issue of closed societies is that of propaganda. Not only were there negative controls, but also events were manipulated positively as well. Japanese respondents recalled that during the Second World War, there was no officially sanctioned news from Europe; the only news on radio concerned the War of Japan, and even then, "it was only that we were winning"; "that we were losing was not reported at all" (Japan, Cohort 1). Recalling the lantern and flag marches with which the attack on Pearl Harbor was celebrated, they denounced these activities as "falsehoods." The Japanese researcher notes that this particular generation was strongly skeptical about the news they obtained in their youth, and further, even fifty years later, they were very reticent to discuss these matters.

The German cohort of the same age was aware that it was not only the news that carried particular propagandistic messages; entertainment, and specifically narrative films, was also heavily encoded. The newsreel and the fictional film, which were shown at the same viewing, complemented each other to reinforce a single, coherent ideological position: "The feature film conveyed the overall ideology. Of course, always in relation to the newsreel. This way, the newsreel showed what was actually going on, whereas the film submitted the overall ideology" (Germany, Cohort 1).

While propagandistic media frequently are implicit in the everyday experiences of a nation, and therefore appear to be concealed, or at least not appreciated as propaganda at the time, there are occasions when it is obvious even to those to whom it is directed at the time. In the South African second cohort, discussion ranged around a five-minute propaganda slot after the radio news each morning. "I do remember listening to it, and I do remember my father listening to it at the same time, and getting extremely angry with it. I remember wondering why he was so angry, but clearly I didn't understand it." This prompted a second respondent to note that: "Personally it was the huge revulsion to what was called 'current affairs,' which when it come on, I would switch off the radio . . . because we know it was the government trying to justify the unjustifiable."

Family

The previous mention of the father's reaction to the propagandistic broadcasts, and the son's reflection on that, brings to the fore the crucial role of the family in response to the media held by youth across all countries and all cohorts. The interaction of the triad of media, memory, and historical events operated at least three levels: children and young people tended to consume the media, particularly news media, favored by their parents; parents acted as gatekeepers or censors, controlling the kind of programming they thought was suitable for their children; and finally, the "meanings" or the value systems, through which children made sense of the news events.

Beginning with the oldest cohort, many of the respondents recall not only listening to the news on radio, but also the social interaction that accompanied them. One German respondent mentioned the reaction of an uncle to a speech given by Hitler; another recalls modeling school essays after the style adopted by the radio commenter (Germany, Cohort 1). A South African respondent claims not to have heard of the abdication of Edward VIII from the media, but rather that he heard the news from his father. Family radio listening was something that was remarked on by the first cohort in all countries, and was also a factor in the later cohorts too. Children watched what the family watched, and took their cue from the parents: "My parents watched the news every evening and I stayed with them and watched it too" (Austria, Cohort 3). When asked about the Iraq war of 1990, a Czech respondent replied, "All I can remember is Saddam Hussein, since my parents were speaking about it" (Czech, Cohort 3). An Austrian respondent echoed similar sentiments: "I still can remember when the United States took the offensive against Iraq [in 1990]. Because we had watched that all together at home and my brother thought that now the third world war would start. But nobody believed that" (Austria, Cohort 3). Going back to the reception of the Rajiv Gandhi assassination, each of the young respondents mentioned members of family in recounting their personal stories: "A gentleman, a lady screamed: Rajiv is dead, Rajiv is dead. My dad was shocked; my mom was shocked. Of course we were also shocked" (India, Cohort 3).

There is repeated evidence of the gatekeeping role played by the family in terms of the access to what was watched or heard. This appears to have happened in the earlier cohorts to a greater extent than the later ones: the first German cohort reported that in a political context, parents chose to act as gatekeepers in order to protect their children from conflicting political developments and to shield them from any "ambiguous news," knowledge that might be viewed as "conspirative" outside the household. This invisible "shield" between the household as the private space of the family and the outside public and politically controlled world was quite obvious to this cohort in their childhood memories. As children they were aware of this "news shield": "I know that my father had a friend, a physician, who risked his life by listening to English programs. We heard from him about some interesting developments. But our parents were in our presence quite careful what they said." Those parents who wanted to control the news inflow into their family did not even purchase a radio at all, as one individual recalls: "They just wanted to be the judge of what we hear and should not hear" (Germany, Cohort 1).

While there were a few examples of this trend within the second cohort, particularly in terms of the television programming children were allowed to watch (see, for instance, the chapter on Austria), the youngest cohort were avid media consumers with little or no parental prohibition on what was watched.

The final aspect is the way in which parents' reactions to events shape the "meaning" of what was happening. These news items were discussed within the family, and the memory of the events was inextricably bound with family responses. Speaking of the Prague Spring, the Czech researchers report that respondents talked of how afraid their parents were in the face of these events, while as children they did not know what was happening (Czech, Cohort 2). A generation later, the South African cohort who experienced the first fully democratic South African elections of 1994 repeatedly referred to the reactions of their parents. The fatalistic sentiments of "My parents thought it would be the end of South Africa and everything would be destroyed" contrasted with more celebratory positions: "I remember my parents and neighbors came over and sat for close to three hours in front of the television, having tea and talking about how they were going to vote. At first I didn't understand how important that voters' day was" and "My parents were also excited when they were watching the news in the morning and [they saw] all these people, especially in the rural areas. They were standing in long, long, lines, but they were also happy" (South Africa, Cohort 3).

Parents acted not only as gatekeepers in the sense of being censors, but more important, by instilling a sense of what was acceptable at an ideological level. One such example comes from South Africa, where despite the Afrikaans heritage of particular families, the parents infused a sense that "the Afrikaans papers at that time were political or party organs." Despite the fact that the extended family would have been reading these newspapers, the respondent was able to articulate that it "was clear that the stance taken by the Afrikaans papers" was not "ours" (South Africa, Cohort 2).

Lifeworlds

The concept of lifeworlds refers to the everyday world as ordinary men and women experience it. The paradigm draws on the tradition of phenomenological sociology pioneered by Alfred Schutz (1972, 1974) for whom the lifeworld is the paramount reality and the main object of inquiry. From a phenomenological perspective, the social world is a world of meaning. Phenomenology insists that meanings do not have an independent existence, a reality of their own that is somehow separate from social actors. They are not imposed by an external society that constrains members to act in certain ways; rather, they are constructed and reconstructed by actors in the course of social interaction.

Jack Douglas (1971) argues that sociologists must "study the phenomenon of everyday life on their own terms. They must preserve the integrity of that phenomenon." While this begs the question of validity, and opens the door to the uncertainty of subjectivities rather than objective "realities," Douglas believes that the "fundamental aspects of everyday life" can be grasped intuitively and the creative insights that result "may someday be made objective knowledge."

At its simplest, associations of lifeworld experiences recall specific historical events. The young German cohort remembered the outbreak of Bovine Spongiform Encephalitis (BSE), more commonly known as "Mad Cow Disease," because it affected some of them directly, as the following exchange illustrates:

A: I was in [England] when that happened.
M: Me too.

A:　　　　　　Yes, it was quite terrible. We went to McDonald's all the time and only could eat McChicken.

Lived experience does not occur in a vacuum—it is connected to our past and our present social context. Memory is the capsule of the past and the major determinant of the future. Specific events are recalled not only in terms of their mediated nature through radio, print, or television, but also in terms of real-life recollections of experiences that happened at the same time. An apposite example is the anecdote recounted in the German study, regarding the attempted assassination of Hitler: "My mother and I went to pick berries in the mountains near Jena. When we returned to the train station . . . they had these loudspeakers . . . and they repeated the message that the group of criminal officers had tried to kill the Führer. However, by providence he is still alive. My mother almost collapsed and I had the feeling that it is a tragedy that this conspiracy was, again, unsuccessful. All this is kept in my memory. However, it was something that we had to hide. At the moment my mother stepped on the train, she had to pretend as if nothing has happened" (Germany, Cohort 3). Volkmer notes that "This deep integration of political events, transmitted by media, in this case loudspeakers, into biographical lifeworld memories, seems to be characteristic for this age cohort," an observation borne out by other country case studies. In South Africa, the centenary of the Great Trek in 1938 sparked numerous personal recollections. One respondent recalled the reenactors of the Trek taking the ceremonial ox wagons far up into the north of the country, the culmination of months of festivities: "all the way up they had celebrations . . . as a kid, I saw them in Ermelo [a small town]"; while another respondent recalled that on the final day of the celebration, her youngest sister was born, and the ward sisters at the hospital dressed the baby in commemorative clothing (South Africa, Cohort 3).

Connecting directly to the concept of proximity discussed previously, is the personal relevance or interest of respondents, that is, media events that are spontaneously recalled and had special significance to an individual in his or her life. In the United States, one respondent recounted the dispute between Tonya Harding and Nancy Kerrigan. As an avid skater herself, she felt scandalized by the news coverage. She had been interviewed about her own local competitions for the local newspaper, but the angle of the story was weighted toward the quarrel between Harding and Kerrigan, rather than the respondent's own achievements. No other cohort mentioned this event; indeed, it is unlikely that even on prompting, many would be able to identify the two protagonists (USA, Cohort 3).

Occasionally, events are remembered almost serendipitously, as was the case of the U.S. respondent who remembered the 1972 victory of the Pittsburgh Pirates baseball team, simply because growing up in the city, she enjoyed listening to the games on her transistor radio (USA, Cohort 2). The OPEC oil crisis was meaningful to Japanese respondents because it resulted in the soaring price of gas, and strangely, the lack of bathroom tissue in stores. For the Czech group, the reunification of Germany was remembered by the exodus of East German residents through Czech territory; while for others in the same group, the Iraq war took on a surreal identity: "It is the fate of our times that an event is viewed as most attractive if it looks more like a videogame than reality" (Czech, Cohort 3).

Triggers

Triggers refer to stimuli that recall particular memories. The more momentous a story or event is in the history of a country, the more it is likely to be included in the collective memory of its people. However, even large stories require a trigger to set off the memory process. While most of the details of a particular event or set of circumstance are lost to memory, ironically it is often the small things that stay embedded in the recollections while the main plot of the story is forgotten. In part this can be explained by the concept of relevance and proximity: those aspects that are of direct relevance to the individual remain in the mind longer, while those parts of the narrative, albeit the more important parts from a systemic point of view, are either forgotten, or more likely, never grasped in the first place. The Vietnam War, for example, remains one of the most significant events to have taken place in the twentieth century, uniting the fates, as it did, of the "West" and the "Orient"; and challenging, for the first time, the might of the industrial world's heartland. Yet for many second cohort respondents outside the United States, the ebb and flow of the war was a blur: what they recall were isolated incidents, high in iconic value, but low in issue-driven strategic terms. South African respondents, for instance, remembered very little of what actually happened in Vietnam, and were hazy about the geography and chronology of the war, claiming they only learned of the details later. However, they remembered seeing video of the Kent State University shooting, an action peripheral to the actual war, since it took place during a university protest march on U.S. soil. This was echoed in an Australian cohort, who recalled the same image. It can be speculated that these two cohorts recalled this protest because it had greater consonance with them at the time—most of the cohorts themselves were at university, and felt a common sense of sympathy with the Kent State protesters. For the South Africans, discussions of Vietnam triggered discussion of the local border war into Angolan territory, and here the connection is stronger, since many of them were either conscriptees, were threatened with conscription, or in the case of the women, had boyfriends or brothers who were conscriptees.

Sometimes memories were triggered by the discussions within the group itself, with one respondent bringing up a subject and others concurring or adding to the stock of recalled narratives. At other times, one set of discussions prompted other associations. In the youngest German cohort, respondents moved directly from the death of Princess Diana to the fatal air crashes at the Frankfurt army base: "I was in bed and my mother came rushing into my room: 'this woman is dead.' I could hardly believe it, and then the air crashes." The same group moved seamlessly from a discussion of a rugby world championship to soccer: "But nobody here knows this, because you all do not play rugby. And other soccer . . ."

The Importance of Images

Images come together in meaningful ways, lending unity, temporal and spatial sequencing, and form. Narratives that persist today bear collective authority, an authority that often emanates from photographic records (Tagg, 1992: 102) Memory is carried through cognitive and social processes, through the words we read and hear, the images we view, and the circumstances in which these happen or are mobilized at a later date. The importance of words, both written, as in headlines, and heard, as on the radio, cannot be overestimated. Yet much of what we remember is derived from images, both still and moving. Barbara Zelizer (1998: 6–7) suggests that if "words function much like the 'index cards' of shared memories . . . [then] images depend on their material form when operating as vehicles of memory." The media provide the materiality for those images—indeed, media acts as the system of both storage and retrieval for huge numbers of people.

A number of groups within the first cohort remarked on films, particularly newsreels, as being of particular importance as facilitators for memories' endurance. The Czech group, along with the South Africans, Japanese, Australians, and Austrians, spoke with affection about the newsreels that preceded the main feature film, a media form that has now disappeared from the screens. The German cohort was acutely aware of the power of newsreel images, noting that they were so vivid that they were still able to share and recall them in the group discussion.

Throughout the discussions, many of the remembered events were marked by a few iconic "moments": a protester standing in Tiananmen Square; Mandela waving to the crowd outside Jan Verster Prison in Cape Town. Referring to pictures of the Berlin Wall, a young South African reminisced: "What I remember are the pictures in the paper. All these weeping people and so on. That is always the image I remember, all these people who were reunited and all that." Many of the images recalled by one group were remembered in other countries as well, often countries divided by entire continents. The Indian, South African, and the Australian cohorts crystallized the Vietnam War in the single image of a naked, napalm-burnt girl running across the screen. Writing of the power of images to evoke memory, Zelizer (1998: 7) comments that:

> Few of us remember the name of the South Vietnamese village where children ran screaming from their napalmed homes into a photographer's field of vision. . . . But its resonance as an image of war atrocity—and invocation by U.S. antiwar groups during the sixties and seventies—stabilized its meaning precisely along its more schematic dimensions. Collectively held images thus act as signposts, directing people who remember to preferred meanings by the fastest route.

Sometimes the image is riveting, despite the fact that it is neither clear nor explicit. The Australian cohort, to a person, recalled watching the moon landing on television, despite the indistinct reception: "It was awful: just this blurry white figure that you could hardly see and had to think this is the man on the moon. "

On occasion, the image itself can be so powerful that is pulled out of context, and recalled ahistorically. During the discussion around the Beijing uprising, the youngest Czech cohort referred to an image of a man standing in front of tanks; however, on probing, it was found that this was not related to the Beijing massacre at all, and indeed, nothing concrete was remembered of the event (Czech, Cohort 3).

Diana, Princess of Wales

To close this chapter, it is useful to survey one quintessential case study that brings together many of the elements above. Leading the two other popularly remembered stories, those of the Bill Clinton–Monica Lewinski affair, and the O.J. Simpson trial, the most ubiquitous of all remembered events among all three cohorts in all the countries surveyed was the death of the

Diana, Princess of Wales. The discussions ranged across several subtopics, following directly on the motor vehicle accident in which she and her companions were fatally injured, as well as the aftermath, including the media reviews and documentaries of her life, covering the gossip and scandals that surrounded her, the period of mourning, and the elaborate funeral ceremonies. All three of the above stories were seen as truly "global" in their reach. As the Japanese researcher in this volume has noted: "With the prevalence of color TV and satellite TV, we noticed that such news as Princess Diana's death and former President Clinton's private life were no longer just an event in a "foreign" country . . ."

A number of interrelated factors account for the ubiquity of memory across these events. First, in terms of all the historical, lifeworld and media events surveyed by the research, these three were among the most recent events, and therefore the level of individual, as well as collective memory, was relatively high. Second, the events scored particularly highly on the newsworthiness grid as outlined by Galtung and Ruge (1973). The unexpected nature of the event also made it stand out as an important news item. A Czech respondent recounts how the usual flow of radio and television programs were interrupted by the "unexpected news."

The stories had a very high threshold of intensity—by any measure, they were large stories. They were stories with reference to elite nations—the United States and Britain, the leaders in the trade of cultural and information exports, both in the English language. They were centered on "elite persons": O.J. Simpson, a renowned African-American football player with a high celebrity profile; Bill Clinton, the president of the most powerful nation in the Western world, and among the most powerful personages on the globe; and Diana, the fairy-princess icon of glamour and scandal. The circumstances for which they are remembered are deeply negative: Simpson was accused and convicted of murdering his beautiful ex-wife; Clinton was embroiled in a scandal that threatened to end his career; and Diana was killed, along with her lover, as the result of an unexpected and violent episode. From a newsworthiness and memorability point of view, these stories ranked as high as it is possible to be. Yet there were other layers of meaning—markers or triggers—that made these stories particularly consonant with the youthful cohorts in the various study countries.

The death of Diana, in a very real sense, was the ultimate Media Event (Dayan and Katz, 1994), beginning with its unexpectedness. Many of the respondents followed the story closely, watching television both on the day of the accident and during the funeral the following Saturday. Many of the respondents spontaneously related how they received the first news of her death from a family member, and watched the television news in a family sit-uation: "I remember, I was up early in the morning and my dad was watching the television. . . . I couldn't believe it; I just sat there watching as well. Then all of us were watching, we were just talking and nobody seemed to be in the right kind of mind." Recalls a Czech respondent: "I can just remember my mother crying—she liked Diana very much" (Czech, Cohort 3). Confirmation of the discursive nature of media memories comes from the Australian group: "Then Mum walked in and I told her. . . . Well, 'cause no one had heard, and I rang up Michael and told him [because] his dad is English"(Australia, Cohort 1). Not only did the young respondents receive the news in the company of others, but subsequently it was discussed and reiterated among their peers. A member of the Austrian group recounted discussion in everyday face-to-face-situations, particularly among school friends: "she still is admired in London, also on pictures. In school we have talked about it and also have seen a film" (Austria, Cohort 3).

The seriality of the event, and its continuity in terms of both prequels (ret-rospective programs on the life of the princess, and the funeral service) were marked by the characteristic remembering of iconic moments, many of them etched in particular photographic or televisual images: the smashed car in the tunnel; the replay of Diana and Dodi walking through the back entrance of the hotel; the funeral with the repeated motifs of the "the altar boys"; "Elton John singing in the Cathedral"; "her brother's speech about how courageous [Diana] was"; "the hearse." Most particularly, it was the flowers that graphi-cally summed up the life, the death, and the funeral of the princess: "After the funeral, they went to an island with all the flowers"; " I remember all the flow-ers"; "the priests, public putting the flowers"; "All the flowers and the roses."

The discussion of Diana precipitated discussions of another death at more or less the same time, that of Mother Theresa of Calcutta. The Austrian cohort in particular made some insightful comments about the different meanings of the death of the two women: "Yes, the cases of Diana and Mother Theresa, I was shocked a little bit. . . . I read it in the newspaper and I thought, 'Is that possible?' I was totally shocked about that, because so many famous people died at once."

Conclusion: Thoughts on Individual and Collective Memory

Halbwachs, like other cultural and sociological thinkers, acknowledges col-lective memory is not a static entity—like identity, it too is negotiated. Depending on the particular historical and sociopolitical moment, "society represents the past to itself in different ways: it modifies its conventions. As every one of its members accepts these conventions, they inflect their recollections in the same direction in which collective memory evolves" (Coser, 1992: 173). A prime example of this is the way in which South Africa's collective memory of racial and social classes has changed over the last two decades. In many ways the nation is exerting concerted energies into reframing its understanding of relationships between individuals, communities, right and wrong. In her discussion of the Truth and Reconciliation Commission, Sarah Nuttall (1998: 88) wrote:

> We are never . . . the first people to know who we are. But if collective memory is the outcome of agency in South Africa it may often seem that we need to approach the construction of memory from the other way round: Is it less, here, that private memories shape collective remembrance than vice versa? Does the challenge then become how we can create a collective memory that is multiple, flickering with the many meanings that individual experience can collectively bring to it?

Nuttall puts her finger on the pulse of South Africa's collective memory, which is multicultural, and radically changing in the post-apartheid era. However, according to Halbwachs's conception of the relationship between the collective and the personal, it is precisely the "other way round" approach that we should always take when revising memory. For in his view, in almost all cases the collective point of view inspires an alteration of the personal viewpoint—this is the result of "interiorisation." However, beyond the directional flow of the change, it is important to note that collective memory constantly revises itself based on the knowledge and power relations of the present moment.

Second, Halbwachs and others (see Edwards and Middleton, 1986) have maintained that language is an important component of the transmission, storage, and retrieval of collective memory. Halbwachs positioned language as the "precondition for collective thought" (Coser, 1992: 173), stating that "it is language, and the whole system of social conventions attached to it, that allows us at every moment to reconstruct our past" (Coser, 1992: 173). Derek Edwards and David Middleton carry through this point in their analysis of joint remembering in which they hold that symbolic communication through language makes our memories "uniquely human" (1986: 424). Through verbal transmission in a commonly understood language, the collective viewpoint influences the personal. Not only is memory verbal, it is also visual, and the ramifications of the role of images in and on memory are explored in this chapter.

Writing on the role of photography in producing a collective memory of the Holocaust, Barbara Zelizer (1998: 3) observed that

> unlike personal memory, whose authority fades with time, the authority of collective memories increases as time passes, taking on new complications, nuances and interests. Collective memories allow for the fabrication, rearrangement, elaboration and omission of details about the past, often pushing aside accuracy and authenticity so as to accommodate broader issues of identity formation, power and authority and political affiliation.

In this view, memory is not a simple act of recall; it is dependent on social, cultural, and political action at its broadest level—as well as individual life circumstances.

Bibliography

Barthes, R. (1972). *Mythologies*. Translated by Annette Laver. London: Gentry Books.

Boyd-Barrett, O., and Rantanen, T., eds. (1998). *The Globalization of News*. London, Thousand Oaks, and New Delhi: Sage Publications.

Connerton, P. (1989). *How Societies Remember*. Cambridge: Cambridge University Press.

Coser, L. (1992). *Maurice Halbwachs on Collective Memory*. Chicago: University of Chicago Press.

Dayan, D., and E. Katz (1994). *Media Events: The Live Broadcast of History*. Cambridge, MA, and London: Harvard University Press.

Douglas, J. (1971). *Understanding Everyday Life*. London: Routledge and Kegan Paul.

Edwards, D., and D. Middleton (1986). "Joint Remembering: Constructing an Account of Shared Experience through Conversations Discourse." *Discourse Processes* 9: 423–459.

Galtung, John, and Mari Ruge (1973). "Deviance, Social Problems, and the Mass Media." In *The Manufacture of News*, ed. Stanley Cohen and Jock Young. London: Constable.

Gans, H. (1980). *Deciding What's News: A Study of CBS Evening News, NBC Nightly News, Newsweek and Time*. New York: Vintage.

Glasgow Media Group (1976). *Bad News*. Routledge: London.

Halbwachs, M. (1980). *The Collective Memory*. New York: Harper and Row. (Trans. from *La mémoire collective*. Paris: Presses Universitaires de France, 1950).

Herman, E.S., and R.W. McChesney (1997). *The Global Media: New Missionaries of Corporate Capitalism*. Washington, DC, and London: Cassell.

Levi-Strauss, C. (1966). *The Savage Mind*. Chicago: University of Chicago Press.

Nuttal, S. and Craig Coetzee, eds. (1989). *Negotiating the Past: The Making of Memory in South Africa*. Oxford: Oxford University Press.

Schiller, H. (1992). *Mass Communication and the American Empire*, 2nd ed. Boulder, CO: Westview Press.

Schutz, A. (1972). *The Phenomenology of the Social World*. London: Heinemann.

Schutz, A., and Luckmann, T. (1974). *The Structures of the Life-World*. London: Heinemann.

Tagg, J. (1992). *Grounds for Dispute: Art History, Politics and the Discursive Field*. Minneapolis: University of Minnesota Press.

UNESCO (1995). *Our Creative Diversity: Report of the World Commission on Culture and Development*. Paris: United Nations Educational and Cultural Organization.

Zelizer, B. (1992). *Covering the Body: The Kennedy Assassination, the Media, and the Shaping of Collective Memory*. Chicago and London: University of Chicago Press.

———(1998). *Remembering to Forget: Holocaust Memory through the Camera's Eye*. Chicago and London: University of Chicago Press.

·GLOBALIZATION, GENERATIONAL ENTELECHIES, AND THE GLOBAL PUBLIC SPACE·

Ingrid Volkmer

Reviewing some of the key concepts of globalization that have provided the coordinates for the understanding of global processes in the perspective of sociology, economy, and political science, it can be argued that each of these concepts represents various "segments" of an increasing complexity of this new sphere.

The first of these globalization-approach segments, which in fact initiated a post–Global Village discourse, represents what I would call "macroframe" concepts. For instance, Wallerstein's theory of a "world-system" was one of the early macroframe analyses, considering the flow of global capital as a system of new relations (Wallerstein, 1974). Other key macroframe approaches considered globalization as a new "agent of transformation" of modern societal and social structures. Globalization was viewed as "the intensification of worldwide social relations which link distinct localities in such a way that local happenings are shaped by events occurring many miles away" (Giddens, 1990: 6). Globalization in this sense has been sometimes viewed in a "modern" perspective, referring to the endangering of the nation-state on one hand (for instance, core realms of national sovereignty), and on the other, to the notion of nationality as such (Wiley, 2004).

Within this macroframe analysis, the globalized societal structure is perceived around discourses of disassociations and disconnections of modern "place-space" structures, the disembedding of cultures, the disconnection from conventional format of identity, and so on (Beck, 1987). We should keep in mind that globalization debates in these early years of an interdisciplinary context attempted to describe globalization in theoretical (modern) terminology; however, the field of analysis chosen for these debates was primarily the globalizing societies of the West. I should also mention that these discourses did not argue that the nation-state would disappear, but that the nation-state would undergo a transformation of power structures, for instance that transnational and international organizations gain increasing influence, on former core realms of national sovereignty—for instance the World Trade Organization (WTO), OECD, and the European Union.

Parallel to these macroframe concepts, "mesoframe" debates began, which focused not so much on broad, but specific disassociations and disconnections, or to use another terminology, on new forms of "particularism" within the (universal) globalization process. These debates discussed, for instance, the "disembedding of cultures and societies," in view of new categories of (national) deterritorialization and (transnational) reterritorialization. Besides classical modern theories of *Gesellschaft* and *Gemeinschaf* (Toennies, 1887, 1963), one of the first approaches within the globalization debate of the early nineties is Arjun Appadurai's theory (1990). Appadurai detects issues of "de-location," but also new transnational structures of "relocation," which he describes as "scapes," for instance, "ethnoscapes," "financescapes," and "mediascapes," as altogether new transnational social segments of globalization (Appadurai, 1990). Other mesoframe debates highlight new transnational connections, creating transnational mobility (Hannerz, 1990). Roland Robertson has provided very substantial new terms for these processes, which he describes as a parallelism of global/local, and in an advanced, more abstract, and dislocated sense, as "universalism" and "particularism" (Robertson, 1992). He consequently argues in favor of a new relativistic globalization approach, that is "intimately related to modernity and modernization, as well as to postmodernity and 'postmodernization'" and that is concerned with "the concrete structuration of the world as a whole" (Robertson, 1990: 20) and requires new terminologies:

> globalization refers . . . to the coming into, often problematic, conjunction of different forms of life . . . simply as an aspect of outcome of the Western "project"

of modernity. . . . In an increasingly globalized world there is a heightening of civilizational, societal, ethnic, regional and, indeed individual, self-consciousness. There are constraints on social entities to locate themselves within world history and the global future. Yet globalization in and of itself also involves the diffusion of the expectation of such identity declarations."(Robertson, 1992: 27)

Within this discourse of relativization, it became obvious that "modern" approaches to globalization seem to fail to detect arising transnational structures. In consequence, new transnational "spaces" came into debate, which began to highlight the influence of globalization not only on advanced globalizing, that is, Western-type societies, but also in other world regions, where "globalization" is associated with a different meaning (see Jameson and Miyoshi, 1998). A paradigm shift from modern concepts of globalization, across relativistic approaches to the theory of the Network Society, finally inspired new debates in the late nineties, which highlight new transnational social structures, around the "self and the Net," which then, *in reverse*, reconstruct conventional societies and nation-states (Castells, 1996), eroding former concepts of time and space, that is, distance and proximity, in a new multidirectional stream of "flows." These concepts raise new questions of dominance and power, of access and participation, of democracy and public discourse in a (global) network society; the Net is not only a technology but also a metaphor for transnational social structures (Castells, 1996).

The third segment of globalization discourses, which I describe here as "microframe analysis," has been developed particularly since the second half of the nineties of the last century. These microframe discourses tend to focus on the subject in relation to particular globalization "micro" forces. Globalization is considered to be a new cultural space, providing new modes of "mediation" and "proximity" (Tomlinson, 1999), around cultures of consumption, media imaginary, technology, and the media (see for instance, Wilson and Dissanayake, 1996). These approaches consider the individual, the subject, as a central aspect of globalization. For instance, approaches review the impact of fragments of globalization, such as deterritorialization on the individual, and conclude:

What is relevant for aspects of deterritorialization is the ever-broadening horizon of relevance in people's routine experience, removing not only general "cultural awareness" but crucially, the processes of individual "life-planning," political identity from a self-contained context centered on physical locality or politically defined territory and leading to "the extension of an individual's phenomenal world. (Tomlinson, 1999: 115)

These three segments of discourse reveal not only the complexity of today's globalization process, but also construct new infrastructures of connectivity in the virtual reality of a globalized symbolic territory.

A globalized symbolic territory transforms the entire dimension of the Habermasian public sphere by mediating new formats of public discourse, involving profound transformations of communication and discourse. As Garnham argues, "what also became mediated is the content of communication and the subject of debate, or to use Habermas's terminology, the experience of the lifeworld" (Garnham, 1999: 364). In my view, one of the widely overlooked new dimensions of mediation, within this complex globalization process, are transformations in regard to transnational political phenomena, that is, the transformation of the *coordinates* of Habermas's groundbreaking theory of the "public sphere." Various transformations of this key dimension of nation-state constructions on one hand, and of the global civil society on the other, could very well be described in view of the above-applied macro-, meso-, and microanalyses.

Just to outline relevant globalizing macroanalytical factors of the transformation of the public sphere, the following can be argued: New worldwide flows of information—the overall satellite infrastructure—allowing point-to-point delivery directly to households and point-to-multipoint program delivery to media outlets, provide a new globalized notion of life events. It could be argued that these events, categorized as "contest," "conquest," and "coronation" (Dayan and Katz, 1992), become "collective moments" within the dimension of the global public. The moon landing—not so much Armstrong's first steps on the moon's surface, but the first glimpse of planet earth from the moon—provided one of the first experiences of globalization for television audiences worldwide. President Kennedy's funeral, the Vietnam and Gulf Wars, Princess Diana's death, as well as the events associated with 9/11, are all in line as globalizing factors of world images. However, as we will see in the microanalytical debate, these events involved globalizing factors with very distinct meaning from the view of lifeworlds embedded into different cultural contexts.

One other aspect of macroanalytical scale is the information economy of globally operating media companies, providing fragmented program flows, CNN, BBC, and more recently, Al Jazeera. These flows are shaping supra- and sub-national communities and undermine the national public sphere with conflicting images and new political contexts. These channels have already created new power structures, which go far beyond former models of media imperialism. For instance, they have created a new "co-orientation" hierarchy among the news media, and centralized (to a certain extent) the process of agenda setting. A study carried out in 1993 revealed that in the newsrooms of public service broadcasters in Europe (European Broadcasting Union), CNN is constantly monitored in their newsroom "to see what is going on in the world" (Volkmer, 1999). The macroanalytical view also reveals that the role of these channels goes beyond being simply news channels; they act as "mediators of the world" for multiple global spheres: for political spheres in conjunction with media diplomacy; and for shaping a new supra-national sphere of political communication involving mediated actions and reactions, for instance in the relativity of global capital markets, and also for lifeworlds. We also tend to overlook that these multiple mediation roles have their own dynamic; they operate in two modalities: in "peace" and "crisis" modes. Crisis situations particularly enforce new mediation structures, as exemplified by 9/11 and the war in Iraq. Both of which have created new crisis modes, involving new (for instance, "embedded") journalism formats as well as supra-national contextual frameworks, such as around Arab media (see Volkmer, 2002). The Arab news channel, Al Arabya, was deliberately established right before the war in Iraq began in 2003. Journalism, in particular formats of foreign journalism, also requires refinement within this macroframe dimension of the global public, because the network structure of information flow refines former internal versus external flows in regard to the nation-state. Furthermore, new technologies enable simulcasting (for instance via CNN)—distributing crucial national affairs to the national as well as the global audience and eliminating former aspects of national and foreign.

On the mesoanalytical level, it can be claimed that the phenomenon of the global public directly impacts the lifeworld. In previous times of primarily home-audience distribution, news was domesticated in national newsrooms. Today, the lifeworld is directly targeted by niche programs, fragments, or even by the totality of global information flows. Given the advanced globalization process, it can be argued that it colonializes the lifeworld in complex new ways. Media, particularly satellite television and the Internet, have already transformed, if not sometimes removed, national/statist public spheres in Habermas's sense. The national focus of media for national debates, in the Habermasian rational and enlightened ideal-discourse mode, are transformed into formats of mediation within the dynamics of new supra- and sub-national political spheres.

I would like to emphasize, however, the influence of these new infrastructures of political information on the level of microanalysis, on the lifeworld level, and on the level of the "Net and the self," which represents not only the relationship between technology and identity but also the existentialist relation of the self to the virtual world. Castells claims that "When critics of electronic media argue that the new symbolic environment does not represent reality, they implicitly refer to an absurdly primitive notion of 'uncoded' real experience that never existed. All realities are communicated through symbols. . . . In a sense all reality is virtually perceived" (Castells, 1996: 373).

It is precisely this virtual perception of the world that constitutes the microanalytical level of the new dimension of the global public, and highlights the fundamental shift of the ontological ground from the place of the nation to the space of the globe—in view of globalization debates, of the virtuality in Castells's view, and "the world" in a phenomenological sense. In this angle, the analysis of world knowledge or the perception of the world becomes an interesting segment of a new approach to determining what the dimension of the global public could mean.

Viewed from this subjective angle, the global public involves new structures of information, of knowledge, and of world perception. It also provides new notions of connectivity and community. The "Net and the Self" seem to refine Heidegger's distinction between "Being" and "*Dasein*" (German for "existence").

Generational Entelechies in the Global Public Space

The ontological inclusion of "the world" is not new to our network society and has already been a component of German Idealism. Kant's notion of cosmopolitanism, which he articulates in his broadly overlooked work on "Perpetual Peace" (1795, 1881), relates to "world knowledge" in the sense of reason and rational debate, and Hegel's "Spirit of the World" considers the world as an ontological place.

The reconstruction of the phenomenological perception of the world, however, reveals a new dimension in conjunction with the network approach, given the fact that media have entered the lifeworld space and create, refine, and encourage a new order of meanings for things in relation to an extended world horizon. It is this "order of things" that has transformed the notions not only of the self and the Net in Castells's terminology, but also in regard to the categories of place and space.

In Husserl's terminology, the order of things represents the "world of natural experiences," as Husserl argued in his "Thing and Space" lectures (1907):

> In the natural attitude of spirit, an existing world stands before our eyes, a world that extends infinitely in space, that now is, previously was, and in the future will be. . . . We ourselves fit into this world; just as we find the world,

so we find ourselves, and we encounter ourselves in the midst of this world . . . we find ourselves to be centers of reference for the rest of the world. . . . The environing Objects, with their properties, changes, and relations, are what they are for themselves, but they have a position relative to us. (Husserl, 1997: 2)

It is, however, Heidegger who laid the foundation for a new understanding of the crucial relation of the (factual) world (be it the place-bound nation-state era, or the space-bound network society) and the self, as we would argue today, or in his terms of "Being" and "Dasein as it actually is" in its relations to the things in the world. (Heidegger, 1949: 33). Heidegger also argues that Dasein is integrated into the broader category of "fate," which relates individual Dasein notions in the sense of "togetherness in the same world." This can be compared to Mannheim, who argued and concluded that "the inescapable fate of living in and with one's generation completes the full drama of individual human existence" (see Mannheim, 1952: 282).

Mannheim's theory of the sociology of knowledge emphasizes this collective, generational perception of Dasein as one key aspect of a society (and, in fact of societal order). In his view, "individuals" share a "common location in the social and historical process." Such a common location limits them "to a specific range of potential experience, predisposing them for a certain characteristic mode of thought and experience, and a characteristic type of historically relevant action" (Mannheim, 1952: 291). "The fact that people are born at the same time, or that their youth, adulthood, and old age coincide, does not in itself involve similarity of location: what does create a similar location is that they are in a position to experience the same events and data, etc. and especially that these experiences impinge upon a similarity 'stratified' consciousness" (Mannheim, 1952: 297).

Such a generational unit was not possible in the limited world horizons of place, with limited means of international communication, for instance in previous centuries, in the era of place-based nation-state structures: "No one, for example, would assert that there was community of location between the young people of China and Germany about 1800. Only where contemporaries definitely are in a position to participate as an integrated group in certain common experiences can we rightly speak of community of location of a generation" (Mannheim, 1952: 298).

Within this framework, he argues,

The human consciousness, structurally speaking, is characterized by a particular inner 'dialectic.' It is of considerable importance for the formation of the consciousness which experiences happen to make those all-important 'first impressions,' 'childhood experiences' . . . and which follow to form the second, third, and other 'strata.' Conversely, in estimating the biographical significance of a particular experience, it is important to know whether it is undergone by an individual as decisive childhood experience, or later in life, superimposed upon other basic and early impressions. Early impressions tend to coalesce into a natural view of the world (Mannheim, 1952: 298).

Mannheim employs Wilhelm Pinder's term of "entelechy" in order to describe the phenomena of "stratified consciousness" and the "similarity of location." In this sense, it can now be argued that each generation builds an entelechy of its own world perception, which characterizes and stabilizes a generational identity. In Mannheim's argumentation, it is precisely this "link of contemporality" that defines generations. In this sense, the term entelechy stands for this mode of contemporary consciousness of first impressions of the world during childhood and youth years.

Returning to our initial debate about globalization discourses, it seems that there must be a framework for further microframe analysis of the impact of globalization, not only of media infrastructures, that is, world-wide available channels as well as new modes of communication by the Internet, but the analysis of the mind-set of individuals living in their own lifeworld of "meaning of the world." In this framework, global as well as local, universal and particular things are integrated in a subjective order, and lay the ground for a perception of the world that is not only crucial for today's globalization process, but also for participation in the global public sphere within a global civil society.

In our project, we have made the attempt to focus on this aspect in a very simple way: by asking for (a) perceptions of the media environment, (b) memory of media-related news, and (c) the spontaneous recalling of prompted events during childhood and youth years. Given the qualitative nature of the study, various lifeworld logics of the order of things, as well as their meaning, have been expressed rather extensively.

Whereas many of the aspects have already been described in the articles focusing on national results, I would like to emphasize some overall aspects, which could indicate (and illustrate) generational-specific entelechies of the three generations in the nine countries involved in this study.

As the study revealed, the drastic expansion of the media environment from the oldest to the youngest generation has already produced very similar overall entelechies of media perception (see also Slade's chapter "Perceptions and Memories of the Media Context"). In the oldest generation, the newspaper and radio were available, but only directed toward adults. Children's media experiences were located *outside* the house, in movie theaters and occasional escapist media adventures. In the middle generation this changed, with the advent of television (except for India and South Africa, where television was introduced much later), and new (U.S.-made) programs began to specifically target children and youth. It was also the time when media were relocated from the family center stage into individual bedrooms. Whereas family life centered on the media in the oldest generation, and still somewhat in the middle generation, this had completely changed in the youngest generation, whose media environment was not only completely individualized, but also highly differentiated.

However, besides these common perceptions of similar media technologies, it also seems to be the case that media experiences have conveyed very particular entelechies *within* each of the three generations. Given the debate of place and space in globalization theory, I would argue that these categories define the world perception of each of the three generations, however with varying meanings. The oldest generation can be described as a place-based generation, where physical presence and identity are bound to a geographical lifeworld context (almost referring to Harold Innis' [1991] terminology of time- and space-based cultures). However, this oldest generation also experienced their own entelechy of space through a limited amount of media, which allowed occasional views into an outside world.

The youngest generation, however, can be described as a space-based generation, where the physical place is less important than the virtual presence. It can also be argued that within this generation, the place-world is defined through the space-world perception.

Based on our results, this distinctive difference can be described by the example of the generational-specific entelechy of distance and proximity. In the following, I illustrate these points by using examples of the three generational world perceptions. I will compare the Australian, German, Indian, and Mexican results of our project.

Entelechy: Distance and Proximity

I would argue that each of the three generations perceives a very particular notion of place and space. In the oldest group, space is represented in very distinctive relations to the world, that is, international events and news. Within each of the countries, however, this place-space relation is different.

For the German focus group of the oldest generation, the radio represented the main medium of Nazi propaganda. For this reason, the medium itself became an ideological world. Although this oldest-age cohort does not recall direct access to political propaganda in their childhood, they clearly recall the music, which was used as the lead-in to the daily Wehrmacht report. The focus group remembers Liszt's *Le Prelude* as well as the lead-in image, an eagle, to the newsreel reports in movie theaters. Within this closed political news infrastructure, remembered events were not political, but rather human-interest stories, for instance sport events, or international events that obviously passed the censorship.

The male focus-group members particularly recalled details of a variety of sports events, which took place internationally but in which successful German champions participated, such as the famous German boxer of those days, Max Schmeling. As one individual recalled:

> My father woke me up in the middle of the night and we went to an uncle to listen to the radio. The most fascinating thing for me as a child was to be woken up by my father in the middle of the night, and then to listen together. The tone was quite unclear and a lot of noise disturbed the reception . . . and then the imagination that this happened far away in New York, and we were able to listen live what was going on. (30)

This sporting event was one of the rare occasions when the Nazi propaganda system allowed a glimpse into the outside world. This German age cohort grew up in an otherwise closed, news vacuum, as one individual stated: "when U.S. forces dropped leaflets after the capitulation, which read, 'It will be over soon,' all of the sudden the whole world opened up."

In Australia, the radio was primarily a medium for national affairs. However it also had a significant role as a communication channel for the mother country, Great Britain. The dialectical space between distance and proximity was close, and was viewed under a broad framework of Commonwealth values and culture.

The oldest Mexican focus group recalled a quite different sense of dialectic between distance and proximity. Due to its proximity to the U.S., Mexico had already experienced a communication revolution. As one Mexican recalled: " . . . it was the time when the influence of communication exploded . . . it was then, when cars actually began to cross Mexico . . . going to Acapulco was a two-day journey, there were no telephones, telegraph, or highways in many places . . . suddenly, communication began, and it began to change the people's mentality" (See Maass p. 142 in this volume).

Radio was integrated into these new symbolic worlds of U.S. movies and music. The family listened to radio novellas together and by doing this, shared the symbolic spaces, and but also the notion of distance. Beyond this new symbolic world, influenced by U.S. media, access to other international programs was only possible through amateur radio receivers: "We built the receiver. At three in the morning, we were connected to see if we could hear Argentina, Spain, Cuba . . . to us, that was a marvel" (18).

Whereas the German cohort experienced a "closed" ideological world, the Mexican cohort had access to cultural images that were contrary to their own, which had an impact on identity within this generation.

In India, the radio was also regarded as a centerpiece of the media world. However, in terms of distance and proximity, it was perceived as a voice of the colonial government. As expressed by Kumar in the chapter on India, listening "was a social experience, associated with important political events, such as the end of World War II, and Mahatma Gandhi's assassination. Social experience meant: to listen with around ten other people, family and neighbors." (See Kumar, p.99 in this volume)

In Australia, international news flow within the oldest generation was limited, due to technological limitations, or political ideology. However, if political news was remembered, it was highly explicit, and involved an almost "homogenous" collective meaning. Although the radio was perceived as the key medium, international events were in many cases remembered in pictorial images, such as detailed images of WWII. As one Australian stated: "I can remember a picture of the front page of the *Advertiser* that I have never forgotten. It was a picture of an Australian airman with his hands tied behind his back, beheaded by the Japanese." (See Slade, p. 25 in this volume)

In Germany, Australia, and Mexico, distance and proximity were defined through a distinct relation to the U.S.A in the middle generation. In these countries, the middle cohort grew up with American mass media, which created a transnational youth culture, based on movies, TV programs, Disney cartoons and characters (such as "Fury" and "Lassie") as well as rock music, which was sometimes translated and reformatted for local cultures. Categories of distance and proximity were reversed in this cohort. The U.S. media, with its pop-culture content, provided proximity and the indigenous culture provided notions of distance.

The Vietnam War and the related student protests formed a political identity. These events created a new generational-defining dialectical space between the experienced proximity to the U.S. and the distance to the unfolding political conflict. As a member of the German focus group stated: "I think I was twelve years or so. . . . I thought it was just brutal, the police violence against protesting students . . . we have discussed all this during the family dinner, my father had a completely different opinion" (7).

This cohort has a much broader range of memories of international events than the oldest generation. Generation-defining events, that is, a common view of space in all countries involved, were the moon landing,

President Kennedy's assassination, the Vietnam War, and the OPEC crisis. These events, however, were mediated by national mass media. Another observation of this generation is that international political news not only served as information but also as a source in the process of defining an individual political identity—quite distinct from their parents.

In the youngest cohort, not only media but also notions of distance and proximity in this space-based generation seemed to be highly individualized. Typical for this generation is the statement of a Mexican: "I believe that you can identify much more with an Australian who is your age and who likes the music group you like, and who likes to ride a skate board like you, than your neighbor, who is Mexican, who is a guy that likes heavy metal rock . . . you can identify much more with someone from another country who is your age and has ideas like you, than with a Mexican, who not because he is Mexican, he is automatically your friend." (Maas, 2000)

Whereas, again, the Indian cohort had a very specific notion of distance and proximity, which is tied to Indian events and its relationship to Pakistan; in Australia, Germany, and Mexico, these categories seem to be reversed in the sense of being generationally specific: "Proximity" does not necessarily relate to the local culture, but to familiar "mediated" characters, personalities, and events.

Entelechy: Analogue and Digital Knowledge

In the youngest generation, media were viewed as a "seamless web" (see Slade, p.23 in this volume) without even knowing where events have been mediated. In this space-based "Network Generation," media merged and represented "background noise." It seems that our view of communication studies, as relating to particular media, should be overcome theoretically, by emphasizing the Web character and by defining new categories of media analysis.

What also become apparent when reviewing the results of this study is that the perception of the world, the memories of news and political events, were stated in very distinct formats in the oldest and the youngest generation. These findings could be related to the fact that the oldest generation still lived in a world as a place, where political information (and news) were embedded into the geographical place. In this process, the perception of the world is described in "analog" terms, i.e., as being embedded in the actual material world.

It can be stated that World War II dominated the news memory of the oldest generation in Australia and Germany. The Indian focus group recalled primarily national political events, and the Mexican group recalled those events that were related to the political tensions with the U.S. If events are recalled, they were recalled in great detail and in depth. Where news memories in the youngest generation were primarily associated with the media, news memories in the oldest generation were strongly associated with social circumstances and—this observation applies to all countries—tended to trigger elaborate descriptions, not so much of the media-related memories but of the social context. This could be described as "analogue knowledge." One reason for this detailed recall of structural news memory might be that national or regional political-news events often affected the immediate life-world context of the oldest generation. An example is a recollection of a member of the Indian focus group: "He recalled vividly the page layout of the *Lokshati* [a Marathi daily], which carried the news about the bomb explosion during a prayer meeting led by Gandhi. . . . He also remembered the tense situation in his hometown when Gandhi was arrested during the 'Quit India' movement. He recalled, how pamphlets were widely distributed" (7). (See Kumar, p.101 in this volume)

The German group also had very vivid memories of their immediate social circumstances in conjunction with important political events. One member described at length the social context when she heard of the death of Hindenburg in 1934: "My first media-related memory is the death of Hindenburg, all the lowered flags people had to hang outside their houses, I had never seen anything scary like that. I just returned home with my caretaker. My parents had traveled to Leipzig for some days. The caretaker's name was Christel and I asked 'What is going on?' All these lowered dark flags made me curious that something important has happened. And I asked Christel 'What has happened?' And she said 'Hindenburg has died' . . . of course I did not have a clue who Hindenburg was, but the whole atmosphere made me quite sad. Not so much that he had died, but that my parents were not there when all this happened and I was left alone with the caretaker" (31).

In Australia, war-related news had a strong impact because of strong pictorial and other media-induced images, as exemplified by the by the man who recalled the picture of the Australian airman who was beheaded by the Japanese.

In Mexico, WWII–related events were viewed from a distance. One Mexican remarked: " . . . we went to the movies two or three times a week . . . we were very interested in war adventures, in action . . . we watched the great stories of the atomic bomb, the end of the war, the beginning of the War in Abyssinia . . . all those stories were very vivid to me." (Maass, p.153 in this volume)

In this middle cohort, media-related political memories were already becoming less explicit and collective. Whereas the oldest generation in India mainly recalled national events, international news events were just as relevant to the middle cohort.

When memories were recalled (see Slade, p.26 in this volume), however, they were associated not only with lifeworld or social circumstances, as was the case in the oldest generation, but seemed to refer to what I would describe as a "cross-media reference." The references included other programs, print media, or radio, which seemed to have reinforced the memory and the importance of the event. Whereas in the oldest generation, lifeworld impressions provided the contextual atmosphere, which then reinforced memory—the media themselves seem to take this role for the middle cohort.

As can be observed in the Australian cohort, the memory of events was vague:

M:	I can remember quite a few from the Vietnam War, but not only the war but also the anti-war protests in North America, the Kent State University things. Those images are very strong.
C:	Can you remember the context of that memory, I mean, where, where you saw them?
M:	The napalm.
R:	The napalm.
Others:	Yeah, the napalm kid. Yeah. (See Slade, 26 in this volume)

It can be argued that this middle cohort had a strong collective memory of a small number of international subjects, which were remembered not so much in terms of social and cultural, that is, place-based perspectives, but because of their media-related aspects. They were recalled in very vague terms, representing the remembered media image.

One Indian stated: "International events? Especially, I remember Vietnam. Watergate, of course, but not much, but then I followed it up later on the BBC, when they telecast it just before the Clinton scandal; they had carried a series of shows on TV, as to how Watergate took place."

For this cohort, the political generational-defining events included the moon landing, President Kennedy's assassination, the Middle East conflict (including the terrorist attacks during the 1972 Olympics in Munich), and Vietnam. This generation grew up in a multimedia environment, but not in a multichannel environment. These events, aired live on public-service TV, had instantaneously a meaning of importance, which also created a certain cross-media atmosphere. As one German remembers the Kennedy assassination: "For instance, I remember a neighbor shouting, 'Kennedy is dead.

Kennedy is dead.' I was quite young and had the feeling of a catastrophe, which went on for days."

In the youngest space-based generation, memories tended to be deeply embedded into the media world itself, which also provided contexts and meaning. It seems, as a hypothesis, that media and news-related memories are recalled in "digital" terms, i.e., image-units, in many cases visual, which have a meaning in themselves, and can be viewed as fixed images. These findings illustrate the transformations from the world of international media to the Network Society.

The young shared almost no collective memories, except for spectacular events, such as O.J. Simpson's trial, the Clinton-Lewinsky affair, and Princess Diana's death. Whereas in the middle cohort, collective images were recalled by the reaction of their social context to media-related images, in this generation, the cross-media reference, the mediation of events, seemed to be complete: images of the above-mentioned events were recalled in an almost identical iconographic terminology. The Gulf War was recalled as a fragmented pictorial image, which reflected the simplistic and special-effect–type media coverage. The Gulf War was remembered as "tanks in the desert" by the German group, "firing missiles" by the Indian cohort, and all remembered the name of Saddam Hussein.

News seemed to be integrated into an overall entertainment flow, as just another entertainment format, as one Australian states:

B:	I listen to the radio all the time.
C:	So, you get news that way?
B:	Yep.
C:	On the hour or half hour or whatever?
B:	Yep.
C:	And what do you listen to?
B:	Triple J.
C:	They do news every.
B:	Every hour.
C:	Every hour. How long? A couple of minutes?
B:	Three to five minutes, I suppose. (See Slade, p.24 in this volume)

Media memories rarely trigger interaction within the social context. The only event, in this generation, which has—at least some—relation to social interaction, was Princess Diana's death. An example is this description by a German participant: "Ok, Lady Di. I don't know, I was lying in bed and my mother came rushing in . . . 'the woman is dead!' I couldn't believe it and then also Rammstein, these airplane crashes during an air show. I remember it clearly. We sat in front of the TV and they have shown all the pictures. I remember that" (32).

These generational entelechies have relevance for the dimension of the global public, the political symbolic territory, or the space of the global civil society.

Returning to our initial discussion of globalization segments, it seems that along with an extended media infrastructure and fresh coordinates for news and information flow, "world knowledge" and "world perception" have become particularly crucial aspects for defining the meaning of news and information in this new global sphere. I claim that these processes, within the political global space, unbalance conventional national public spheres. These processes alter established balance because they shape, on the individual level, political identities and notions of citizenship in a new political vacuum. World knowledge and world perception have an increasing influence on the balance between the global and the local, between universal and particular contexts, and between the longitudes and latitudes of a network infrastructure.

Although issues of collective memory have been discussed in social sciences for quite some time (see for instance, Middleton and Edwards, 1990), only a few studies have focused on the general issue of news memory, in conjunction with a cross-cultural reception analysis. Jensen and Mancini's (1998) study is an exception.

Jensen's research focused on the reconstruction of recent news, "news media" being understood as "sources of meaning that help to orient the distributed localized action of action of citizens, which, in the aggregate, constitutes political and other social institutions" (Jensen, 1998: 16). Our study also considered news (and news media) as a source of meaning, which is, however, closely tied into the symbolic lifeworld universe.

Based on this assumption, and given the transformation of the "global village" to a "network society" in recent years, the lifeworld universe has been colonized by (news) media with the consequence that the parameters of the "construction of meaning" (or the encoding and decoding processes) have changed.

Bibliography

Appadurai, Arjun (1990). "Disjuncture and Difference in the Global Cultural Economy." In *Global Culture: Nationalism, Globalization and Modernity*, ed. Mike Featherstone. London, Newbury Park, New Delhi: Sage.

Beck, Ulrich (1986). *Risikogesellschaft: Auf dem Weg in eine Andere Moderne. [Risk Society: On the Way to a Different Modernity].* Frankfurt/Main: Suhrkamp.

Castells, Manuel (1996). *The Rise of the Network Society.* Oxford, UK: Blackwell.

Dayan, Daniel, and Elihu Katz (1992). *Media Events: The Live Broadcasting of History.* Cambridge, MA: Harvard University Press.

Garnham, Nicholas (1999). "The Media and the Public Sphere." In *Habermas and the Public Sphere,* ed. Craig Calhoun. Cambridge, MA: MIT Press.

Giddens, Anthony (1990). *The Consequences of Modernity.* Cambridge, MA: Polity Press.

Hannerz, Ulf (1990). "Cosmopolitans and Locals in World Culture." In *Global Culture: Nationalism, Globalization, and Modernity,* ed. Mike Featherstone. London, Newbury Park, New Delhi: Sage.

Heidegger, Martin (1949). *Existence and Being.* Chicago: Regnery.

Husserl, Edmund and Richard Rojcewicz (editor and translator) (1997). *Thing and space: Lectures of 1907.* Dordrecht, Boston: Kluwer Academic Publishers.

Innis, Harold (1991). *The Bias of Communication.* Toronto: University of Toronto Press.

Jameson, Frederic, and Masao Miyoshi (1998). *The Cultures of Globalization.* Durham, NC: Duke University Press.

Jensen, Klaus Bruhn (1998). *News of the World: World Cultures Look at Television.* London: Routledge.

Kant, Immanuel (1795, 1881). *Zum Ewigen Frieden. [To Eternal Peace].* Leipzig: Reclam.

Maass, Morgarita (2000). Mexico. Paper on the Medjentorum Colojne. June 4–7.

Mannheim, Karl (1952). *Essays on the Sociology of Knowledge.* London: Routledge & Kegan Paul.

Middleton, David and Derek Edwards, eds. (1990). *Collective Remembering.* London, Newbury Park, New Delhi: Sage.

Robertson, Roland (1990). "Mapping the Global Condition: Globalization as the Central Concept." In *Global Culture: Nationalism, Globalization and Modernity,* ed. Mike Featherstone, 15–30. London, Newbury Park, New Delhi: Sage.

Robertson, Roland (1992). *Globalization: Social Theory and Global Culture.* London, Newbury Park, New Delhi: Sage.

Toennies, Ferdinand ([1887] 1963). *Gemeinschaft und Gesellschaft: Grundbegriffe der Reinen Soziologie. [Community and Society: Basic Terms of Pure Sociology]* Darmstadt: Wissenschaftliche Buchgesellschaft.

Tomlinson, John (1999). *Globalization and Culture.* Cambridge, MA: Polity Press.

Volkmer, Ingrid (1999). *News in the Global Sphere: A Study of CNN and Its Impact on Global Communication.* Luton, UK: University of Luton Press, John Libbey.

Volkmer, Ingrid (2002). "Towards a New World News Order? Journalism and Political Crises in the Global Network Society." In *Journalism after September 11*, eds. Stuart Allen and Barbie Zelizer. London, UK: Routledge.

Wallerstein, Immanuel (1974). *The Modern World-System*. New York: Academic Press.

Wiley, Stephen B. Crofts (2004). "Rethinking Nationality in the Context of Globalization." *Communication Theory*, February, 78–96.

Wilson, Rob and Wimal Dissanayake, eds. (1996). *Global Local: Cultural Production and the Transnational Imaginary*. Durham, NC: Duke University Press.

About the Authors

Thomas W. Bohn is Dean of the Roy H. Park School of Communications, Ithaca College, New York.

Andres Hofman is a student in the Master's Program in Communication Studies at Iberoamericana University, Mexico City, Mexico

Theo Hug is Associate Professor of Educational Science and Media Education at Innsbruck University, Austria. He is also Head of the Research Studio eLearning Environments, Research Studios Austria.

Jan Jirak is Associated Professor at the Department of Media Studies at the Faculty of Social Sciences and its Centre for Media Studies, Charles University, Prague, Czech Republic. He is author of the project of media education adopted by Czech educational system and co-author of textbooks of media studies and media theory.

Keval J. Kumar is Professor and Director at the Symbiosis Institute of Mass Communication, Pune, India. He retired from the University of Pune in early 2003. He was Visiting Professor at the University of Siegen, Germany, prior to his joining Symbiosis. He has also taught at Ohio State University, Bombay University and the Bahrain Training Institute. He is the current President of the Media Education Research Section, International Association of Media and Communication Research (IAMCR).

Margarita Maass Moreno has been Head of Communication B.A. (1997–1999) in the Faculty of Communication in Iberoamericana University, Mexico City, Mexico. where she has also been a member of the Interdisciplinary Research Division (1999–2003). She is a founding member of LabCOMplex (Laboratarorio de Comunicación Compleja), at UNAM (Universidad National Autónoma de México).

Matthew D. Payne is an independent radio and film producer, Secretary to the Board of the Association of Independents in Radio, and Coordinating Producer and Marketing Manager of Murray Street Productions in New York City. A graduate of Ithaca College's Roy H. Park School of Communications.

Daniela Rivera is a student in the Master's Program in Communication Studies at Iberoamericana University, Mexico City, Mexico

Gebhard Rusch teaches since 1991 at the Institute for the Empirical Study of Literature and the Media (LUMIS), and since 2002 at the Institute of Media Research, University of Siegen, Germany.

Reiko Sekiguchi is Professor at Otsuma University, Tokyo, Japan. She taught at Toshokan Joho University; at Kyoto University, Japan, and at the University of Calgary, at Winser University, Canada. She was the Acting Director of the Centre for the Teaching of Japanese Language and Culture of the University of Alberta, Canada, in 2000.

Christina Slade is Professor and Dean of Humanities at Macquarie University, Syndey, Australia. She has taught at the University of Canberra in the Faculty of Communication, at New York University in the Department of Culture and Communication and at La Universidad Ibero Americana and the ITESM, Xochimilco in Mexico City. She is currently Professor of Media Theory, University of Utrecht, the Netherlands. She has published widely on issues of philosophy of communication, such as *The Real Thing. Doing Philosophy with Media.* New York: Peter Lang, 2002.

Jill Dianne Swenson has been Associate Professor in the Roy H. Park School of Communications, Ithaca College, New York. She has held faculty positions at University of Georgia, University of Wisconsin and University of Chicago. She is now retired.

Ruth Teer-Tomaselli is Professor at the Department of Cultural and Media Studies of the University of Natal, Durban, South Africa. She is a member of the Board of Directors of the South African Radio Station SABC and has contributed significantly to the renewal of Public Broadcasting's concept. She is also UNESCO Chair.

Ingrid Volkmer has been Professor of Media Studies in Germany and teaches now at the University of Otago, New Zealand. She is also Fellow at the Amsterdam School of Communication Research, Universiteit van Amsterdam, the Netherlands and has been Fellow at the John F. Kennedy School of Government, Harvard University. She is Associate Editor of the Encyclopedia Globalization (Routledge) and on the Editorial Board of the Journal Global Media & Communications (Sage).

Tables of Focus Groups

Australia

Australia—Table 1: Cohort 1 (70–75)

Name	Age	Gender	Place of Birth	Parents' Occupation	Family	Education	Media Equipment
Georgie	75	F	Port Pirie, S.A.	Father: Teacher, Mother: Housewife	2 females 2 males	Tertiary	1 radio, papers
James	75	M	Adelaide, S.A.	Father: Civil Servant Mother: Housewife	1 male 2 females	Tertiary	1 radio, crystal set, papers
Hilda	74	F	Adelaide, S.A.	Father: Senior Manager Mother: Housewife (died while H was young)	1 female	Tertiary	1 radio, papers
Charles	72	M	Adelaide, S.A.	Father: Businessman Stepfather: Architect Mother: Housewife	1 male 1 female	Tertiary	1 radio, papers, crystal set
Eva	73	F	Adelaide, S.A.	Father: Civil Servant Mother: Housewife	1 male 2 females	Secondary	1 radio, papers, crystal set
Donald	75	M	Adelaide, S.A.	Father: Farmer Mother: Housewife	2 males 1 female	Secondary *military	1 radio, connected through grand-parents' papers, crystal set

Australia—Table 2: Cohort 2 (40–45)

Name	Age	Gender	Place of Birth	Parents' Occupation	Family	Education	Media Equipment
Ric	45	M	Bateman's Bay	Father: Fisherman Mother: Housewife	1 male 1 female	Tertiary	first TV in street, radio, crystal set
Anna	45	F	Young	Father: Teacher Mother: Housewife	1	Tertiary	radio, papers
Mat	42	M	Perth	Father: Accountant Mother: Housewife	6 children	Tertiary	TV, radios
Meg	43	F	Sydney	Father: (n.a.) Mother: Housewife	1 male 1 female	Secondary	TV (first in street), radios
Bill	40	M	Sydney	Father: (n.a.) Mother: Housewife	1 male 1 female	Tertiary	TV, radios
Belinda	43	F	Sydney	Father: (n.a.) Mother: Housewife		Secondary	TV, radios

Australia—Table 3: Cohort 3 (15–20)

Name	Age	Gender	Place of Birth	Parents' Occupation	Family	Education	Media Equipment
Esther	15	F	Canberra	Father: Civil Servant Mother: Academic	1 male 1 female	At School	2 TV's, 4 Computer, Internet 4 radios, papers
John	15	M	Adelaide	Father: Teacher Mother: Veterinarian	3 males	At School	4 TV's, 4 computer, Internet many radios, papers

Australia—Table 3 *(continued)*

Beth	19	F	Adelaide	Father: (has died) Mother: Legal Secretary	2 females 1 male	University	2 TV's 1 computer many radios, papers
Jill	15	F	Adelaide	Father: Bus Inspector Mother: Housewife		At School	2 TV's, computer, many radios, papers
Sam	16	M	Adelaide	Father: Consultant Mother: Travel Agent	2 males 2 females	At School	2 TV's, computer, many radios, papers
Adam	15	M	Adelaide	Father: Fireman, Mother: Nurse	1 female 2 males	At School	2 TV's 2 computer many radios, papers

Austria

Austria—Table 1: Cohort 1 (70–75)

Name	Age	Gender	Place of Birth	Family Structure	Education	Media Equipment
Anna	70	female	Innsbruck	five children,	College	Radio, newspaper
Helga	71	female	Innsbruck	Only child	Business College	two radios, newspaper
Sabine	74	female	Innsbruck	two children	Teacher College	radio, newspaper
Albert	73	male	Innsbruck	seven siblings.	apprenticeship	Radio, newspaper

Austria—Table 1 *(continued)*

Bernd	70	male	Innsbruck	six children,	College	Radio, newspaper
Robert	70	male	Innsbruck	father and mother, no siblings	Teacher College	Radio, newspaper

Austria—Table 2: Cohort 2 (40–45)

Name	Age	Gender	Place of Birth	Family Structure	Education	Media Equipment
Beate	45	female	Innsbruck	(n.a.)	Business College	radios, newspaper
Andrea	43	female	Innsbruck	(n.a.)	Academy	radio
Paul	41	male	Innsbruck	one brother	College	TV, radios, newspaper, stereo set, record player, tape recorder
Markus	41	male	Innsbruck	one brother and one sister	Academy	radio, newspaper
Maria	44	female	Innsbruck	one sister	Apprenticeship	Radio, Newspaper, record player
Christian	40	male	Vöcklabruck	one sister	Academy	TV, radios newspaper, record player

Austria—Table 3: Cohort 3 (15–20)

Name	Age	Gender	Place of Birth	Family Structure	Education	Media Equipment (in the first ten years)
Beatrix	17	female	Innsbruck	three children	At School	three TV sets, six radios, newspaper; two computers (without Internet access); video recorder; cell phone; stereo set; gameboy; tape recorder; tamagochi
Christa	16	female	Innsbruck	three children	At School	TV, five radios, newspaper, one computer (without Internet access); video recorder; cell phone; stereo set, tape recorder, video games, gameboy
Nora	19	female	Innsbruck	five children	Apprenticeship	one TV set five radios, newspaper, two gameboys, record player, tape recorder, stereo set, walkman

Austria—Table 3 *(continued)*

Anton	16	male	Innsbruck	one child	At School	one TV set, five radios: newspapers, tape recorder; stereo set; record player
Bernd	17	male	Innsbruck	two children,	vocational school	two TV sets, four radios newspaper;
Paul	16	male	Innsbruck	he has three older brothers and one younger sister	vocational school	One TV set, five radios, newspapers, one computer (without Internet access), game-boy, stereo set

Germany

Germany—Table 1: Cohort 1 (70–75)

Name	Age	Gender	Place of Birth	Parents' Occupation	Family	Education	Media Equipment
Ursula		female	Mikultczyce, Silesia, Ger-many		Five siblings	High School Degree	Radio, news-paper, journals for chil-dren, books, newspaper, cinema
Irene		female	Barcelona, Spain	Father: Manager Mother: (n.a.)	Three siblings	High School Degree	Radio, books, gram-phone

Germany—Table 1 *(continued)*

Erwin	male	Ostpom-mern		1 sister	University	radio, newsreel, newspaper, books
Karin	female	Jena		five siblings	College	newspaper, books, gram-phone, radio
Klaus	male	Wuppertal,		father, mother and son	University	radio, newsreel, movie detector, news-paper, books, gram-phone
Martin	male	Hannover	Father: Professor	two brothers and one sister	University	radio, cinema, journals, books, magazines, gram-phone

Germany—Table 2: Cohort 2 (40–45)

Name	Age	Gender	Place of Birth	Parents' Occupation	Family	Education	Media Equipment
Jan	43	male	Detmold	Father: Butcher Mother: (n.a.)	three children	University	books, tape recorder, record player, TV, new-paper, radio
Susanne	39	female	Bielefeld		Only child	University	TV, books, tape recorder,

Germany—Table 2 *(continued)*

Name	Age	Gender	Place of Birth	Parents' Occupation	Family	Education	Media Equipment
							record player
Ulrich	43	male	Detmold	Father: Civil Servant, Mother: Housewife	a younger sister	University	transistor radio, tape recorder, books, record player, TV, cinema, journals, newspaper
Claudia	41	female	Bielefeld	Father: (n. .a.)	Only child	University	Tape recorder., radio, books, TV, news-paper, cinema
Angela	39	female	Bielefeld,	Father: Entrepreneur, Farmer Mother: Housewife	one elder sister	University	Radio, tape recorder, TV, books, newspaper
Mark	43	male	Duisburg,	Father: Manager	two younger sisters	College	radio, TV, record player, computer, daily news-paper, xxbooks

Germany—Table 3: Cohort 3 (15–20)

Name	Age	Gender	Place of Birth	Parents' Occupation	Family	Education	Media Equipment
Katarina	16	female	Rheda-Wieden-brück	Father: Joiner, Mother: Teacher	one brother	At School	TV, tape recorder, stereo set, PC

Germany—Table 3 *(continued)*

Kristina	17	female	Rheda-Wieden-brück,	Father: Trader; Mother: Pharmaceutical Assistant	2 elder siblings	At School	TV, stereo, tape recorder, comics, movies, video recorder
Andre	17	male	Rheda-Wieden-brück,	Father: Physicist, Mother: Housewife	2 elder siblings	At School	TV, tape recorder, Comics, PC and stereo set
Dirk	18	male	Rheda-Wieden-brück,	Father: Manager, Mother: Housewife	2 younger	At School	Tape recorder TV, Comics
Marcel	18	male	Rheda-Wieden-brück,	Father: Manager, Mother: Business Assistant	Only child	At School	TV, Comics, Video
Niklas	17	female	Rheda-Wieden-brück,	Father: Business-man,	Two younger siblings	At School	Tape recorder, Comics, 4 TV sets, 4 stereo sets, 4 PCs, 2 cell phones

India

India—Table 1: Cohort 1 (70–75)

Name	Age	Gender	Place of Birth	Mother Tongue	Religion	Education	Media Equipment
Chavan	70	M	Pune	Marathi	Hindu (Brahmin)	Graduate	News-papers, folk media

India—Table 1 *(continued)*

Dandekar	77	M	Pune	Marathi	Hindu (Brahmin)	Graduate	News-papers, folk media
Kamla	75	F	Pune	Marathi	Hindu (Brahmin)	High School	News-papers, folk media
Seema	75	F	Pune	Marathi	Hindu (Brahmin)	Graduate	News-papers, folk media
Joshi	71	M	Pune	Marathi	Hindu (Brahmin)	Graduate	News-papers, folk media
Vaidya	78	M	Pune	Marathi	Hindu (Brahmin)	High School	News-papers, folk media

India/Bahrain—Table 2: Cohort 2 (40–45)

Name	Age	Gender	Place of Birth	Mother Tongue	Religion	Education	Media Equipment
John	44	M	Cochin	Malayalam	Christian	Ph.D.	News-papers, magazines, radio
Khan	43	M	Bangalore	Kannada	Muslim	Ph.D.	News-papers, magazines, radio
Shoba	40	F	Bangalore	Kannada	Hindu	Post-Graduate	News-papers, magazines, radio
Uday	45	M	Bangalore	Kannada	Hindu	Post-graduate	News-papers, magazines, radios

India—Table 3: Cohort 3 (15–20)

Name	Age	Gender	Place of Birth	Mother Tongue	Religion	Education	Media Equipment
Dev	19	M	New Delhi	Panjabi	Sikh	Under-graduate graduate Student (Law)	News-papers, TV, radio, Internet
Yashwant	19	M	Calcutta	Bengali	Hindu	Under-graduate Student (Commerce)	News-papers, TV, radio, Internet
Meeta	19	F	Calcutta	Bengali	Hindu	Under-graduate Student (Law)	News-papers, radio, TV, Internet
Nabo	18	F	Calcutta	Bengali	Hindu	Under-graduate Student (Commerce)	News-papers, radio, TV, Internet,
Marie	18	F	Jamshedpur	English	Christian/Roman	Under-graduate Student (Commerce)	News-papers, radio, TV, Internet

Japan

Japan—Table 1: Cohort 1 (70–75)

Name	Age	Gender	Place of Birth	Parents' Occupation	Family	Education	Media Equipment
Morio	70's	male	city	Father: Farmer Mother: Housewife	Extended family, multiple siblings	8-year elementary school	News-paper, radio, movie
Sadao	70's	male	city	Father: Farmer Mother: Housewife	Nuclear family, multiple siblings	8-year elementary school	News-paper, radio, movie

Japan—Table 1 *(continued)*

Yoshio	70's	male	city	Father: Farmer Mother: Housewife	Nuclear family, multiple siblings	8-year elementary school	News-paper, radio, movie
Chicko	70's	female	city	Father: Farmer Mother: Housewife	Nuclear family, Multiple siblings	Secondary school	News-paper, radio, movie
Motoe	70's	female	village	Father/ Mother Shop-keeper	Nuclear Family, Multiple siblings	Secondary school	News-paper, radio, movie
Kimie	70's	female	village	Father/ Mother Shop-keeper	Nuclear Family, Multiple siblings	Post-secondary school	news-paper

Japan—Table 2: Cohort 2 (40–45)

Name	Age	Gender	Place of Birth	Parents' Occupation	Family	Education	Media Equipment
Jiro	40's	male	city	Father/ Mother: Farmer	Three-gene-rational family	Post-secondary	News-paper, TV, radio
Taro	40's	male	city	Father/ Mother: Farmer	Three-gene-rational family	Post-secondary	News-paper, TV, radio
Kazuo	40's	male	city	Father/ Mother: Farmer	Three-gene-rational family	Post-secondary	News-paper, TV, radio
Ginko	40's	female	city	(n.a.)	Nuclear family 2–4 siblings	Post-secondary	News-paper, TV, radio

Japan—Table 2 *(continued)*

| Hisako | 40's | female | city | (n.a.) | Nuclear family 2–4 siblings | Post-secondary | News-paper, TV, radio |
| Ikuko | 40's | female | town | (n.a.) | Nuclear family 2–4 siblings | secondary | News-paper, TV, radio |

Japan—Table 3: Cohort 3 (15–20)

Name	Age	Gender	Place of Birth	Parents' Occupation	Family	Education	Media Equipment
Umeo	17	male	city	Father: Doctor Mother: Housewife	Nuclear family	At School	News-paper, muliple TV sets, multiple radio,
Kunio	17	male	city	Father: Doctor Mother: Housewife	Nuclear family	At School	News-paper, muliple TV sets, multiple radio,
Nobuo	17	male	city	Father: Civil Servant Mother: Housewife	Nuclear family	At School	News-paper, muliple TV sets, multiple radio, Internet
Itsue	17	female	city	Father: Doctor Mother: (n.a.)	Nuclear family	At School	News-paper, muliple TV sets, multiple radio,
Kiyoe	17	female	city	Father: Civil Servant Mother: (n.a.)	Nuclear family	At School	News-paper, muliple TV sets, multiple radio,

Japan—Table 3 *(continued)*

Ochie	17	female	city	Father: Company Employee Mother: (n.a.)	Nuclear family	At School	News-paper, muliple TV sets, multi-ple radio,

Mexico

Mexico—Table 1: Cohort 1 (70–75)

Name	Age	Gender	Place of Birth	Parents' Occupation	Family	Education	Media Equipment
Gloria	70	F	Monterrey, Nuevo León	Father: Merchant Mother: (has died)	Only Child	Tertiary	1 radio, books, papers
Guada-lupe	74	F	México D.F.	Father: Business-man,	4 males 4 females	Tertiary	Books
Roberto	75	M	Habana Cuba	Father: Engineer Mother: Housewife	2 males and 1 female R. eldest	Doctor	2 radios, books, papers
Teodoro	71	M	México D.F.	Father: Employee Mother: Housewife	2 males T. is eldest	Engineer	1 radio, books, papers
Eduardo	73	M	México D.F.	Father: Engineer Mother: Housewife	2 males and 1 female E. is 2nd.	Engineer	2 radios, books, papers
Rebeca	71	F	Saltillo, Coahuila	Father: Auditor, Mother: Housewife	1 male and 1 female R is eldest	Tertiary	1 radio, books, papers

Mexico—Table 2: Cohort 2 (40–45)

Name	Age	Gender	Place of Birth	Parents' Occupation	Family	Education	Media Equipment
Rebeca	41	F	Saltillo, Coahuila	Father: Auditor, Mother: Housewife	1 male and 1 female R is eldest	Tertiary	1 radio, books, papers
Teresa	40	F	México D.F.	Father: Physician	1 male and 5	University	1 radio, 1 TV,
				Mother: Housewife	female		books, papers
Gilberto	46	M	México D.F.	Father: Businessman Mother: Housewife	2 males and 2 females	University	1 radio, 1 TV,
Lilly	45	F	México D.F.	Father: Engineer Mother: Housewife	2 males and 1 female	University Art.	1 radio, 1 TV, books, and papers
Elsa	41	F	México D.F. 15	Father: Employee Mother: Merchant	2 females	University	1 radio, 1 TV, books, and papers
Rafael	40	M	México D.F.	Father: Professional Mother: Housewife	2 males and 1 female	University	1 radio, 1 TV, books, and papers
Román	41	M	Necaxa, Veracruz	Father: Employee Mother: Housewife	3 males	University	1 TV, books, and papers

Mexico—Table 2 *(continued)*

Mexico—Table 3: Cohort 3 (15–20)

Name	Age	Gender	Place of Birth	Parents' Occupation	Family	Education	Media Equipment
Monse-rrat	20	F	Chile	Father: (has died) Mother: Professional	2 females M. Is the first	University Law	Television, video, radio, computer, Internet, papers
Carlos	20	M	México	Father: Professional Mother: Housewife (divorced)	1 male and 1 female	University	Television, video, radio, computer, Internet, papers

Mexico—Table 3 *(continued)*

Name	Age	Gender	Place of Birth	Parents' Occupation	Family	Education	Media Equipment
Facundo	20	M	Argentina	Father: Professional Mother: Merchant (divorced)	2 males	University. Advertis-ing,	Tele-vision, radio, computer, Internet, papers, nintendo
Esmer-alda	19	F	México	Father: Employee Mother: Housewife	1 female 2 males	University Advertising	Television, video, radio, computer, Internet, papers
Ana Luisa	16	F	Chile	Father: (has died) Mother professional	2 females	Preparatory School	Television video, radio, computer, Internet

South Africa

South Africa—Table 1: Cohort 1 (70–75)

Name	Age	Gender	Place of Birth	Parents' Occupation	Family	Education	Media Equipment
Joseph	75	male	Johannes-burg	Father: Manu-facturer's representative; M: Housewife	1 male 1 female	Secondary	radio, cinema, news-papers
George	70	male	Durban	Father: Bricklayer Mother: deceased young.	Only child	Primary military	No radio until the war, news-papers
Mary	70	female	Durban	F: Clerk M: House-wife	2 females 1 male	Secondary	2 x news-papers, radio, cinema
Joyce	72	male	Hiedleberg (Transvaal)	Father: Motor-garage owner, Mother: (n.a.)	3 females	Tertiary	Many news-papers, radio, imported magazines
Dawid	73	male	Vryheid (Natal)	Father: Farmer Mother: Teacher	2 females 3 males	Tertiary	Battery-powered radio, news-paper
Stuart	74	male	Belfast (Natal)	Father: Diary Farmer M: Housewife	1 male 2 females	Secondary	Wind-powered radio, news-papers, imported magazines
Herm-anus	72	male	Greytown (Natal)	Father: Farmer Mother: Nursing sister	3 males	Secondary	Radio, news-paper

South Africa—Table 1 *(continued)*

Cornelia	70	female	Durban	Father: Electrician Mother Hairdresser	3 males 1 female	Secondary	Radio, news- papers

South Africa—Table 2: Cohort 2 (40–45)

Name	Age	Gender	Place of Birth	Parents' Occupation	Family	Education	Media Equipment
Charles	45	male	Durban	Father: High School Principal Mother: High School Teacher	2 female 1 male	Tertiary	news- papers, radio, magazines, cinema
Paul	40	male	Johannes- burg (Transvaal)	Father: Bank teller Mother: Administrative Clerk	1 female 1 male	Tertiary	news- papers, radio magazines cinema
Edward	45	male	Stilfontein (Transvaal)	Father: Miner Mother: Housewife	3 females 1 male	Tertiary	news- papers, radio, magazines, cinema
Gray	45	male	Johannes- burg (Transvaal)	Father: Professor Mother: Housewife	2 males 1 female	Tertiary	news- papers, radio, magazines, cinema
Nancy	44	female	Durban	Father: Carpenter Mother: School Principal	2 females	Secondary	news- papers, radio, magazines, cinema
Jimmy	45	male	Durban, boarding School in Kimberley (Northern	Father: Business- man Mother: Housewife	Only child	Tertiary	Daily and weekly news- papers, radio,

South Africa—Table 2 *(continued)*

			Cape)				magazines, cinema
Mavis	40	male	KwaMashu (near Durban)	Father: Delivery Driver Mother: Factory Worker	3 males 2 females	Secondary	Radio, news-papers
Lindiwe	41	female	Emangani (northern Natal)	Father: School Teacher Mother: Nurse	3 females, 1 male	Secondary	Radio, news-papers

South Africa—Table 3: Cohort 3 (15–20)

Name	Age	Gender	Place of Birth	Parents' Occupation	Family	Education	Media Equipment
Janey	17	Female	Durban	Father: Insurance Executive Mother: Dressmaker	1 male 1 female	(n.a.)	Radio, satellite television, Internet
Kumi	16	Female	Durban	Father: Clerical administrator (retired) Mother: Housewife	3 females 4 males		Radio, satellite television
David	17	male	Durban	Father: Academic Mother: teacher	2 males		Radio, satellite television, Internet
Thokoza	17	Female	Durban	Father: Taxi Owner/ Driver Mother: domestic worker	3 female, 2 2male		Radio, FTA tele-vision
Jacinta	18	F	Grahams-town (Eastern Cape)	Father: Academic Mother:	1 male, 1 female		satellite television radio Internet

South Africa—Table 3 *(continued)*

Baree	16	M	Durban	Father: Computer Programmer Mother: Housewife	2 female 1 male	satellite television, radio, Internet
Mark	17	M	Vryheid (Natal)	Father: Tiler (build-ing trade) Mother: Housewife.	5 males	radio, television
Sanjev	16	M	Durban	Father: Marketing Representative Mother: Housewife.	2 males only	radio, satellite television
Bongi	18	F	Empangeni (Natal)	Father: Postal Clerk Mother: Factory Worker	2 female 2 male	radio, television

USA

USA—Table 1: Cohort 1 (70–75)

Name	Age	Gender	Place of Birth	Parents' Occupation	Family	Education	Media Equipment
Gertrude	74	Female	Wellsboro, PA (RURAL)	Mother: Farmer	1 older brother	High School	Radio, comm-unity movie theatre
James	72	Male	Buffalo, New York (URBAN)	(n.a.)	1 sister	College	Radio, news-papers, weekly movie
Robert	75	Male	Rural North Carolina	Mother and Father: Farmers	multiple siblings;	College	Phono-graph, news-paper, radio

USA—Table 1 *(continued)*

Jason	73	Male	Brooklyn, New York	(n.a.)	3 siblings	College	Radio, news-papers
Michelle	73	Female	Montreal, Canada	n.a.	multiple siblings	College	Radio, movies
Kath-leen	74	Female	Cape Cod	Father: Telegrapher Phonograph	only child	College	Radio, news-paper,

USA—Table 2: Cohort 2 (40–45)

Name	Age	Gender	Place of Birth	Parents' Occupation	Family	Education	Media Equipment
Gwen	43	Female	Central New Jersey State	N/A	2 sisters	College	Record player, TV, books, news-papers, magazine
Steve	41	Male	Concord, Mass-achusetts	Father Professor	2 older sisters	College	Stereo set and amp-lifier; TV, books, news-papers, magazines
Julie	42	Female	Pittsburgh, Penn.	N/A	only child	College	TV, radio, stereo and amps; news-papers and magazines
Tom	42	Male	Tompkins County, New York	Father: Machinist Mother: Homemaker	8 Siblings;	High School	Radio, TV cinema
Sally	43	Female	Ithaca, New York	(n.a.)	1 brother	College	Record Player, TV, Radio; Drive-In Movies

JUSA—Table 2 (continued)

| essica | 44 | Female | Newton Center, Massa- chusetts | Father: Foreign Service Mother: Homemaker | 2 sisters | College | TV, radio, books |

USA—Table 3: Cohort 3 (15–20)

Name	Age	Gender	Place of Birth	Parents' Occupation	Family	Education	Media Equipment
Bree	16	Female	Ithaca, New York	(n.a.)	younger brother, older sister	At School	Computer with Internet; VHS play- ers, multi- ple TV sets; stereo with CDs; multiple papers and magazines
Lind- sey	17	Female	Ithaca, New York	(n.a.)	older brother	At School	Computer with Internet; VHS play- ers, multi- ple TV sets; Stereo with CDs; multiple papers and magazines
Simon	17	Male	Ithaca, New York	Father: College Professor Mother: Computer Sales	2 brothers	At School	Computer with Internet; VHS players, multiple TV sets, stereo with CDs; mul- tiple papers and magazines

USA—Table 3 *(continued)*

Chris	17	Male	Ithaca, New York	Father: College Administrator Mother: Homemaker	1 brother 2 half-	At School	Computer with Internet; VHS players, multiple TV sets, stereo with CDs; multiple papers and magazines
Kathie	18	Female	New Jersey; England; Seattle; Ithaca, New York	Father: Satellite Launch Engineer Mother: Homemaker	older sister; younger brother	At School	Computer with Internet; VHS players, multiple

USA—Table 3 *(continued)*

				Mother: School Librarian			TV sets, stereo with CDs; multiple papers and magazines
Roy	17	Male	Rural Central Penn.; Ithaca, New York	Father: Nursing Home Administrator Mother: Teacher	older brother	At School	Computer with Internet; VHS players; multiple papers and magazines

Notes

Notes to Australia—Christina Slade

1. I refer here to the admirable summary made by Toby Miller in his chapter, "Radio" in *The Media in Australia: Industries, Texts, Audiences,* ed. S. Cunningham & G. Turner, 47–69 (Sydney: Allen & Unwin 1997).
2. Canberra has roughly 300,000 inhabitants and Adelaide one million. In the 2001 census, more than 50 percent of Canberra residents had a home computer and more than 60 percent had used the Internet in the previous week.
3. This may be a failure in the choice of category—student protest was a far wider category than some of the others. However, the outbreak of WWII is similarly broad, yet most of the senior cohort remembered specifically hearing it on the radio.
4. In Australia, the bombings in Bali on October 12, 2002, had an even greater impact, bringing terrorism home.
5. We can find this view in Poster (1994: 177–178); Postman, passim; and Rushkoff (1997: 66), among others.

Notes to Austria—Theo Hug

1. RAVAG is an acronym for the company name "Österreichische Radio-Verkehrs-AG," or "Austrian Radio-Business-PLC."
2. In Vienna, the Americans and the British set up additional stations.
3. The first TV test programs were already broadcast in 1955.
4. For details, see http://www.media-analyse.at. Further details about the Austrian media landscape including aspects of media culture and media policy are discussed in Fabris & Luger (1988); Sieder, Steinert, and Tálos (1995); Geretschläger (1997); and Günther & Hüffel (1999).
5. All focus-group discussions took place in this town with the help of students. The exact dates are: February 17, 1999 (Cohort 3, 15–20 years old); March 18, 1999 (Cohort 2, 40–45 years old); and April 29, 1999 (Cohort 1, 70–75 years old); special thanks to Angelika Grabher, Daniela Löffler, Thomas Lotter, and Elke

Schratzer. For some pictures and basic information about the town, see http://www.innsbruck.at/.

6. Totzenhacker was a radio program that was broadcast for about 20 years, from the beginning of the '70s to the end of the '80s. During the program, people had the chance to tell about their readiness to help others in a certain situation or it was reported how people had done a favor for someone. These helpful acts were rewarded with a special *Totzen* called *hrentotzen*, a Totzen for honor. A kind of musical fanfare was played for the helper. Negative reports were mentioned and presented, too, as in, for instance, a quarrel between neighbors.

Notes to Czech Republic—Jan Jirák

1. The following overview is based mainly upon: Jirák, *Dejiny zemí koruny ceské II*, Praha: Paseka, 1992 (chapters 4–7); Kaplan, *Pravda o Ceskoslovensku 1945–1948*, Praha: Panorama, 1990; and Mencl et al., *Kri ovatky 20. století*, Praha: Naše vojsko, 1990.

2. We use here the expression "Soviet model" referring to "four theories of the press" (Siebert, Peterson, and Schramm, *Four Theories of the Press*. Urbana: University of Illinois Press, 1963), which is the desired role of media in totalitarian regimes.

3. The project "Media Generation 2000" was included into research activities of the Faculty of Social Sciences, Charles University. In cooperation with Barbara Köpplová, the Head of the Centre for Media Studies (CEMES), a seminar "Media Generation 2000" was established within the framework of the Media and Society course in spring semester 1998/1999. With the support of 12 master's students of media studies, a moderating guide was prepared, and finally three focus groups were arranged according to criteria discussed by international project group in spring 2000 and other two groups in the fall 2000. Students were divided into three teams, each responsible for one age group. Each question and each topic was tested in the class of bachelor students of journalism and in a special course for seniors offered to retired people. In fall 1999, the project with preliminary results was introduced to the academic board of the faculty of Social Sciences, Charles University, and was appreciated as a respectful topic and included into the research plans of the faculty. The official title of the research plan is "Czech Society at the Beginning of Third Millennium."

4. Titles for farmers were connected with the activities of the Farmer's Party (Agrární strana), a right-oriented political body, quite strong during the two decades between World War I and World War II.

5. *Rudé právo* daily was the party paper published by the Czechoslovak Communist Party. It was the biggest and probably the most influential paper

in the country. It was highly ideologized and was part of the propaganda system of the country.

6. *Lidová demokracie* daily was the party paper of Czechoslovak People's Party (which collaborated with the Communist Party within the postwar historical framework of the "National Front"). This party was supposedly more orientated toward religious people and developed into the Christian Democratic Party after 1989. *Vecerní Praha* daily was an evening regional paper published in Prague dealing mostly with local and regional events.

7. *Mladá fronta Dnes* daily (*Young Front Today*) is a descendant of a pre-1989 daily. Nowadays it is among the three biggest national daily newspapers according to circulation (with *Právo* and *Blesk*). *Mladá fronta Dnes* is a semi-tabloid medium with a heavy dose of political news, as well as a lot of infotainment. The daily probably belongs among few media in CR that can be characterized as opinion makers.

8. "Section" in this case is not a precise expression. A sports section or cultural (art) section is usually represented by 1–4 pages and is part of the main folder.

9. *Lidové noviny* daily is a traditional title that was reestablished in the late '80s as *samizdat* ["samizdat" is a common term for "illegally published title"—the word itself comes from Russian] and has become daily in the '90s. Nowadays it is a mixture of typical tabloid infotainment with some more intellectual weekly sections. The circulation is not very high but is increasing and the paper is popular mostly among inhabitants of Prague and some other big cities.

10. The necessity to save fuel was one of the most typical images of the oil crisis. It was part of the propaganda and its purpose was to show the instability of life in the West in comparison with the safe and stable situation in the East (where there was no shortage of fuel in that period).

Notes to Germany—Gebhard Rusch and Ingrid Volkmer

1. The German study of this international research project took place in Bielefeld, an industrial city in the northern part of Germany; in Siegen, a university town close to Cologne; and in Rheda-Wiedenbrück, a smaller town close to Bielefeld. The focus-group interviews of the oldest and the middle cohort were conducted in Bielefeld, and the session of the young cohort in Siegen and Rheda-Wiedenbrück. This study would not have been possible without the support and help of many students at the University of Siegen and the University of Augsburg. Ingrid Volkmer would like to thank in particular Florian Deffner, Daniel Erhardt, and Richard Rössler for their careful reviews of the quite extensive focus-group transcriptions; and Alexander Arndt, Anika Kimmerle, and Julia Knoller for their detailed research of his-

torical sources of different decades of media development in Germany. Gebhard Rusch owes thanks to Silvia Pillai and Henning Groscurth, University of Siegen, who substantially supported the focus-group data analyses. Both authors would like to thank all focus-group participants for their willingness to take the time and effort to participate in this research. Their candid and open remarks have provided this study with important insights.

2. This is a concept similar to the Volkswagen, which was introduced in Berlin at the Automobile Exhibition in 1936.

3. The first phase of internationalization began after WWII, when books, newspapers, records, and radio programs were brought into the divided Germany.

4. This term does not refer to Habermas's definition of "the public" as an ideal platform of rational discourse and debate with a democratic (modern) society (see Habermas, 1992). The term here refers to the general notion of the public in the sense of the public eye within a totalitarian state, not in the sense of free discourse. "Public" in this sense was perceived in the oldest focus group as having been distinct from the private family sphere, where debates were possible.

Notes to India—Keval J. Kumar

1. The focus group with the over-70-year-olds was conducted in Marathi by Vishram Dhole, lecturer in the Department of Communication Studies, Pune University. This section was written in collaboration with him.

2. The names of all participants in the focus-group discussions have been changed. However, suitable pseudonyms (first names only) have been selected so as to reflect the religious and community identities of the participants.

Notes to Japan—Reiko Sekiguchi

1. First names of interviewees are cited parenthetically.

2. Flooring. The floor of a room is covered with tatami like a carpet.

Notes to USA—Mathew D. Payne, Jill Dianne Swenson, and Thomas W. Bohn

1. The interaction of lifeworld and mediaworld will be looked at repeatedly during the course of this paper. Lifeworld can be understood as the everyday reality experienced by ordinary people. Schutz's *Commonsense Knowledge* can be

extended for a definition of mediaworld. Mediaworld is the everyday mass-mediated reality experienced by ordinary people. The mediaworld encompasses all that is taken for granted and considered unproblematic in one's mediated environment.

2. In Mannheim's "Problem of Generations" he writes, "Not every generation/age group creates original collective impulses and formative principles. When it does happen, it is a realization of potentialities inherent in the location and connected with the tempo of social change. When the tempo moves so quickly that traditional patterns of experience can't be used, there is a new generational entelechy (style)." (1952: 309)

Notes to Construction of Memory—Keval J. Kumar, Theo Hug, and Gebhard Rusch

1. See, for example, Winter (2002), who discusses questions of public commemoration as an impulse to reflection on memory, referring to the Holocaust and World War II.

Notes to Memory and Markers—Ruth Teer-Tomaselli

1. The section on collective memory was written in conjunction with Deanne Peters (nee Powers). The work contributed to her dissertation "Television, Memory and Identity: An Analysis of South African Youth and Fictional Programs," in partial fulfillment toward her master's degree in cultural and media studies, University of Natal, Durban, 1991.

2. A table summarizing these factors is reproduced below.

SUMMARY OF FACTORS AFFECTING THE SELECTION OF EVENTS AS "NEWS ITEMS"

1. Frequency
2. Threshold
   i. Absolute Intensity
   ii. Intensity Increase
3. Unambiguity
4. Meaningfulness
   i. Cultural Proximity
   ii. Relevance
5. Consonance
   i. Predictability
   ii. Demand

6. Unexpectedness
  i. Unpredictability
  ii. Scarcity
7. Continuity
8. Composition
9. Reference to Elite Nations
10. Reference to Elite Persons
11. Personification
12. Reference to the Negative

3. By the early 1950s, news flow was dominated by the "Big Four" Western agencies: Agence France-Presse (AFP, French), Associated Press (AP, American, English language), Reuters (British and Commonwealth, English language), and United Press International (UPI, American, English language). The Russian agency, TASS, and the Chinese Xihnua served their allies in the Eastern Bloc and communist Asia respectively. While all of these services ran subsidiaries in other languages, English, and to a lesser extent French, remained the important languages of internationalization. Today, the picture is more complex. In the notable processes of concentration, deregulation, re-regulation, privatization, and commercialization, new agencies have been founded, while those previously under the control of centralist states have been transformed. The emphasis in international media trade has moved, at least in part, from print to television, with the concomitant growth in mega-corporations such as Cable News Network (CNN), Bertlesman, and News Corporation, part of the Murdoch empire. Nevertheless, the old patterns of geographic, language, and political hegemony remained remarkably well intact: two of the three leading video news players formed significant affiliation with existing global print agencies (Reuters Television and AP Television), and the third, World Television Network (WTN, previously UPITN) evolved from a partnership in which one of the previous Big Four had played a significant part (UPI) (Boyd-Barrett and Rantanen, 1998: 11).

Index

-A-

Allan, S., 4
Ammon, R., 4
analogue knowledge, 263
Anderson, S., 13, 14
Appadurai, A., 252
appropriation, 198–200
Assman, A., 215, 218
Assman, J., 215, 218
audience divide, 92
Australia
   generational media experiences and,
      25–30, 30–33
   history of media in, 19–20
   media environment in, 21–22
   media interaction in, 22–25
Austria
   generational media experiences and,
      44–48, 48–51
   history of media in, 35–36
   media interaction and, 41–44
   perception of media environments in,
      37–41

-B-

Baacke, D., 2

Baldasty, G. J., 5
Barthes, R., 227
Bartlett, F. C., 212
Beck, U., 252
Being, 256, 257
Bernhurst, K. G., 96
Baudrillard, J., 2
Bennett, L. W., 3
Berg, K., 80
Bhasin, K., 96
Bourdieu, P., 196
Boyd-Barrett, O., 5, 234
Brown, J. L., 95

-C-

Carlsson, U., 95
Cary, J., 1
Castells, M., 2, 253, 255, 256
ceremonial journalism, 90
chronology of memory, 211
closed societies, 236, 237–38
cognitive structures, 212
collective elaborations of memory, 214
collective memory, 225, 226–28, 246–48
collective memory construction, 217
collective remembering, 213

communication
  development, 2, 3
  media-influenced, 41
  mediated, 2
communicative action, 2
communicative competence, 2
communicative memory, 217
Connerton,
conquest, 254
contest, 254
conversational elaboration of memories,
  214
conversational rules, 214
conversion, 198, 200–202
Coser, L., 226, 227, 247
coronation, 254
cosmopolitanism, 256
critical incidents, 228
cultural idealism, 232
cultural memory, 217, 218
Cunningham, S., 4
Curran, J., 3
Czech Republic
  generational media experiences and,
    62–68
  history of media in, 53–59
  media environment in, 59–62
  media interaction in, 59–62

-D-
Dasein, 256, 257
Davidson, A., 4
Dayan, D., 1, 90, 170, 245, 254
de-location, 252
diasporic groups, 4
digital divide, 3
Dissanayake, W., 253
Douglas, J., 240
driving forces, 214

-E-
Ebbinghaus, H., 212
Edwards, D., 14, 213, 214, 215, 247, 266
Eisenstein, E., 32
elaboration, 212
Elgin, C. Z., 50

entelechies, 7, 190, 251–56, 258
  analogue knowledge, digital knowl-
    edge, and, 262–66
  distance, proximity and, 259–62
Entman, R., 3
Esteinou, Madrid, F. J., 142
ethnocentrism, 235, 236–37
ethnoscapes, 252

-F-
Feierabend, S., 80
Feilke, H., 51
Fejes, F., 3
Festinger, L., 214
financescapes, 252

-G-
Galtung, J., 229, 230, 231, 232, 235, 245
Gans, H., 232
Garnham, N., 254
Gemeinschaf, 252
generational units, 219
generations, theory of, 6
geography of memory, 211
German Idealism, 256
Germany, 90–93
  generational media experiences and,
    72–80, 80–85
  history of media in, 69–72
  media memories in, 85–90
Gesellschaft, 252
Giddens, A., 251
Gilboa, E., 4
global journalism, 2
global knowledge, 50, 51
global media
  Australia and, 19–20, 21–22, 22–25,
    25–30, 30–33
  Austria and, 35–36, 37–41, 41–44, 44–48,
    48–51
  Czech Republic and, 53–59, 59–62,
    62–68
  Germany and, 69–72, 72–80, 80–85,
    85–90, 90–93
  India and, 95–97, 97–98, 98–101,
    101–107, 107–115, 115–118

Japan and, 119–21, 121–24, 124–30, 130–34, 134–37
Mexico and, 139–42, 142–44, 145–47, 147–51, 151–55, 155–56
South Africa and 159–60, 160–65, 165–73, 174
USA and, 177–79, 179–80, 180–84, 184–90, 190–91
Global Media Generations project, 6
global media relativism, 3
Gülich, E., 214
Goodman, N., 50
Green, L., 198

-H-

Habermas, J., 2, 4, 162, 254
habitus, 195
Hachten, W., 4
Halbwachs, M., 217, 226, 227, 246, 247
Hannerz, U., 252
Hargrave, A. M., 95, 96
Hegel, G. W. F., 256
Heidegger, M., 7, 189, 256, 257
Herman, E., 234
Hirsch, E., 15, 195, 197, 198
Hug, T., 50, 60
Husserl, E., 190, 256

-I-

incorporation, 198, 204–205
India
    generational media experience and, 107–115, 115–118
    history of media in, 98–99, 101
    media environment in, 97–98
    media history in, 95–97
    media interaction and, 98–101, 101–103, 103–107
Innis, H., 259
instant knowledge, 50
inszenieren, 216
interpenetration, 4, 6

-J-

Jameson, F., 253
Japan

generational media experience and, 130–34
    formation of knowledge and, 134–37
history of media in, 119–21
media environment in, 121–24
media interaction in , 124–30
Jensen, K. B., 266
Johnson-Laird, P. N., 213

-K-

Kant, E., 256
Katz, E., 1, 90, 170, 254
Kiefer, M.-L., 80
Klingler, W., 80
knowledge, 49

-L-

Lees, T., 95
Lerner, D., 2, 3
Levi-Strauss, C., 228
lidatic abstraction, 190
life marker, 189
lifeworlds, 225, 240–42, 254
Loftus, E., 218
Lull, J., 3

-M-

Maass, M., 260, 263
Mancini, _____, 266
Mannheim, K., 6, 7, 190, 217, 219, 257, 258
marker events, 228, 229–30
Mattelart, 3
Maturana, H., 212
McChesney, R., 234
McKenzie, W., 213
McLeish, J., 164
McLuhan, M., 32, 210
media context, 195–97, 209–10
    appropriation and, 198–200
    conversion and, 200–202
    incorporation and, 204–205
    objectification and, 202–204
    "sacred relics" and, 196–98
    technology, personhood, and, 205–209
Media Event, 170
media imperialism, 3

media memory divide, 92
media relativism, 32
media violence, 96, 97–98
mediascapes, 252
memory
    chronology of, 211, 218–21
    cognitive aspects of, 212–13
    collective, 225, 246–48
    communicative, 217
    construction of, 211
    contemporary and subsequent, 231–35
    cultural, 217, 218
    family and, 238–40
    geography of, 211
    images and, 243–44
    lifeworlds and, 240–42
    mapping, 221
    marker events and, 228, 229–30
    newsworthiness and, 229
    politics of, 211, 221–23
    processing, 226
    proximity and, 235–36
    prompted, 211
    social aspects of, 213–18
    triggers and, 242–43
Menon, R., 96
mental models
Mexico, 155–56
    generational media experience in, 147–51, 151–55
    history of media in, 139–42
    media environment in, 142–44
    media interaction in , 145–47
Meyer, W. H., 3
Meyrowitz, J., 32, 157, 196
Middleton, D., 14, 213, 214, 215, 247, 266
Miller, G. A., 212
Miyoshi, M., 253
modernity, 2
Morley, D., 15, 195, 197, 198
Mowlana, H., 4
multimedia generation, 49

-N-

Network Generation, 262
Network Society, theory of, 253, 265

New World Information and
    Communication Order, 3, 233
Nordenstreng, K., 3
Norris, P., 3
Nuttall, S., 247

-O-
objectification, 198, 202–204

-P-
Park, M.-J., 3
particularism, 252
Perger, J., 50
personification, 232, 233
Pinder, _____, 258
politics of memory, 117, 211
prompted memories, 211
public sphere, 162, 254

-R-
Raboy, M., 4
Ralph, S., 95
Rantanen, T., 234
regulated media, 46
relativization, 253
Robertson, R., 2, 252
Robinson, P., 4
Ruge, M., 229, 230, 231, 232, 235, 245
Rusch, G., 50, 60, 212, 214

-S-
Said, E., 3
Schiller, H. I., 3, 234
Schlesinger, P., 96
Schramm, W., 3
Schuman, H., 217
Schutz, A., 189, 240
Scott, J., 217
Scotton, J. F., 4
Sekiguchi, R., 15
Semo, E., 140
Silverstone, R., 15, 195, 197, 198
Sinclair, J., 4
Slade, C., 46, 258, 261, 262, 264
space-based cultures, 259
sociology of knowledge, 257

South Africa
    generational media experience in,
        165–73, 175
    history of media in, 159–60
    media environment in , 160–65
Spigel, L., 195
symbolic content, 155

-T-
Tagg, J., 243
Thompson, J. B., 146, 155
Thussu, D., 3
time-based cultures, 259
Tinchon, H. J., 213
Toennies, F., 252
Tomlinson, J., 3, 253
Turkle, S., 32, 42

-U-
Uchida, R., 96
universalism, 252
USA
    demographics of, 177–79
    generational media experience in,
        184–90, 190–91

media context in, 177–79
media environment of, 179–80
media interaction in, 180–84
political context of, 177–79

-V-
variations concept, 50
verbalization, 213, 217
Vitouch, P., 213
Volkmer, I., 3, 255
von Feilitzen, C., 95

-W-
Wallerstein, I., 251
Wartella, E., 96
wet ware, 212
White, K., 2
Wiley, S. B., 252
Wilson, R., 253
world knowledge, 256
world-system, 251

-Z-
Zelizer, B., 4, 228, 243, 248
Zillmann, D., 92

Toby Miller
General Editor

Popular Culture and Everyday Life is the new place for critical books in cultural studies. The series stresses multiple theoretical, political, and methodological approaches to commodity culture and lived experience by borrowing from sociological, anthropological, and textual disciplines. Each volume develops a critical understanding of a key topic in the area through a combination of thorough literature review, original research, and a student-reader orientation. The series consists of three types of books: single-authored monographs, readers of existing classic essays, and new companion volumes of papers on central topics. Fields to be covered include: fashion, sport, shopping, therapy, religion, food and drink, youth, music, cultural policy, popular literature, performance, education, queer theory, race, gender, and class.

For additional information about this series or for the submission of manuscripts, please contact:

Toby Miller
Department of Cinema Studies
New York University
721 Broadway, Room 600
New York, New York 10003

To order other books in this series, please contact our Customer Service Department:

(800) 770-LANG (within the U.S.)
(212) 647-7706 (outside the U.S.)
(212) 647-7707 FAX

Or browse online by series: www.peterlangusa.com